THE KOEHLER METHOD OF

Guard Dog Training

by W. R. Koehler

An effective and authoritative guide for selecting, training and maintaining dogs in home protection and police, security, sentry, and military use. Photographs by the author and others.

1978—Eighteenth Printing

HOWELL BOOK HOUSE INC.

230 PARK AVENUE

NEW YORK, N.Y. 10017

To Margaret Pooley

ACKNOWLEDGMENTS

I wish to express my deepest appreciation to the following people for their help in the preparation of this book:
Dick Koehler
Betty Regan
Police Chief Ray McLean of the Montclair, California, Police Department
Jack Felton
Bob Henry
Miss V. E. Meyers.

CONTENTS

SECTION 1

I. The Personal Protection Dog

II. The Police Dog

III. The Plant Security Dog

IV. Military Dogs

SECTION 2

Care, Housing and Obedience Training

PREFACE

If you consider the manner and number of crimes of violence which shame our society, you will be convinced that there are more areas of need for dogs at this time than ever before. With the awareness of a need that a dog can fill in a singular way, there comes a multitude of questions. Police chiefs and others, who on the one hand are responsible for the effectiveness and economy of their administrations, and on the other hand must maintain good public relations, need solutions, not mere answers, to forestall the problems that often becloud the survey, procurement, and training factors of installing police dogs in a department. Similarly, those individuals in business and industry who have been harassed by vandalism and theft have asked how dogs can meet their specific needs and how to establish such a service for plant protection.

The military has encountered many problems of security as the strategic importance of new electronically-oriented installations increases. In addition to such security values, the dog is being considered as an aid to certain types of combat operations.

The constant security and peace of mind that a dog of proven reliability can bring to a home has caused thousands of family heads to ask how they may procure and maintain dogs of predictable effectiveness for the protection of home, yard, automobile, and boat.

This book is specifically designed to provide the solutions to these problems.

AFFIDAVIT

Burbank, California
May 12, 1967

TO WHOM IT MAY CONCERN:

I, Raymond E. Shultz, residing at 732 Screenland Drive, Burbank, California, do hereby certify that the following information, pertaining to the experience and accomplishments of W. R. Koehler, of 5059 State Street, Ontario, California, is factual.

According to War Department Credentials, Mr. Koehler served as a dog trainer at the Pomona Ordnance Base, and was transferred from that Base to the War Dog Reception and Training Center, San Carlos, California, where he served as a Principal Trainer. Further evidence establishes, that in addition to instructing officers and enlisted men, Mr. Koehler did training of a specialized nature.

From July 1946 through this date, Mr. Koehler has served as Chief Trainer for the obedience program of the Orange Empire Dog Club, the largest open member-ship dog club in the United States. Statistics show that during this period more than 14,000 dogs participated in the obedience classes sponsored by the above organization. He also conducted classes in tracking and specialized training for that club.

From 1946 through 1957 Mr. Koehler served as Class Instructor for obedience classes sponsored by the Boxer Club of Southern California. Club records show that during that period more than 1100 dogs participated in these classes.

Mr. Koehler served as Instructor for obedience classes sponsored by the Dober-man Pinscher Club of Southern California. During the period of his instruction, 90 dogs participated in these classes.

From 1954 through 1960, Mr. Koehler served as Instructor for the Field Dog Classes sponsored by the Irish Setter Club of Southern California, which are open to all pointing breeds. Records show that 140 dogs have received instruction in this specialized training program.

Additional classes, for which the number of participants has been substantiated, bring the total number of dogs trained in Mr. Koehler's classes to well over 15,700.

The following innovations have been accredited to Mr. Koehler's work in the field of obedience classes:

Introduction of foundation work with a longe line, in conjunction with a complete absence of oral communication, as an emphatic means of instilling attentiveness into a dog.

Introduction of a system of gradually diminishing the length of a light line, used in conjunction with other equipment, as an assurance of a dog's reliable off-leash performance.

Development of more widely applicable methods of rehabilitating fighters, biters, and other major offenders. There is no record of his ever having refused a dog the opportunity for rehabilitation for any reason.

Establishing class procedure which demanded that all class participants make emphatic corrections, and which ruled out tentative, nagging corrections on the premise that an indefinite approach to animal handling constituted a major cruelty. Later this contention was supported with evidence supplied by an internationally accredited scientist who revealed that the use of electro-encephalograph equipment, of the same type used by the medical profession, showed that the training efforts of an indeterminate person cause great emotional disturbance to a dog.

Following are some of the accomplishments resulting from Mr. Koehler's efforts in the field of obedience classes:

The rehabilitation of an unsurpassed number of problem dogs, many of which were referred to his classes by humane organizations and law forces as a last hope to avoid destruction.

The generating of competitive obedience dogs, outstanding in numbers and quality even in the Los Angeles area, which, according to The American Kennel Club statistics, is by far the greatest obedience center in the United States.

A record of effectiveness and provision for the physical welfare of dogs that has caused his formats and training methods to be adopted by more obedience clubs than those of any other trainer in this region.

Three of the owner-handled dogs from his Field Classes have become Field Champions and many others have won points.

I have viewed letters from law forces in evidence of his personal experience in the areas of police work and tracking with dogs.

As an indication of the standard of performance exhibited by motion picture dogs he has trained, four of the number have been selected as deserving of the Achievement Award by the American Humane Association. "Wildfire" received the award for his performance in the picture "It's a Dog's Life," presented for the outstanding animal actor in 1955. The honor went to "Chiffon" for his performance in the picture "The Shaggy Dog" in 1959. "Asta," trained by Mr. Koehler and handled by him and his associate, Hal Driscoll, received the award for best television performance by an animal because of his work in the series, "The Thin Man." "Big Red," trained by Mr. Koehler, received the award for 1962.

My qualifications for the aforementioned statements are as follows:

1. Obedience Chairman—Boxer Club of Southern California, Inc. (5 years).
2. President—Boxer Club of Southern California, Inc. (1 year).
3. Delegate to the Southern California Obedience Council (5 years).
4. President—Southern California Obedience Council (2 years).
5. Vice President—Hollywood Dog Obedience Club, Inc. (2 years).
6. President—Hollywood Dog Obedience Club, Inc. (2 years).
7. Chairman of an Advisory Committee to the Southern California Obedience Council (2 years).
8. Director—German Shorthaired Pointer Club of Southern California (1 year).
9. Presently serving as President of the German Shorthaired Pointer Club of Southern California.

Raymond E. Shultz

Subscribed and sworn to before me this _12th_ day of _May_, 1967.

Dorothy T. Hoffman

DOROTHY T. HOFFMAN

My Commission Expires November 3, 1969

INTRODUCTION

You charged the author with a great responsibility when you bought this book for a definite use. Service and safety demand that the instruction for training police and protection dogs be executed with the utmost accuracy and penetration. In order to accomplish this I have treated the three categories of use separately by placing all information pertaining to each category in an individual section, except for a few parts that can be applied without modification to more than one type of dog. This has been done to prevent diffusing the reader's focus as well as to make it less likely that a user will try techniques that are irrelevant and harmful to his particular training needs. Unless you are referred to such material by the section treating the kind of dog you need, leave it alone. You will borrow trouble if you borrow that which does not concern your dog.

I. The Personal Protection Dog

1. A WARNING

You might make one of the most costly mistakes of your life within the next hour. Your failure to accept the truth of this chapter can hang you up for the most thorough bleeding imaginable. Show my statements to a lawyer and ask him if I exaggerate when I say that there is being created in this country a most inviting field for exploitation. Further, get his opinion on why a certain type of dog can be a real "stopper," giving the maximum degree of personal protection with a minimum of legal risk.

It is a fact that the opinions of the public and the courts have often been colored by an unjust classification of dogs, sometimes favorably and sometimes unfavorably, but never logically. Experienced veterinarians and professional dog men can tell you that from 1945 until about 1955 the two breeds most commonly accepted as "good family dogs" were the leaders in the percentage of indiscriminate biters per existing numbers of all the breeds combined. One of the two breeds charmed its beholders with appealing puppiness and surprised them later with puddling shyness and "fear biting." The other, regarded as heroic from its representation in many novels, saddened many homes by showing hysterics instead. Although judicious breeding has brought the two breeds to a level of good temperament, the same individuals who accepted them solely on reputation as being "good" now reject them solely on reputation as "bad."

Let's see how illogical prejudice affects other areas of the dog's relationship with man. There are sections of our country where a dog found roaming at large in the vicinity of pastured livestock can be shot without risk of legal redress, even if it could be proved that his liberty was caused neither by intent nor carelessness and that the dog had never chased any stock. The fact that the dog might have been a top hound with a record of winning tree-hound purses would not alter the case. The same courts that would order a road department to replace a cow killed by careless weed-spraying because the animal "contributed to a farmer's livelihood" would reject claims for a dog worth five times the cow's cash value.

With dogs guiding the blind, doing police and guard work, herding stock, hunting, retrieving, and doing other jobs, it is certain that more dogs than horses are working in useful occupations, but the horse, as livestock, still enjoys a legal status that the dog does not have.

In some areas there is a "three-bite rule"—not officially, but as a matter of custom. A dog whose first bite is shabby, indefensible attack will often be permitted two more bites, though circumstances show him so unpredictable that his career should have ended with the first offense. Another dog may exhibit admirable patience around a bunch of senseless humans, score three justified nips in as many years, and then be automatically classified as one who will "have to go."

You might have noticed "Beware the Dog" signs are being replaced by signs that say such things as "Dog—Do Not Open Gate." Such words as *beware* and *mean* have often been used as evidence by "innocent victims" who enter yards in "moments of emergency" and receive bites that cause "great physical suffering and long periods of expensive mental anguish." Now let your lawyer friend tell you how much fun an attorney for a plaintiff would have with the fact that his poor client suffered irreparable damage at the teeth of a dog that had been "formally trained to attack human beings." All present in the court would be moved by evidence that "a trained attack-dog" had been kept in a position to injure anyone who might seek help in an emergency. It is almost inevitable that the current propagandizing and promotion of "attack-trained dogs for home protection" will provide oportunities for the "innocent" to become injured and enriched.

2. ATTACK-TRAINED vs. NATURAL PROTECTOR

Cheer up! Even if you are convinced that the classification of "attack-trained" could make a dog into quite a liability, you can still have the right guard dog whether you need a reliable alarm or a physical protector. Whatever little protection you require from a dog, you will profit from comparing two classifications of dogs at the highest level of guard work, which is man-stopping. One of these is the attack-trained dog who has been expertly agitated to a point where he identifies persons who act in a certain way, or enter certain places, as human varmints whom he should attack. The second kind is the natural guard dog who is motivated by inherent temperament traits to accept responsibility for the protection of persons and property and to use the proper amount of force to do that job.

The *advantages* of an attack-trained dog are:

1. Agitation can sometimes put suspicion into an overly trusting dog, stiffen up an indecisive dog, or break the "taboo" a dog might have against biting a person, thus making possible varying degrees of usefulness in dogs who could not otherwise qualify for guard dog work.
2. Attack training makes it easy to set up test situations in which

a dog can demonstrate his readiness to bite a person who acts in a certain way.

3. An attack-trained dog may make an all-out assault more certainly in some situations than would a natural guard dog.
4. His reputation of being attack-trained may discourage intruders.

The *disadvantages* of an attack-trained dog are:

1. In the event of law suits, his classification of "attack-trained" would prejudice a court.
2. He can be stimulated to attack under the most regrettable circumstances by a person who may innocently act like an agitator.
3. The patterns of reaction that trigger him will often override his discernment and good judgment.
4. Although the suspicious moves of an agitator can be purposefully related to trespassing, the theft of garden tools, or threats to a person, and can result in a dog clobbering people who "make the wrong moves," they can never provide the fine discrimination that is based on a sense of responsibility.
5. The impression made by attack training will often give undeserved accreditation to an inferior dog.
6. A dog that needs to be shut away for the protection of the innocent will probably not be close at hand when he is needed.
7. He can be teased into a booby trap much easier than a natural guard.
8. If lightly agitated in the apparent hope that he will "bite lightly," he will have a half-hearted attitude that will soon fade to nothing.

The *advantages* of a natural guard dog are:

1. Motivated by a responsibility for what is his, he won't leave his own property to bite someone who happens to act in a certain way.
2. He is more completely aware of his surroundings and less subject to distraction than an attack-trained dog would be.
3. His judgment is better: He won't leave the baby and run out toward the road to investigate the waving motions of a surveyor.

4. He is discriminating in his enforcement as well as in his decisions. It is not uncommon for him merely to warn friends who try to come near his baby but attack a stranger who takes the same liberties.
5. In the case of a bad bite under doubtful circumstances he will be regarded in court as a dog who did "what came naturally" instead of as a dog "trained to attack human beings."

The *disadvantages* of a natural guard dog are:

1. He is much more difficult to obtain.
2. Because he is motivated to protect something by "what he feels" rather than to fight something because certain patterns tell him to do so, he is harder to test and demonstrate.
3. He may have less psychological effect than a dog reputed to be attack-trained.
4. In some situations he may only warn or threaten, where the agitated dog would make an all-out attack.

If, after reading these comparisons, you decide you want a dog to make an all-out attack each time he is stimulated, and you are going to be with him every moment he is on duty, as with the police dog, you will find instructions for that type of training in the Police Dog Section. You may decide that, since you are without acquaintances who would ever call on you, the dog most useful to you would be one who uses force on everyone who enters his premises. The section on plant-protection dogs will take you to such a goal. Talk to your lawyer before you decide on either of these two types of dogs for personal protection, and get costs from an agent on how much liability insurance you should carry.

In the name of sweet reason, do not try to reduce the risk of having an attack-trained dog by giving "light agitation" with the thought that your dog will only bite lightly. As for that smooth-sounding asininity, "attacks only on command," what sort of a nut would want a dog who would not defend him when he was asleep or voiceless from a case of laryngitis?

You may conclude, after weighing the foregoing caveat, that some kind of a natural guard dog would be the best kind for you.

3. WHICH KIND?

Your first step toward acquiring the right type of personal protection dog is to examine your own needs and environment carefully before you look at a dog. Next, consider the three definite categories of personal protection dogs and align your efforts accordingly. They are:

1. The dog whose sole function is to give alarm.
2. The dog who gives alarm and offers some physical threat to an intruder.
3. The real man-stopper, whose temperament and physical qualities make him a game and capable fighter.

Your correct choice of a dog will be determined in great measure by the type of protection dog you need.

Right Ones and Wrong Ones

Whatever kind of dog you seek, you will find it interesting and helpful to consider the following comparison of two types of prospects: the qualified and the unqualified. This information is not intended to suggest that at the present time you can find a breeder producing dogs for your specific purpose, but rather to prove to you that *there are indissoluble differences in the quality of dogs which cannot be minimized by training and environent.* The facts on this comparison are found in a book entitled *The New Knowledge of Dog Behavior,* by Clarence Pfaffenberger (Howell Book House).

While dog trainers had long been aware of the great variation in ability between individual dogs, it remained for Mr. Pfaffenberger and those who worked with him to substantiate that difference with statistics. Knowledgeable professionals have accepted the book's evidence as fact. You can avoid wasting a great deal of time by joining in that acceptance. The material is based on the results obtained by Mr. Pfaffenberger and his associates through their work at the Roscoe B. Jackson Memorial Laboratory, Bar Harbor, Maine, and at Guide Dogs For The Blind, Inc., San Rafael, California, in initially adapting the best dogs they could find to guide the blind and later breeding their own candidates especially for guide dog work. When their procurement program consisted of acquiring the very best prospects from the most favorable sources available, only 9 percent of the trainees completed the program successfully. During a 14-year period, which encompassed a program of study and purposeful breeding, they learned to produce a strain of puppies of which 90 percent have made successful guide dogs. The program therefore resulted in an improvement of one thousand percent! The purposeful breeding instilled in the puppies a sense of responsibility and other qualities essential in guide dogs.

These startling results are not offered to suggest that you must find a purposeful breeder who is producing dogs for your particular needs. Rather, the two-fold objective of these truths is to impress upon you the great difference in potential between one dog and another, even when they are of the same breed, and to help you realize that you must find a "right one" even though he is the result of chance and not the predictable product of a dedicated breeder. This necessity applies to each of the three categories of personal protection dogs. Whatever kind of dog you need, your evaluations must be made among dogs that are at least one year old.

4. THE ALARM DOG

His Job

The job of an alarm dog is to detect and announce any person approaching the area he serves. He is useful in situations where an alarm is needed but where biting, or even the threat of biting, could not be permitted. Examples are places where the proprietor needs to know of each arrival but, because the callers are few, does not spend time watching the entrance.

Qualifications

Because such a dog need not offer the threat of physical protection, there are no minimum requirements for size and strength. One of the small breeds can be as good an alarm dog as the largest dog. There are obvious advantages to a smaller dog in some situations. The smaller dogs are usually longer lived than the larger ones and often have more robust constitutions, as a veterinarian will tell you. Even the Toy breeds come in such a variety of coats that they can take all extremes of temperature and weather, from the coldest and wettest to the hottest and driest. In Chapters 7–10 you will find information common to many breeds of protection dogs.

Checking Prospects

When you have learned of a good prospect, try to make your first visit to his home a surprise so that you can see the dog as he usually acts and discover things which you may not see if special arrangements were made for your visit. Note carefully where he is kept, how he alerts, whether he barks too much or not enough, and other factors that might be important to you. Don't overlook a bad fault and then complain about it later. For example, determine if he is such a constant barker that he would have to be confined where he would do you little good. Observe whether his alertness is solely the result of a panicky shyness. Undeniably, a shy dog motivated by uncertainty will sometimes make a useful alarm dog, but a dog that is sound in temperament can do the job better and is more pleasant to be near.

As you talk, watch for any peculiarities the owner may have which would make you question his opinions. Emphasize that you will provide full measure of care and kindness for any dog you select but it will be kept only if it fills your need for an alarm. Such a condition will tend to keep accurate the claims made for a dog.

Testing

There is a simple test you can use to check an alarm dog that seems worth further consideration. Arrange to call again at the dog's home accompanied by two other persons, who will wait a short distance from the house until after you have been admitted. Not only will you get a second chance to study how the dog reacts to your approach, but it will give you the opportunity to see whether the dog is so distracted by your presence that the individual approach of the other two "strangers" will go unnoticed. If the dog shows enough responsibility to concern himself with each separate arrival, he is worth a trial if you've found that he qualifies in other respects.

Before you bring a dog home for a trial, prepare for the right start by studying Chapter 11.

5. THE THREAT DOG

His Job

You would not be afraid of a dog who turns tail and runs from you; neither would anyone else. The dog who barks and runs away from the advance of a stranger may make a good alarm dog, but he could hardly be suitable candidate for the second classification of a personal protection dog, the dog who provides a threat as well as an alarm.

Qualifications

Although the threat dog should not be overly aggressive, he must have the courage to stand his ground staunchly against anyone who tries to bluff his way past him. This need for courage and alertness means that much care must be used in selecting the dog.

In considering first the general type of dog for the job, remember that, in posing a threat, a dog's attitude is more important than his size. True, there is something impressive about a large dog standing firmly in the path of an intruder. But there is something equally impressive about the right kind of a small terrier who appears ready for violent action.

You would kick a small terrier out of the way? You would walk right over him? I know of bears that have been detained when they tried just that. However, size itself can be quite a deterrent and, if a smaller dog is your choice, it is doubly important that he be right physically and temperamentally. For an example of how structure can make a great difference between two breeds of dogs of similar size, compare the Pug with one of the smaller terriers. The Pug's head, while large for his size, has such a flat face and small teeth that it would not scare a determined intruder. When the terrier snarls he reveals a well-equipped mouth that is big enough to grab a lot of leg, pants and all.

You will find further information common to all types of protection dogs, and methods of finding them, in Chapters 7 through 10.

Testing a Threat Dog

You have at least tentatively made the preliminary decisions on the breeds which seem suitable to your purpose and the age of the prospects you will seek. Those sources of information mentioned in Chapter 10 will soon supply you with enough leads to make a start.

The following step will save you much time. If possible, before you go to look at a prospect, phone its owner and explain that you need a dog with enough courage to stand up to a person who will try to bluff him down. Make it clear that you will want to watch while a stranger does the testing. If an owner objects to such a proposal, eliminate his dog. Without a test for this essential quality, there is no reason to consider any other virtues the dog might have.

When you have obtained an owner's consent to test his dog, arrange to have someone who can follow directions capably to do the testing while you watch from a concealed place. The dog should be tested in as close to the normal home situation as possible, but he must be within a fence, or tied, while the test takes place so that there is no danger of a bite. The owner should not be within sight when the testing is done, as his presence may encourage the dog to react differently.

Your tester should have a burlap sack and a cap gun to snap, with or without caps. If the dog is shy, he'll back up from the clicking. Ask the tester to walk in a normal manner to a point where the dog will alert, and then to proceed to within a few feet of the dog where he should make a threatening swing with the sack and snap the gun two or three times. If the dog continues to oppose your helper's entry after the sack is swung toward him and the gun is snapped, the tester should turn and leave the area. The dog should indicate by his actions that he has sufficient staunchness to discourage most intruders, which will serve your purpose.

If your situation is one in which a dog would have to exercise discretion and be easily controlled, another simple test, which you can give personally, will be required. By arrangement with the owner, visit the dog's yard or household when the dog is at liberty to stop you, and see how much difficulty the owner has in bringing him under control so that you can be admitted. In short, is the dog staunch enough for your purpose, and yet controllable enough so that you wouldn't have to confine him in such a way that he would be useless?

Before you bring a dog home for trial, carefully read Chapter 11 on "Starting Right."

6. THE MAN-STOPPER

His Job

A true man-stopper does not merely show a willingness to fight. His job is to stop a man, if necessary, by winning a fight.

Qualifications

A strong sense of responsibility. Unless he feels responsible, a dog may be easily distracted from his purpose of physical defense.

Awareness. He must be keenly alert and aware of situations that develop.

Decisiveness. It is not enough for him to be aware and concerned. He must act with sufficient force.

Courage. He must be able to stand up to threat and pain.

Capability. He must have the mental and physical abilities to be a formidable opponent.

Reasonableness. When you admit someone to your premises, your dog should respect your judgment but remain alert. The maniacal, uncontrollable dog is not only dangerous—he's useless, being shut away much of the time when his presence would be a comfort.

To find a dog who meets the above requirements and can then

reorient these qualities to another master can be very difficult. Generally, a pup with such potential is more adaptable to a household than an adult would be. However, you will probably find that, since the methods for seeking and choosing an adult are the same as for finding and accrediting a pup, through the performance of his relatives, you can start looking and let your decisions be influenced by the best that is available.

You will find further information common to all types of protection dogs, and methods of finding them, in Chapters 7 through 10.

Checking Prospects

Use all available information so that you will have a full perspective on what is obtainable. Keep in mind all the breeds mentioned as suitable, instead of one or two. Truly, handsome is as handsome does in the case of a man-stopper. Regardless of what he looks like, the most beautiful dog you will find is the one who would give his life to save yours.

The following suggestion may help you acquire additional facts about the dogs to which your leads may take you. From some of the breeders you will meet, or from the pages of dog magazines, you can obtain the names of the secretaries and other officers of regional and national breed clubs. These officers, along with the writers of the breed columns, often possess quite a knowledge of the accomplishments of various breeding programs. Although it's true that there is a degree of "kennel blindness" in the dog fancy, it is just as true that a person who would fault a rival's dog as not being of the "right type" will concede the same dog's superiority in demonstrated characteristics such as protectiveness and trainability. When they learn that you need a dog for such an exacting task as maximum protection, they will try to tell you of a person who, either by intent or by chance, produces dogs that are conceded to be the best for your needs. They realize that in questions of performance, unlike those of eye-appeal, comparison is generally conclusive.

If your discussions turn up any information on people who have been active in obedience work, talk with them. They are interested in temperament and may be able to tell you about common faults and virtues that they have observed in certain lines of dogs. Both professionals and amateurs may be of help in this respect.

You will find that your leads to dogs and information will generate more leads, and you will eventually have some prospects worth testing. The tests are surprisingly simple.

The Responsibility Test

The first is a test to see whether a dog will stay with a person or property by his own free choice when there are obvious and inviting opportunities to leave. Remember that *no guard dog is any good when he's gone.* Even more important is the truth that a dog who lacks the responsibility to stay with his charges rarely makes a good protector when he is with them. Conversely, a dog who concerns himself with staying where he belongs is one who will act effectively when his charges are threatened. These facts emphasize the foolishness of skipping this test merely because there seems to be no possibility of your dog escaping from confinement. Apply the test in the same manner to adult prospects and to the parents or close relatives of any puppy prospect you might consider. The best possible way of determining the traits a family of dogs possesses is by observing those traits in dogs of that family.

You will soon see that an explanation of how you intend to test prospects will cause many owners to retract their statements on their "great" dogs, thus saving you much time. Have the owner of each dog you test take him by car away from his premises, and, in a strange area, free him from any restraint. Without commanding the dog in any way, the man should walk slowly along. From a distance, watch to see whether the dog is so distracted or tempted by his new surroundings that he forgets all about his master. A dog with the qualities of a good guard dog might drift around a bit, noticing all things in his environment, but he would show concern with his master's whereabouts, and at definite intervals would swing back close to him to demonstrate his responsibility. Such a dog would be worthy of further consideration. If, when he is not restrained, a dog finds his new surroundings so interesting that he forgets to keep track of his master, you had better look elsewhere for a natural protector.

As previously stated, merely considering such a test will cause many owners to withdraw their dogs with such excuses as, "He's had no training," or "He's never been out of the yard." You'll gain more than you'll lose from these withdrawals.

The second step in testing is to arrange with the dog's owner for a demonstration of what happens when a gate or door is accidentally left open. Watch the proceedings from a distance so that you will be of no interest to the dog. A dog who is accustomed to confinement is sometimes slow to notice an opportunity to leave an area, so be sure that your prospect makes a choice between staying and leaving. The owner should remain concealed and quiet so that he does not influence the situation.

Ideally, a responsible dog should be concerned with staying on "his" property. Don't write him off completely if he saunters outside his area and putters around in a way that demonstrates he is still more concerned with home and fireside than with the call of the open road. However, if he shows that his heartstrings are but frail threads against the pull of adventure, and with his unconcern indicates that you could steal the house from behind him, you'd better say "Thanks, but no thanks." What makes such a dog appear to be a demon guard when confinement forces him to confront an intruder is not the thing that will make him a dog to ride the river with.

The Capability Test

The nature of this test may frighten off another block of owners. Again, good riddance—you claim you want a real "stopper."

For this very careful procedure, you will need complete understanding and coöperation from the dog's owner and assistance from a well-coördinated man who will follow your instructions carefully. Your helper should be equipped with a burlap sack and a gun for blank-firing.

Even if you were willing that your helper be bitten, you would find no volunteers, so in order to protect the man, you will have to choose between having the dog securely chained or confined and having him wear a safe muzzle. Though it will confuse some dogs, the muzzle is by far the better choice. See that the owner of the dog you are considering has an opportunity to familiarize his dog with the muzzle by having him wear it during short periods for two days before the test.

Meet with the owner and your helper in a place where the dog cannot see or hear any of you talking together, and arrange to have the dog muzzled and in a definite place so that your "heavy" can force an entrance and make the test. Explain to the owner that the place of the test must provide a means of your watching the action without attracting the dog's attention, and permit him to be close at hand for any emergency, yet out of the dog's sight. All concerned should realize that there should be no oral communication between any of you, because at best it's difficult to create a test situation that will ring true to a good dog. Be definite about the time of entry and the signal that will tell the man that the muzzle is in place and all is ready. The lighting of a light or the closing of a drape are easy ways of signaling.

When he gets the signal, the "heavy," gun in one hand and the sack in the other, should approach the point of challenge, which will probably be the door or gate. Regardless of whether the dog meets him head on or hangs back a bit, the heavy should move steadily toward him. The man should snap the cap gun a couple of times, hit the dog with a hard swipe of the sack, and retreat from the area, shoving the dog back away from him if necessary so that the gate or door can be closed. If the muzzled dog tries to fight the man in the face of the gun and club-like sack, there should be little doubt that he would make things rough for an intruder. If he stands his ground while trying to free himself of the muzzle, you can logically conclude that he would fight effectively without that handicap. Muzzled or not, if he shows he would sooner retreat than fight, he's not the kind of dog you need.

The foregoing tests will reveal whether or not a dog has the qualities that will make him a good personal protector. However, there are other factors that can determine how acceptable he may be in your situation. Your own observation of the physical situation in which he lives can tell you much about a dog's living habits. A thorough questioning of the owner will give you more information. Remember, many undesirable traits are definitely inherited and you should check for their existence in the relatives of a puppy prospect as well as in an adult.

Before you bring any dog home, carefully read Chapter 11.

7. PUREBRED OR CROSSBRED?

As any professional trainer will tell you, there are many factors that favor a purebred, the most important of which is that it is possible to predict his development with considerable accuracy because you can get information about his family characteristics. Make use of such information because, as you have seen from the experience of Guide Dogs For The Blind, Inc., there is a great deal of variation even within a single breed. As examples of this variation, the little Miniature Schnauzer and the impressive Doberman Pinscher, two breeds that are considered quite suspicious, will produce occasional individuals who would not react to the approach of a Frankenstein. So, after you have decided on the size and general physical type to suit your home area, you will have to start the interesting but exacting task of finding prospects in that general category.

To prevent the selection of your dog from being influenced by sentiment and eye appeal, continue to regard each prospect primarily as a potential implement until you have located a usable dog.

8. BREEDS

The logical way for you to begin a search for any of the three types of protection dog is by giving thought to those breeds with the greatest number of dogs most apt to qualify physically and mentally for your purpose. For your convenience in seeking such information, it is advisable to consider dogs according to the groups to which they belong.

GROUP 1: SPORTING DOGS

Do not bypass the sporting dogs with the idea that they are limited to hunting and companionship. Those of us who worked with some of them in the World War II Dog Program are still wondering who it was that had the sporting dogs surplussed en masse because they were "too birdy" to make war dogs. Some of them showed exceptional ability. Supposedly, it was thought that some of the foreign game birds they might encounter would divert them from their purpose, so they were returned to their homes, including some who had demonstrated exceptional ability prior to the issuance of the surplus directive. One of that group was "Shorty," a purebred English Setter who hunted men with an intensity and finesse such as his ancestors had visited on quail. Since the time of that conclusion, two of the retriever breeds,

Labrador and Golden, have distinguished themselves by guiding the blind on city streets where pigeons putter enticingly a few feet away and through parks where game birds are common. Some of the other sporting breeds show outstanding qualities of concentration and responsibility in the way they work on a specific quarry, ignoring cats, rabbits, and other distractions, and in handling birds in a way that requires the utmost in control. These facts do not contradict the advocacy of breeding for a purpose—they support it. The sense of responsibility instilled by breeding for one purpose occasionally finds expression in another field.

While generally easygoing, some of the sporting dogs have a raw, primitive courage that comes as quite a shock to those who have had no experience with them. True, there is no obligation on the part of the breeders of these dogs to produce guards, but don't write off a prospect without a test merely because he's a sporting dog.

There are four sporting breeds that show more than the average responsibility for guarding a variety of things, from automobiles to families. Physically, they combine size and soundness in a way that qualifies them to be threat dogs and man-stoppers, but makes them unsuited for alarm dogs, where a big dog, even if friendly, might be offensive to some timid souls who would be kept away by anything larger than a Toy breed.

Chesapeake Bay Retriever

A large percentage of Chesapeake Bay Retrievers have the protectiveness and determination to be man-stoppers as well as the physical ability to do a good job. An outstanding constitution and a harsh, weather-resistant coat enables the Chesapeake to live and work under climatic conditions that would be a hardship to most other breeds. He needs a lot more obedience training than the average sporting dog, and for best results it should begin as soon as he is six months old. Such training will develop qualities that come as a surprise to those who have assumed that he was only an exceptionally rugged retriever.

Height: Many big males will stand 25 to 27 inches at the shoulder, and females a few inches less.

Weight: Males can carry 80 pounds or more in hard condition, and females about 65 pounds.

German Shorthaired Pointer

This breed can be a fine all-purpose gun dog as well as a home and car protector. However, while there are many with alertness and suspicion, there are fewer who have the courage to be a man-stoppers. In fact, some of the families of the breed have been plagued with a form of timidity that has been well-described as "situation shyness." Such a dog, though he may have no fear of a gun, will be frightened by such things as the sight of a judge in a field trial or another hunter in the field. But when he is of good breeding and has been properly exposed to lots of strange sights and·sounds, the German Shorthaired Pointer can serve you well.

> *Height:* The Standard gives the shoulder height as 23 to 25 inches for males and 21 to 23 inches for females.
> *Weight:* Males, 55 to 70 pounds; females, 45 to 60 pounds. There is a current tendency to breed dogs heavier than these weights.

German Wirehaired Pointer

This breed is not sufficient in numbers to permit wide observation, but a high percentage of those observed seem to be protective and courageous. These dogs have exceptional strength and agility and it's wrapped up in a coat that gives them lots of protection.

> *Height:* Males, from 24 to 26 inches at the shoulder; females, a bit less.
> *Weight:* No weight is specified by the Standard, but many males exceed 80 pounds, and almost never does such size bring unsoundness, as is the case with some breeds.

Weimaraner

This dog was introduced to this country in accordance with plans intended to protect him from casual breedings. Unfortunately, as is often the case with a new breed, novelty seekers acquired some of the stock and careless matings were made, resulting in a regrettable variation in temperament types. Soon the Ymar, as he is called, was

A good German Shorthaired Pointer will protect your equipment as well as work for you in the field.

A determined Boxer can stop the "foot in the door" approach.

being disparaged for lacking drive and intensity in the field and being without the intelligence claimed for him. However, his loyal supporters prevailed over his detractors, and quite a few of his breed have demonstrated ability as upland hunters, retrievers, and trackers of game and men. His record in the obedience ring is outstanding.

Although he has proven his usefulness, he often shows a paradoxical quality which demands much care in his selection. Ymars are one of the better breeds for "staying home," but some individuals protest against staying alone by doing a lot of barking and destructive chewing, clinging to these bad habits with awesome obstinacy. Nearly always, when one has the breeding and rearing to be free of this fault, he is qualified for a lot of jobs, including that of a man-stopper.

Height: Males, 25 to 27 inches at the shoulder; females, slightly smaller.

Weight: The Standard specifies no weight, but males commonly reach 80 pounds, females somewhat less.

GROUP 2: HOUNDS

The hound group is greatly varied in appearance and size, ranging from the Dachshund to the Irish Wolfhound, tallest of dogs, but the scant sprinkling of protective individuals within this group does not make it a good hunting ground for guard dogs. The one exception to this generality is the Dachshund. When his bark is accompanied by a wagging tail, he makes an inoffensive little alarm dog who isn't likely to frighten timid callers. But when he's really protective, he can back up a threat with a lot of mouth and a hard bite, as some intruders have learned quite suddenly. Short of leg though he is, he can move a few feet in a hurry.

GROUP 3: WORKING DOGS

This group varies in size and purpose from the small dogs that were developed for herding to the biggest breeds in dogdom. More dogs suitable for police work, guard duty, and personal protection are found in this group than in any other. Don't assume that you will not find the less common breeds near you just because you have not heard of them.

The following working breeds are well worth considering for threat dogs and man-stoppers.

Belgian Sheepdog

He is a dog of very convenient size for home and car and is intelligent and very discriminating.

> *Height:* Males should be about 24 to 26 inches at the shoulder, females generally under 24 inches.
> *Weight:* 55–65 pounds.

Belgian Tervuren

In character, structure and size he is almost identical to the Belgian Sheepdog.

Bouvier des Flandres

He has quite a background in many different jobs. At present, some are doing a fine job in police work in Canada. Males average about 27 inches at the shoulder and will weigh over 90 pounds in good condition. Females are only slightly smaller.

Boxer

A good Boxer who has had the amount of obedience training necessary to bring about his full development can be a companionable dog with the courage and substance to be a man-stopper. Certainly he is one of the most reliable with children. He must be chosen carefully, as many of his breed are too naïve and good-natured to be guard dogs.

> *Height:* Males will average 24 inches at the shoulder; females are slightly smaller than males.
> *Weight:* Males will average close to 65–70 pounds, females about 55–60 pounds.

Briard

A good Briard has a strong sense of property boundaries and can do an authoritative job of protecting them. However, to acquire a dog of

In his native country, Belgium, the Bouvier cannot win his championship unless he has also won a prize in working competition as an army, police, or defense dog.

The Great Dane's size alone should discourage any intruder.

his physical ability that is the least bit timid can be a distasteful experience. The Briard has an interesting history of use but, unfortunately, his breeders too often offer glowing tales of his past instead of demonstrations of what he can do now. When considering a Briard for a demanding job such as man-stopping, believe what you see and not what you are told.

Height: Males, 23 to 27 inches at the shoulder; females, about an inch less than males.

Weight: There seems to be more variance in the weight of Briards than in other breeds. One dog that stands 27 inches at the shoulder may weigh 90 pounds, while another of equal height and in the same condition may be no more than 75 pounds.

Bullmastiff

He can be as determined as he looks, and when he's in hard condition can back up his opinions with enough physical force to stop a man cold. The fact that he is almost never noisy makes him a good choice for a city home.

Height: Males often stand as high as 27 inches at the shoulder, which is about an inch higher than the females' height.

Weight: A good average is 115 pounds for males and 100 pounds for females.

Collie

A good one can be very sagacious, a poor one very giddy and noisy. On the physical side, the percentage of present-day collies with defective vision is shocking.

Height: Males will average about 26 inches at the shoulder; females run approximately two inches less than males.

Weight: Males, about 65 pounds, females between 50 and 60 pounds.

Doberman Pinscher

One of the best choices. Breeders have done an excellent job of stabilizing temperament in the Dobe. At the present time there are many families of the breed that are trustworthy and discriminating, as well as being among the most fearless and capable of man-stoppers.

Height: 26–27 inches.
Weight: 70–85 pounds.

German Shepherd

There is not a finer working dog than a good German Shepherd. His temperament, physical ability, and wonderful coat equip him for all kinds of jobs in as many places. But when stricken with shyness, as many of his breed are, the German Shepherd can be the most useless of dogs. Choose carefully, lest you come up with a "protection dog" who would run from a cap pistol.

Height: A good working size for the male is 25 inches at the shoulders, females two inches lower.
Weight: About 85 pounds, females 10 pounds less.

The current tendency to breed oversized Shepherds is resulting in unsoundness and clumsiness. Don't mistake bigness for quality.

Great Dane

His size does not prevent him from being one of the best housedogs, and he has the ability to take care of his home. The Great Dane does the job of keeping things under control without being trigger-happy.

Height: The Standard sets the minimum height of 32 inches for the male and 30 inches for the female.
Weight: 135 pounds for males, 115 pounds for females.

Great Pyrenees

Well able to take extremes of weather, the Great Pyrenees makes an excellent guard, excepting those individuals who seem utterly lacking in responsibility to guard their homes, much less stay there.

Height: The male will average above 30 inches at the shoulder, and the female several inches less.

Weight: Males will often weigh more than 120 pounds, and the females about 90 to 110 pounds.

Kuvasz

With a very limited number of this breed to observe, it would seem that the percentage of good guards among them is high.

Height: Males will average close to 27 inches at the shoulder; the females are slightly smaller.

Weight: An average male in good condition will weigh 80 to 95 pounds, the female about ten pounds less.

Newfoundland

A quiet and responsible home protector. He is outstanding with children.

Height: Males 27 to 29 inches, and females about 3 inches less.

Weight: Males, about 145 pounds; females, as much as 30 pounds less.

Rottweiler

A dog of great physical force and exceptional biting power, a Rottweiler can hurt a man badly in a brief encounter.

Height: Males, 26 to 28 inches at the shoulder, and females about 2 inches less.

Weight: The Standard demands that the dog give the impression of tremendous power combined with freedom of movement for his height.

Saint Bernard

When a Saint Bernard qualifies in the tests for protectiveness, he's a lot of dog to push out of the way.

The Newfoundland is a black shadow but a comforting one.

Height: 27½ inches minimum for males, 25½ for females.
Weight: 110 pounds for females and up to 185 for males.

Standard Schnauzer

One of the smallest of the working group to be used as a man-stopper, he is strong and extremely agile. A good one has the faculty of doing the right thing in a fight with a human. Quite a few of the breed have interesting records in police and protection work.

Height: Males 20 inches, females about 19 inches.
Weight: His weight must provide exceptional sturdiness with flashing agility.

GROUP 4: TERRIERS

The advantages of some of the larger terrier breeds as compact-sized man-stoppers are well worth considering.

Airedale

The Airedale has been used as a conventional police dog in England and Europe, and for many years he was regarded as one of the best all-round dogs in this country. However, during World War II very few of the breed had the qualities needed for military use, generally failing to respond to agitation. In fact, it would seem that there is now an almost total lack of working ability in some strains, which means that an Airedale that is intended for use must be very carefully selected.

Height: Males about 24 inches at the shoulder, and females a bit less.
Weight: 55 to 65 pounds.

It is in the area of personal protection where a dog must combine a degree of friendliness with an ability to sense animosity that some of the terriers excel. Although the faculty for sensing a threat is possessed by terriers in general, it is seen in the fullest measure in the descendants of dogs that fought in the dog pit. Because the reason for this pronounced ability is often unrealized, it is well to explain it in some detail.

In order to survive, a working pit-dog had to be more than game. Some of the conditions for his survival were his ability to judge his opponent's intent instantly and accurately, his fighting strategy, and his great physical power. For generations the fighting breeds featured some families wherein every parent was of proven capability. Fortunately, some of these good qualities have filtered down to an occasional individual, and the sense of evaluation and capability that made great pit-dogs are used to determine and thwart the intent of threatening humans.

The next three breeds mentioned have at least some heritage from the dog-pit.

Bull Terrier

In either the white or colored variety a Bull Terrier, with his inherently good muscle tone, is a tremendous amount of dog for his size. However, while some American breeders have bred more for functional correctness and utility value, in England the concentration in recent years has been entirely on producing show dogs. This means that anyone considering a Bull Terrier for use should ask what his family has done, not what it looks like.

Height: Males of a good working size and type should stand 18 or 20 inches at the shoulders, and females about two inches less.
Weight: Males, 50 to 60 pounds; females, 45 to 50 pounds.

Kerry Blue

The Kerry is smaller than the other man-stopping terriers, but he has a demoralizing agility that can make a person look ridiculous.

Height: Males of good size will stand 20 inches at the shoulder; females are only slightly smaller than males.
Weight: Males will weigh from 35 to 40 pounds, and the females will average a bit less.

48

Bull Terriers have a knack of getting there at the right time.

The essence of power and courage, a Staffordshire Terrier can be trained to ignore other dogs.

Staffordshire Terrier

The "Staff" is another one of those breeds that is brought to the highest levels of usefulness by obedience training. When he has had such training, he is one of the greatest of all dogs. To the great surprise of those who regard him only as a "fighting dog," he accepts the presence of other animals and will focus his outstanding abilities on the job of being a companion and protector. He has the senses, intelligence, and strength to do many different jobs. No other breed has such a documentable record of gameness. Because of his overall strength and hard bite, a Staffordshire can be much smaller than the averages given below and still be all the dog needed to be a man-stopper.

Height: Males, 18 to 20 inches; females a bit less.
Weight: Males, 50 to 60 pounds; females, 50 to 55 pounds.

There are more than a dozen other terriers, varying in size from the Irish Terrier, which stands about 18 inches at the shoulder and weighs close to 30 pounds, down to breeds the size of the Australian Terrier, which is about 10 inches tall and weighs from 12 to 15 pounds.

The fact that the ancestors of all of these breeds were rugged fighters of such animals as the fox and badger makes it easy to understand why they have lots of ability. Being small, when these terriers bark, they do not usually frighten callers, so they can qualify nicely as inoffensive alarm dogs. But when one is highly protective, he can back up his oversized mouth with a courage that is equally large and spell trouble with an authority that makes him double as a threat dog.

You will get the greatest satisfaction from one of these terriers if he is selected from a line in which working ability has been favored.

GROUP 5: THE TOYS

The Toy breeds have advantages that are often overlooked. They possess exceptionally keen senses which make them excellent alarm dogs; and, because of their small size, they can be used in places where any real threat to callers could not be permitted. Some Toys have exceptionally tough constitutions, are long-lived, and the rough-coated ones can take extremes of temperature as well as most dogs.

50

This Australian Terrier has plenty of courage and the teeth to match it.

A Toy can announce a customer's arrival without frightening him.

The way to find a good, sensible Toy dog is by contacting good, sensible breeders.

Group 6: Non-Sporting Dogs

Chow Chow

In some situations this breed is one of the best of personal guard dogs. For reasons of exceptional loyalty and strong habit patterns, adults do not usually adapt well to change. He who chooses a Chow should start with a pup.

> *Height:* 17–21 inches.
> *Weight:* 45–65 pounds.

Dalmatian

This breed is well worth testing for personal guard dog purposes. He has enough speed and strength to do the job, fits well into a house or car, and is generally very clean.

> *Height:* 20–25 inches.
> *Weight:* 55–65 pounds.

While these figures are slightly higher than those given in the Standard, many breeders maintain that few Dalmatians bred today are as small as the Standard recommends.

The recommendations in this chapter are backed up by extensive experience and research in the areas of obedience classes, field dog classes, kennel operations, and discussions with knowledgeable persons. They are intended to refer you to where the hunting is best, not as absolutes. If chance takes you to an individual dog of an unmentioned breed who seems to be a good prospect, give him a try. The techniques you will use in finding and testing prospects will accredit the good dogs and eliminate those that are unsuitable.

So that you will be reminded that your probability of developing an effective guard dog depends more on the selection of a suitable prospect than on your way with dogs, review Chapter 3 on the experience of the trainers at Guide Dogs For The Blind.

9. AGE AND SEX

The following two questions are common to the selection of any type of protection dog, regardless of breed.

The Best Age?

Here are the most significant advantages of an adult prospect:

1. He can demonstrate his ability to you.
2. In most cases, he will be ready for use sooner than a puppy would.
3. He requires less care than a puppy.

The most significant advantages of a puppy prospect are:

1. In a complex home situation, a puppy will often adjust more satisfactorily.
2. You will find more pups than grown dogs available.
3. A pup will have a longer use potential than a grown dog would.

Any exceptions to these generalities will be explained in the proper places.

Which Sex?

You will be wise to choose a prospect on the basis of merit rather than because of its sex. Unless you have a particularly difficult situation, the seasons of a female will cause no problems that cannot be met by a little common sense and suggestions from a pet shop. Spaying is not an answer; it nearly always lessens a female's effectiveness. Again, concentrate on finding the best prospects for protection work, whether male or female.

10. LEADS TO DOGS

The sources you may use to obtain leads to both adult and puppy prospects are the same for all three types of protection dogs. Because you should consider only prospects whose backgrounds can be readily checked out in some detail, such sources as pounds and animal shelters, where for good reasons the names of former owners are not revealed, can be eliminated. Start your search by contacting persons who may be able to refer you to the owners of available dogs about which full information is obtainable. Among the good places for leads are veterinary hospitals, the lists of breeders in pet shops, boarding kennels, and breeding kennels. People in such places know of dogs and pups which their customers regard as desirable enough to deserve the best in food and care, but which for some reason must be sold. Dog magazines can supply additional information. There is an outside chance that the classified section of your newspaper may mention a dog worth checking. It is possible that an ad of your own, giving your needs and the fact that such a suitable dog will be greatly appreciated, will interest a reader who has a good dog to place. This emphasis on "purpose" will weed out owners who may wish to unload undesirable pets. The American Kennel Club (51 Madison Avenue, New York, N.Y. 10010) and the Canadian Kennel Club (667 Yonge St., Toronto, Ontario) can supply you with the names and addresses of breeders near you.

You will find that your leads will speedily multiply, and very soon you will have an interesting fund of information gleaned from the people you'll meet and the books you'll find in your local library and other places.

In addition to the procedures for finding a dog, there is another area of interest common to all types of protection dogs. This is the possibility of an undesirable feature which might make an otherwise good dog unsuitable for a particular situation. For example, an excellent guard dog whose one fault is chewing shrubs may be valuable to a machine shop but hardly acceptable in a nursery.

Here are some of the faults to check against your own requirements:

Excessive barking.
Hole digging.
Destructive chewing.
Unclean house habits.
Over-exuberance.
Over-aggressiveness.

All further appraisals and decisions must be made on the basis of the particular service that the dog is expected to supply. As you have seen, specific instructions for testing and choosing each kind of dog have been included in the material on its own category.

A reminder: Regardless of how healthy the pup or dog of your choice appears, one condition of final acceptance should be the approval of a veterinarian.

11. STARTING RIGHT

In the case of a good dog, where loyalty is strong, adjustment to a new master may take several months or more, which from the standpoint of urgency gives the adult only a slight advantage over a pup. Trying to shorten the period of adjustment by forcing yourself on the dog will only jeopardize your chances of establishing the best relationship with him. Any capable, courageous dog will have to be introduced to a new house more carefully than would a mere pet. You can't show him a receipt for payment and expect him to transfer his strong loyalties to you instantly.

There is a procedure which will give you the best chance of successfully installing a dog in your home. Begin by making enough visits to the prospect's owner at his home to cause the dog to regard you with some familiarity. It's hard to butter up a good dog, and his acceptance of you will depend more on his master's honest interest in talking to you than on any cajoling. When and if the dog seems to feel that your moves are pretty much beyond suspicion, you can do a few little things for him in a casual, not bribing, manner, such as opening a door or putting a pan of water down for him.

There is a simple routine which can do much to help you earn the trust of a strange dog. I have used it in those cases where it has been necessary to borrow a dog for an incidental scene in a motion picture. Simply walk somewhere with the owner and his dog; then, when the owner hands you the leash, wait until he has had enough time to walk out of sight to a predesignated spot, and then take the dog to him. You will be amazed to see how rapidly this combination of the owner placing the dog in your care and you justifying his confidence by taking the dog to him can increase the dog's trust in you.

By your own observations and the answers to your questions, learn all you can about the dog's habits and reactions in various situations. Find out the amount of obedience training he has had. Plan on duplicating some of his schedule and environment for at least the first few weeks he is in your home to give some familiar feeling to his new surroundings. Have his quarters ready before you bring him home so his new situation will have a good, permanent feel. Check to see that his area of confinement is secure, because until he's "your dog" he will try to head back to his former home. Chapter 1 in Section 2 has much information that will be useful to you, particularly if your dog is to live outside. *The section on poison-proofing will help you foil those who would harm your dog.*

Take the dog to your place when your schedule will permit you to spend at least a couple of days with him without having to leave for more than a few hours. Don't force yourself on him to the point where he feels you are a pest who will give him no privacy. Instead, make a lot of contacts with him as a logical part of feeding and caring for him so that he will feel you are a sensible as well as an authoritative person. Let him have several days to look things over at his own tempo; then start doing a few routine things with him while he is on leash. Lots of practice in handling a dog correctly is a prerequisite to authority during times of excitement, as well as a means of building a bond between him and his new owner.

Rarely will an adult dog who shows strong protectiveness in his home transfer his attention equitably to all members of a new family, and chances of success are not increased by goodies and games. *Have it understood that no member of the household cancels out your good work by handling him improperly. Don't make the mistake of trying your dog with mock tests. Inviting friends over to see how your dog protects you will only confuse and blunt him.*

After the dog becomes accustomed to his change of homes, some further training can be used to bring about the fullest acceptance of his new master. In addition to providing closer orientation with his household, obedience training will increase the dog's composure, thus making him more aware of what's right and wrong with his surroundings.

Do It Right

You would be inviting trouble by not recognizing the need for following the correct procedures when installing any courageous dog in your home—particularly one who is protective. A dog who has demonstrated a willingness to fight a man is not the best thing to have around if he is uncertain or uncontrollable. *If there is anything that might keep you from installing an adult protection dog properly, do the sensible thing: Start with a pup.*

12. TRAINING

You have carefully selected your dog for those natural qualities of temperament that are useful to your particular purpose, so he will start to function in his new environment without any specialized training or encouragement from you. However, there are several things that obedience training can do to increase your dog's value as a useful, happy companion.

First of all, it is a lot less discouraging to a dog to give him training that will enable you to bring him under control with a command after you have admitted someone to his presence, than to bluntly shut him off from the sight of each caller you welcome. Secondly, an obedience trained dog is more composed, thoughtful, and is generally much more aware of his environment. The more emotionally stable a dog is, the more alert and discriminating he will be.

Obedience training can protect both you and your dog. A dog that can convince a caller that he is formidable would convince the police of the same thing. In the case of a bite under questionable circumstances, you may be asked to show just what control you have over your dog. You had better have some.

The obedience section will provide you with any instruction you may need. It covers your obedience training relationship with your dog and will help you correct problems in his conduct should any occur.

13. THE PUPPY PROSPECT

A puppy that is being considered for a specific purpose must be chosen primarily on the promise that his breeding makes, rather than on the impression he makes. Unlike the adult dog who demonstrates what his character is like at maturity, the pup—except one produced by a stable breeding program—is unable to give more than an inkling of his future abilities. Your best indication of what he will be like when grown will come from your knowledge of what his ancestors were like, and particularly what his brothers and sisters from previous litters, if any, are like. Because the qualities that will later make him an effective protection dog will stem from his inheritance rather than from his master's influence, it can be costly for you to make the common mistake of ignoring the probability that a pup will resemble his parents in behavior as well as appearance. These facts add up to one more way of saying that odds favor the purebred.

Each of the chapters dealing with a type of personal protection dog includes suggestions on the kind of dog suitable to its classification. If you have read these chapters carefully, you have probably decided on the classification of dog best suited to your needs and have given thought to the kinds of dogs you would consider. Continue to think of prospects from the standpoint of future usefulness, so that you won't be influenced by that puppy appeal which sometimes promises things that never materialize.

The information contained in Chapters 7 through 10 on dogs and how to find them applies to pups as well as adult dogs.

You will soon be hearing about puppies that are available. Before you look at any prospect, explain to its owner that, because you need a dog for work, you must see evidence that any pup you consider comes from stock with good potential, and that you must obtain such evidence by actually testing one or both parents and other closely related dogs. This proposition will scare away those breeders who have nothing to offer but their own emotions.

Carefully review the instructions on how to test adult prospects for your needs. As has been said before, these tests will be used in exactly the same manner to test the available relatives of every pup you consider. Keeping these procedures well in mind when you talk to breeders will help you explain your needs and make arrangements.

As you look at pups and check out the potential of their breeding, you should keep in mind that you are seeking a future worker, not a pet. Your choice should be based on performance, not prejudice. This means you should consider as many suitable kinds of puppies as are available. The one whose family shows you the most favorable characteristics is likely to be the kind of dog you can use.

Do not make the mistake of settling for a poor prospect that appeals to you personally, because you've kidded yourself into believing that you can substitute your influence for the qualities his heritage did not provide. Do not accept a pup who appears inferior, regardless of what may be claimed for his breeding. Although good breeding produces good results percentagewise, there are variables. Occasionally a pup, or a whole litter, will fail to inherit the good qualities which were sought. Avoid a pup who retreats unreasonably from strange sights and sounds, or who growls or barks from a corner. Such a pup will rarely make a satisfactory protection dog. The ideal prospect would combine boldness with awareness and initiative. The proper reserve will come later.

As to physical soundness, accept no pup until a veterinarian has checked him. You are not equipped to detect some of the troubles which you might acquire in an unsound pup.

Age

The age at which a puppy can best go into a home and begin a useful life has been the subject of many conflicting opinions. It is true that there are advantages in taking a pup between the ages of seven weeks and four months, but a good prospect, who had a favorable puppy experience, can be adapted to a new situation when he is as much as a year old. The best evidence of this fact is probably the success of Guide Dog schools in taking pups, even as loyal as the German Shepherd, that have been raised by 4-H Club members to almost a year, and installing them in training programs preparatory to making another change when they leave the school in the service of the blind. Certainly this long record of success proves that a good pup, who had the proper care and some early training, can be adapted to a new situation when he is as much as a year old.

Housing the Pup

You should decide on how your pup will be housed and confined, and make arrangements accordingly, before you bring him home. If he is to be kept outside, provide a secure area where he will not be subjected to contact with persons other than yourself, whether well-meaning or not, when you are absent. He should have a comfortable house, draft-free and small enough for his body heat to warm it, not one of those monstrosities that are made by wood specialty yards and which are several times too big, with a huge door placed incorrectly. Make sure his shade is adequate during the warm hours of the day. The more care you show in making him comfortable, the more he will feel that he has really "come home."

You may have facilities to house your pup now and when he grows up, but you will get some useful information by carefully reading all of Chapter 1 in Section 2. *The part on poison-proofing applies to pups as well as grown dogs.*

Feeding

Because the brands and types of puppy foods available vary from one locality to another, the best advice on feeding your puppy will come from a qualified person in your area. A successful kennel operator, a veterinarian, or the manager of a good pet shop are some sources of information. A good basic diet for grown dogs and older pups is described in Section 2.

Bringing Him Home

Arrange to bring your pup home at a time of the week that will give you the longest uninterrupted period with him. This will make it possible for you to work out any unforeseen problems of his adjustment by leaving him for varying periods, then returning unexpectedly and quietly to see how he reacts to your absence. Also, the occasions of your return will give him confidence that you will come back to him. There will be benefits from letting him get the full picture of the normal environment and schedule at your place, so spend a lot of time with him but, above all, do not baby him into yakking like a spoiled brat whenever he's left alone.

The Right Start

If he should whine and yelp excessively after he's had five or six days to adjust, you'll have to start correcting him. For a small amount, you can prevent a mistake common even among experienced kennel people, that of making it possible for the dog to run away from correction. By equipping your pup with a snug collar from which a piece of light line is dragging, you can speedily convince him that, if he tries to avoid correction by holing up under something, he'll be brought out rapidly and quite uncomfortably. It's amazing how the presence of this light line can cause a pup to do a bit of reasoning. If the line is of slick material, it will not catch on things, and there's not much chance of your dog being caught and choked by it. Use a line that would not hold the pup's dead weight if you feel your situation would permit such an accident.

After a few times of snarling "out!" at him when he's creating a noise nuisance, he'll respond to your reproof with a show of guilt. From that time on, when he offends, rush back to the line—not the dog—and work your way to the collar; then give him a good shaking and sting his upper thighs a bit with a folded belt. No, such discouragement from a senseless practice will not blunt his alarm potential. And don't worry that he's too young to learn. Regardless of your pup's age, your hand will be forced if you have neighbors.

Your puppy prospect's future good judgment as a personal protection dog will depend considerably on his having a full puppyhood. If he sees quite a bit of what is normal in your environment, he'll be more certain to detect anything that is not normal. Such things as walks and

64

companionship are much better recreation for a puppy prospect than games and toys. Above all, do not play ball with your pup, nor permit anyone else to do so. Ball-playing generally grows into an obsession that can ruin a dog for protection work.

Long before your pup is old enough to begin serious obedience work, he can be helped by a program of planned puppy training. It has now been established that there is hardly a limit to how young a pup can learn. You will accomplish much and risk nothing by studying the obedience section of this book, and then teaching your pup, according to its instructions, all he can learn, omitting any corrections until he is six months old or until he tells you with a show of guilt that he knows he disobeyed. This policy will prevent any possibility of corrections being made too soon.

Beginning on page 183 of the obedience section, you will find methods of dealing with such things as housebreaking, chewing, and other specific problems. Unless the problem is too pressing, you should wait until your puppy has had the benefit of full obedience training before you resort to any strong corrective measures.

In addition to being the basis for preventing and correcting conduct problems in dogs, thorough obedience training gives the dog the stability and composure to keep his mind open to what takes place around him. Nothing can equal obedience training as a means of gaining a complete understanding between master and dog. With the promise of many benefits in mind, be conscientious in your obedience training.

You will use much time and care in the choosing of a pup. It is my hope that you will be rewarded by years of comfort and security which his future protectiveness will provide.

II. The Police Dog

1. INTRODUCTION: THE ATTACK-TRAINED DOG

The attack training of a dog is not accomplished by a process of teaching and enforcement. Instead, learning is caused by supplying experiences that develop the dog's hunting instincts and cause him to classify certain humans as "game" to be hunted and fought. These experiences are described by the term *agitation*.

Agitation consists of systematically offending and teasing the dog in steps that are carefully calculated to cause him to express his resentment, each of which ceases rewardingly the moment the dog reacts properly. For example, at the first session, if a shabbily dressed agitator approaches the dog in a peculiar, uncertain manner, and the dog does no more than show suspicion, the man immediately retreats. Such a cowardly retreat does more than merely confirm the dog's suspicion that the man was a human varmint. Along with the victory, the dog gets a boost in confidence.

The formula of carefully increasing the threat, confirming the dog's judgment, and deepening his confidence with a victory is followed until the dog is fully awakened to the joys of hunting "human varmints," and is confident that he can defeat any one of them he finds.

A dog who experiences this agitation doesn't merely change to some degree: he undergoes a transmutation that lifts him up to a high level of usefulness. Although at times he has been brought up to a point of white-hot anger, he does not become a hater of mankind. He becomes a hunter and fighter of humans who act in certain ways or intrude into certain places.

It is this "varmintiness," instilled through agitation, that becomes the motivating factor in a police dog, a plant protection dog, and in some kinds of military dogs. These jobs vary some in the amount and type of agitation that each will need, but at least the first 4 levels are basic to each of them.

2. TIME-TESTED

No one can state the objectives of the training and use of a police dog without immediately involving himself in the philosophy of police work. He must be able to say that what he proposes is the best in the areas of both effectiveness and public relations. Effectiveness in the mechanics of detecting, pursuing, combating, and transporting a suspect will manifest itself early during the dog's training. The second factor, good public relations, is somewhat less predictable as to the time it will become evident and, in fact, its existence is very much a matter of definition by those concerned. For example, there are many—too many—chiefs of police to whom good public relations means deference to minority groups, small in number but loud in voice. At times when logic and personnel problems have forced action in favor of installing a dog, the attitude of these chiefs shows that they would like a dog that merely barks, or has rubber teeth.

I know of several department heads who, in healthy contrast to the above "public servants," define good public relations in another way. They feel that a choice must be made—and it seems such choices must be made with increasing frequency—in favor of giving the fullest possible public service to the useful citizens who form the quiet majority.

It may be that some of the more timid chiefs who read this will believe that I am not familiar with the complications of their office. In turn, I suspect that many of them have been so nervously occupied with being inoffensive that they have failed to notice that there are departments that have won the endorsement of a decisive majority through bold and definite methods of enforcement.

There is such a chief who heads a dynamic department in a small city completely surrounded by four other cities, two of which are very large. He employs men and dogs in such a fair but positive manner that the undesirable elements respect his town's boundaries in a way that is actually amusing. Citizens proudly compare their community's low crime rate with the rates for the bordering towns. The chief compares them, too—whenever laments are raised against his policies. As he points to the record, he lets one and all know that he'll gladly resign if the community would like to replace him with a more conciliatory man. The voice of approval from the appreciative majority continues to drown out the whines. This chief's good public relations can be explained in a single word—results!

In your task of providing evidence of the success of police dog programs, it will avail little to review the early history of the police dog's employment, because those who need convincing may claim that such functions are inapplicable to modern times. It is also advisable to omit reference to the accomplishments of individuals who have trained and used police dogs because, even though successful, they would not have the official approval of a police force. Instead, references should be confined to modern, organized programs which you can easily verify.

In his book, *Forty Years with Dogs,* Lieutenant Colonel E. H. Richardson describes the use of police dogs prior to World War I by the Queen's Park Division in Glasgow. According to Lieutenant Colonel Richardson, two Airedales were used with great success in the residential district of Pollokshields.

A clipping from a Liverpool, England paper of this same time comments:

> Twenty dogs are maintained and are under excellent control; no person has ever complained of having been molested or frightened by the animals. While speaking of the work of the dogs in the Mersey seaport, the chief constable mentioned that one of the Airedales and a constable were able to effect the arrest of six men who had been attempting to commit a crime.

A statement by the chief constable of Nottingham is evidence that even a mounted patrolman was made more effective by a dog:

> Since taking over the command of the borough constabulary I have found it necessary to have regular mounted patrols in the outlying portions of the borough. These patrols are very useful, and are incentive to reduce the commission of crime. The police dogs are a distinct acquisition to the force, particularly in connection with patrolling the outside districts. They are powerful, sensible animals, and are regularly exercised and trained for police duties. They have proved most useful in finding persons secreted in out-of-the-way places and followed and stopped others at some distance away whom the police were desirous of overhauling, but would have failed to get in touch with without the dogs' assistance. They are valuable companions to constables patrolling lonely beats.

In 1944, a quarter of a century after the above information was released, the London police "discovered that dogs could outrun the thugs that infested such places as Hyde Park. It was found that the shrubbery which screened the lawless from police offered small protection against dogs. Other cities in England have benefited similarly from using dogs."

In the United States, the city of Berkeley, California began using dogs in some areas of special need about 1939. Citizens of that town still remember the time a group of students from the nearby campus staged a predicted rush on a local theatre and were met by two Dobermans. None wanted to be the first to try the dogs. Soon all decided to leave without demanding time for discussions.

In 1957, letters to a Baltimore newspaper by readers, who had read of the effectiveness of Scotland Yard's police dogs, came to the attention of Police Commissioner James M. Hepron. His suggestion that Baltimore try dogs resulted in donations of both dogs and the service of trainers. Before the training of these first few dogs was completed, they helped make a few arrests. The small number of dogs were made to seem like many by shuttling them around to different areas, and their effectiveness encouraged enlargement of the program. By November 1959 this force had 20 dogs covering 92 square miles of problem area with a resultant drop in crime.

In St. Louis, Missouri, men like Major Andrew T. Aylward, Commander of the Bureau of Services, installed a dog program, and, more importantly, gave information and encouragement to other interested police departments.

Salt Lake City, Utah is another city that has used dogs with success, and has shared its fund of information with other organizations.

By 1963, Chicago, Illinois had a dog corps strength of 57 animals. The city's Crime Analysis Bureau evaluates the current crime activity patterns and assigns the dogs accordingly.

In Miami Beach, Florida, dog patrols are used to deter the jewel and fur thieves who descend on this resort town every winter.

The following are additional cities that have used dogs successfully: Newark, N.J.; Cleveland, Ohio; New Rochelle, N.Y.; Camden, N.J.; Englewood, N.J.; Portland, Oregon; and Dearborn, Michigan.

Recently, police departments in many smaller cities have increased their efficiency with police dogs. An outstanding example of a small city operation is that of Hermosa Beach, California. These dogs, trained and installed by Jack Felton of San Bernardino, California, reflect the high standards of law enforcement that characterize Chief Berlin and his force. Chief Ray McClean of the Montclair, California police department was one of the first department heads in the complex Southern California area to make good use of dogs. Chiefs McClean and Berlin are known to be two of the most outstanding police officials in one of America's most heavily populated areas.

In each place where police dogs are used, a significant drop in crime has been reported, which poses some interesting questions. Why, after an initial success, should the effectiveness of a police dog program ever decline? The answer is quite simple. At the start of a program, the personnel involved in the program are interested in learning about this phase of law enforcement. However, as time passes, because of politics or routine replacements in personnel the dogs may be brought under the administration and handling of uninterested or prejudiced persons who feel they need not have any special instruction to administer the program. Never has decline in effectiveness been due to the lessening of a properly handled dog's potential.

Another question often asked is, "Why haven't more cities acknowledged the proven value of dogs?" There are two possible answers to this question: First, a completely illogical prejudice against police dogs, and second, hesitancy on the part of police officials who claim that the guns their officers carry are less offensive to the minority groups than dogs would be. How even the most muddled mind could arrive at the premise that dogs agitated during their attack training by Caucasians could be motivated by prejudice against nonwhites or other minority groups is something that cannot be readily understood.

In Los Angeles, where the use of dogs has been strongly rejected, the point of not offending an individual's dignity has been honored to the ultimate degree. During the city's recent Watts riots, in at least several instances where dogs could have changed the course of action, gunfire provided some individuals with a guarantee that their dignity would be permanently protected against offense. They're dead.

3. PERSPECTIVE

In the preface to this book you read my statement that I am aware of the questions in your mind as you contemplate the use of police dogs. There is a problem, first in order and importance, that has probably not yet occurred to you. If you solve this first problem, your police dog program should succeed regardless of other difficulties. If you do not solve this first problem, your other efforts are doomed to failure.

Simply stated, this problem is one of acquiring a full perspective on police-dog work and being able to communicate it authoritatively to all concerned with the program. From the patrolman who is trying to convince his superiors of the many values a good dog would have on night patrols in parks and problem areas, on up through the chief who must patiently respond to questions on effectiveness and economy in all the operations of his force, the answers must be clear and comprehensive. You will learn quite soon that this demand for information from many areas is inevitable. In response to this civic-accountability, I will try to present the material in a way that will give you a full perspective that is qualified by logic and conclusiveness. Gain and hold this perspective. It is the biggest step you can take in the use of police dogs and in warranting the proud support of understanding officials and a grateful community.

The man sneered out through the window of the general store at the Malamute lying on the front porch. His hand went to his hip pocket and came back with a detective-model .32 caliber revolver with a two-inch barrel. "I've got my dogs right here," he said.

It was more than a sneer the private patrolman had turned on my dog that lit my fuse. I had been talking to the wife of the man who ran the store in the town of Woodside, where I lived while serving as a principal trainer at the War Dog Reception and Training Center, San Carlos, California during World War II. The Dog Center was a subject of interest to most of the people who lived in the area, and the woman had asked the stock question, "How are all the dogs?"

Before I could have answered, the "protection man" had grabbed at an opportunity to express his disdain for the dog family. If I needed more than his tone of voice to tell me he was incompetent, the stubby gun in his hand sufficed. Woodside at that time was on the edge of a primitive area, with houses far apart; any chases were certain to be over a lot of geography and any shots pretty apt to be long ones. Since I had a fairly good knowledge of guns, I knew that any action could better be met by shotgun or rifle, certainly nothing less than a police sidearm of conventional barrel length. Even a competent man could do little with a two-inch tube. And the fact that the man glowering at me would depend on such a weapon showed me he was not competent, so I made my offer:

"Let's find out how my one dog compares with your six," I suggested. "Tonight we'll set up some problems. I'll break and run on ten straight trails. You give me a 30-second start, then try to stop me with your 'six dogs.' Then you make ten breaks, and I'll give you a 30-second start and I'll send my dog. We'll bet ten dollars a break. And just so you aren't worried about your 'deadly weapon' you can use a long-barreled air gun. It won't be deadly, but it'll shoot straighter than that thing."

He looked at the powerful dog and his sneer sagged. He mumbled a hollow "I'd like to, but I couldn't," put his "six dogs" in his pocket, and went out.

It was plain that the "inadvisability" of shooting at anyone with an air gun was not what was in his mind. My offer had crystallized for him what little chance a 30-second start would have given him to outrun the dog.

Though the beautiful Malamute, which I had trained in several war-dog routines, is a cherished memory, the advantages a good dog can bring to many areas of police work are just as significant now as when the above incident occurred. Some of the most discerning men in police work have concluded that the complexities of society are increasing, not diminishing, the number of situations where dogs are needed.

A few moments' thought will show anyone why the speed of a dog can be a tremendous factor, physically and psychologically, in those instances where a suspect must be apprehended while on foot. In addition to the obvious advantages of on-the-scene apprehension, there is another factor in these times of fast cars and crowded streets. Chases that dogs can resolve while the suspects are still on foot often develop into mechanized nightmares when the suspect reaches his or someone else's car ahead of pursuit. Certainly a means of taking a suspect on foot whenever possible is more necessary today than it was when cars were less available.

Parks, railroad yards, and cemeteries are but a few sections of a city where in the event of a chase, the dog's speed would be an asset. In the more congested parts of a city a good dog can stop a running man without any of the hazards to the innocent that gunfire would bring.

More common than the foot chase that ends in a car is the one that begins when a boxed-in suspect abandons a car—his or another's—and takes off on foot. That race will end abruptly when a pursuing policeman opens the door of his own car for an eager dog. As to the psychological effect of a dog riding about town in a prowl car, it is amazing how a dog's presence can discourage the fastest footracers.

For no apparent reasons, police problems seem to feature certain types and patterns peculiar to a time and place. If your community is plagued by delinquents, old or young, who literally try to outrun the law, acquaint yourself with the physical and psychological potential of a good dog.

"How would you take a sentry post covered by a man and a dog?" This question was often asked of rookies at the war dog centers. Generally it brought more questions, instead of answers, to the minds of the listeners. Significantly, the actions of a man are more predictable than those of a dog; because of this, it is quite easy to time an assault on the human sentry but almost impossible to make a simultaneous attack on his dog, who is watching, listening, and scenting with powers much greater than those of mankind. Failure to coördinate such an attack perfectly would result in an alarm, and the sentry post would have fulfilled its purpose.

The virtual impossibility of surprising a man and dog team was a great comfort to soldiers during the war. It can be equally comforting to a policeman who would like to have more than just his own senses while probing along a lonely night beat.

This chapter cannot help you estimate a police dog's effectiveness in areas such as railroad yards, cemeteries, and parks unless we emphasize the potential of one of his senses that is universally unappreciated. This is his sense of smell when applied to the detection of breeze-borne scents. This alerting to the scent of an individual borne by air that is free of other equally fresh human scents describes the function of our military scout dogs. Consider the significance of some of the tests run on these dogs.

Before assigning our dogs to scout-dog duty, we carefully checked the range of their noses. We had dogs capable of pinpointing a man 500 yards away on a mild breeze. A dog that reacted consistently to "a man on the wind" at a distance of 400 yards was only average. There have been countless times when the right dog, "hung on the wind," could have thoroughly scouted out a deserted park in a matter of minutes, saving much of the time wasted by men who had only the senses of sight and hearing to help them.

You can be silent, but have you ever tried to be scentless?

What happens after the detection and successful pursuit of a suspect?

Traditionally, the suspect should submit to custody. We find a growing element that does not respect tradition nor the physical person of a policeman. Resistance to arrest, often with aid from police-hating allies, is becoming quite common. Think of the cases where a policeman, reluctant to defend himself with his gun, has been set upon and severely beaten. Contrast this with the ease with which a policeman, equipped with a dog, has controlled a mob among which no individual is ready to volunteer as the dog's first target. In these successes there is no outnumbered policeman who must wait for the development of exact situations before he dares to draw his gun for so much as a threat. There is no indecision to encourage the pack, only the certainty in the way his alerted dog squares off to meet the first aggressive move.

A good dog is an effective fighter. A top dog, properly trained, is an overpowering fighter. Later we will consider the many elements, physical and psychological, which make a dog so effective in combat against a man.

You may be asking, after reading the foregoing facts, why police dog programs ever fail. Again, it can be said that, regardless of whether a failure appears to be caused by a handler, a dog, or a situation, basically it can be ascribed to inadequate education of some individual.

If the information in this chapter suggests that the police dog could serve your department, proceed with confidence. Be certain that all concerned should know what a good police dog is, how he can be best used, and how he is obtained. The other problems will diminish as you work toward this first objective.

In front or behind, he's a policeman's best friend.

4. FINDING A PROSPECT

What kind of dog makes a satisfactory police dog? How does one obtain a candidate dog for police training? You need more than answers to these questions. You need qualifications for those answers, some of which will be immediately forthcoming. Other qualifications will materialize as you progress with your training program. On the strength of this promise, I am going to ask you to follow my advice without reservation or modification in the task of procuring the best prospects.

Your questions will concern the dog's physical and temperamental qualities. Because it is the more easily accomplished of the two tasks, we will eliminate the physically unsuitable before screening out the dogs who lack the proper temperament.

A physical description of a dog best begins with reference to his breed. Although there are many breeds capable of doing police work, some of the breeds are so few in numbers as to be generally unavailable for testing. However, with the possibility that one or more of them can be found in your locality, I'll mention them along with the more common breeds.

Airedale Terrier
Belgian Sheepdog

Bouvier des Flandres
Boxer
Briard
Doberman Pinscher
German Shepherd
Giant Schnauzer

Other breeds have been used as specialists, such as the Bull Terrier and Staffordshire Terrier, whose heritage of superior courage and fighting ability has qualified them for police work where physical combat was known to be unavoidable. Pages 40 through 50 give brief discriptions of the above breeds.

Most officers and law forces would benefit more by concentrating on the general purpose police dog until such time as experience in training and handling, together with a definite need, warrants the employment of one of the "specialists."

Your search for dogs on the suitable list can be made thoroughly and rapidly if you follow a systematic procedure. Veterinarians, pet supply stores, commercial kennels, and animal regulation departments can give you the names of the breeders of purebred dogs in your area who, though they might not have the breeds you seek, can give you prospective leads. The American Kennel Club, 51 Madison Avenue, New York, N.Y. 10010, can supply you with the names and addresses of breeders near you. Ads in newspapers, dog magazines, and sporting magazines can furnish others.

When you talk to breeders, remember you're asking for help, so don't irritate them by calling their purebred dogs "thoroughbreds." Soon the references and bits of information which these contacts provide will lead you to other breeders who may be active in the suitable breeds and who, if they have no prospects to show you, may know of a grown male that may be available as a candidate.

It is true that "handsome is as handsome does," but it is also true that one factor of a police dog's effectiveness is the impression he makes. A seedy looking dog does not make an authoritative impression on the suspect he confronts, nor on the city officials who appropriate the money for his installation and maintenance. In view of this fact, it might be well for you to equip yourself with a book listing the breed standards of perfection for each of the breeds you examine. Such books are obtainable in all libraries and in most good book stores and pet shops. The standard will provide a convenient checklist for calling attention to factors you might otherwise overlook. Though some parts of a breed's standard are irrelevant to a dog's functional capacity, it does emphasize some points that are fundamental to his physical ability.

5. SCREENING

Unless you have had a lot of experience with dogs, you will find it useful to have someone with a general knowledge of the subject to accompany you on your survey. It would not be feasible to pay for the opinion of a veterinarian or professional dog man until you have located a dog that is worth their consideration.

Most of the dogs to which your chain of referrals leads will be washed out by the tests you'll give them. Don't let this discourage you. Nearly everyone who looks for dogs for police work has to use this "prospecting" method. In other fields where dogs are employed, breeders are engaged in producing dogs for specific purposes, but there has not been enough use of police dogs to interest competent and dedicated breeders in the task of producing them. However, the essential qualities for police work are scattered through each of the breeds I've mentioned, and sometimes fortune favors an individual dog with all the requirements.

Before taking the time to look at a dog, ask whether he meets the age and sex requirements. While there have been some excellent female police dogs, a bitch can be lost to service during the time she is in season, and generally, if spayed, her aggressiveness and physical condition seem somewhat affected. So it is better to devote your time to finding a male. In most cases, a dog of less than a year could not reasonably be subjected to the testing and training for police work.

Unless he is of exceptional quality, or has basic obedience training, a dog older than three years has the disadvantage of a shorter career. If the owner cannot tell you his dog's age, go and look at him for signs which may enable you to estimate it.

When you go to a home or kennel to check a prospect, ask someone who is familiar with the dog to take him, on leash, into an area where there is room and good footing. You can better view the dog standing and moving if he can be maneuvered as you request. Also, some structural weaknesses are more apparent when a dog is walked or trotted on leash than when a gallop blurs the pattern of his action. Point by point, check the items on the following list.

Size. Any candidate you consider should meet the minimum standards of 23 inches at the shoulder and a weight of 65 pounds, or the maximum of roughly 28 inches at the shoulder and a weight of no more than 100 pounds. Probably the average dog you consider will stand close to 27 inches and weigh about 80 pounds. The small advantage gained by height and weight above this average will be offset by a decrease in speed and agility and inconvenience in transporting the dog in a car.

General Conformation. If there is anything freakish about the structure of a dog that makes him move in a clumsy or poorly balanced way, he won't be able to do the job. Ideally, a police dog should be able to travel the roughest ground and scale six-foot fences easily. If your candidate obviously couldn't qualify, rule him out.

Head. For effect as well as combat, big, sound, canine teeth, often dramatized as "fangs," are valuable. Examine them to see that they haven't been broken or worn down. A dog's usefulness will not be impaired by one broken canine tooth, but if more than that are in bad shape, eliminate him for physical reasons, and for other reasons which will be dealt with a bit later. If you are in doubt about the dog's age, check the incisors, the small teeth spaced in between the canines. If they are sharp, the dog is probably not more than two years old. If the edges are well worn, the dog is perhaps too old to warrant further interest.

The biting power of a dog seems to be as much a matter of overall muscle tone as it is structure. Therefore, if he's strong and vigorous he'll have enough "bite," even though he may lack the desirable deep underjaw, which by reason of the added leverage it affords does give some mechanical advantage.

While checking the dog's head, give consideration to his eyes for signs of visual defects. Though you are not prepared to test his hearing for sensitivity and orientation to sound, you can prove that he's not deaf by watching his reactions to a few soft, strange noises.

Legs and Feet. Strong, well angulated legs and firm, resilient feet are very desirable in all working dogs; however, evaluation should be made on the dog's performance, not on his appearance when standing. Persist until you have seen him move at all speeds: walk, trot, and hard-run off leash with quick changes of direction. A slow walk up a long stairway will often reveal a weakness that goes unnoticed when the dog is moving on the ground. Later, if your initial tests find the dog worthy of the expense, an examination by a veterinarian will protect you against unobserved deficiencies.

When the combination of you, your helper, the breed standard, and my suggestions has brought you to the conclusion that the dog qualifies physically, we'll begin the interesting task of testing his temperament.

6. TESTING

You can appraise a dog's qualifications for work more easily if you keep in mind the difference between disposition and temperament, two words that are often misused. Think of disposition as the attitude a dog intentionally expresses toward humans and other living things in situations where he should be compatible. It would refer to his being "sweet" or "grouchy," reliable or unreliable. Temperament is the complex of factors of instinct, emotion, and intelligence that determines a dog's use of the opportunities his environment affords. Certainly disposition is one factor of temperament, but it is only one of a great many factors. A few others are courage, hunting instinct, alertness, and emotional stability. You'll see the need for these and many more as the selection and training of your police dog progresses. For further emphasis on the importance of considering all factors of a dog's temperament, rather than merely that of disposition, let's look at a couple of examples.

I recall a coon hound who was well known for two things: his tremendous cold-trailing ability, and his dislike of nearly all humans. He had the intensity, ability, and persistence to work out a track that left other dogs puttering in a senseless pattern. He was as honest as daylight. When his chop changed to a bawl, you knew the track was straightening out, and when the perfect meter of his tree-bark boomed through the night, you ran towards it. However, unlike most of his breed, he was ready to snap at a stranger who offered a friendly pat. His owner didn't pay much attention to the fault. He counted his coonskins and knew that even though his hound had a bad disposition he still scored pretty high in temperament.

One beagle I recall was quite unlike the coon hound. He had a warm, captivating regard for all humans, and a complete disinterest in the scent of game. I used every trick in a hound man's book to start him, but with no success. He had a wonderful disposition, but a poor temperament.

Often commercial kennels are called by the owner of a dog that has "turned vicious" and which the owner says would probably make a good police dog. How absurd. Though good disposition is but one factor of temperament, it is one of the essential factors in the case of a police dog—one of the many qualities you should look for in the dogs you check.

Actually, you began to learn things about the dog's temperament when you were checking his physical qualifications. If, when the dog was led out for your inspection, he hung back on the leash as though more concerned with avoiding you than staying with his master, you can be sure he would be even more cowardly away from his home. Forget him. If he had to be restrained from attacking you for no other reason than that you were available, and in other ways seemed irrational, try to find out something of his history. If he has a record of indiscriminate biting, don't gamble on him. On the other hand, if his record was not bad, and it seemed as though his handler was an ineffective person, it might be that he could be reclaimed by a proper obedience program and would be worth testing on strange ground. Some dogs that have been nagged into neurosis by ineffectual owners are not basically vicious and respond quickly to positive handling.

Equally as useless for your purpose as the truly "mean" dog is the "shy-sharp" individual. He shows the fangs of a tiger and the heart of a mouse. True, he may be quite alert and, when restrained by a leash, may make a blustering stand; but unrestrained, his character may cause him to hide behind his master or run away. If the situation in which you view him is such that you are unable to get a demonstration of his character, and you feel that he might be worth another look, there will be a way to test his mettle when you try him away from home.

Possibly it appears that the dog you go to see is completely unaware of your presence. Don't rule him out yet. His environment may be so constantly filled with the intrusion of children and neighbors that his awareness of strangers has been dulled. At least he doesn't fear your presence. He's well worth checking in another situation.

If the dog comes into the area, alerts on you, and then turns to other interests immediately, don't let his short attention discourage you. He's shown enough to make him worth another look.

If he comes into your presence alertly and boldly, approaches you with a dignified reserve, and after accepting you continues to be aware of your movements, you may have an outstanding prospect for further testing.

If the dog greets you as though you are an old playmate who has come to romp with him, don't write him off as hopeless. The fact that he isn't afraid of you means he's worth testing in another situation.

You can see that the first check on temperament, just a by-product of the physical evaluation, is treated rather casually. It is no more than an opportunity to eliminate the obviously unsuitable. Don't feel uneasy, thinking that you may be placing trust in a counterfeit. The proper tests for the essentials of temperament will not be casual—don't you be casual in applying them. It is necessary that you follow the exact procedures as they are given for making these tests. Omissions and shortcuts can only bring you expensive embarrassment.

For the first formal test, you'll need a quiet place where you can control what the dog will hear and see. Good examples would be a city yard in which equipment is maintained or industrial yards at times when the employees are not present. A rock and gravel company generally provides a good situation during its quiet hours.

Next, arrange for a man to help you who can follow directions capably, who is well coördinated, and is not known to the dog. In the process of testing, you should be an observer, never a participant. A raincoat and any kind of a hat with a brim will give your helper the appearance of a real "heavy." He should have a double-action revolver, or blank gun of any caliber, for shooting blanks; a single shot will not provide the rapid fire needed. If you have to buy a gun and live in a state with no gun restrictions, you may find a used, practical revolver a better choice than a regular blank gun. Have the cylinder of your gun fully loaded when you give it to the heavy.

You will need the help of the dog's owner, or someone the dog knows equally well, to act as handler. See that he's equipped with a strong collar, preferably of the mettle-training kind, and a heavy leather training leash six feet long.

Take time to plan your setup carefully. Provide a shed or building with a peephole or window near the door which your heavy will work

This test provides the moment of truth in selecting a dog for police work.

out of, so that he can time his assault to the dog's approach without revealing his own position.

To make certain that the dog doesn't see the heavy before the test, and to prevent any conversation between the heavy and handler, arrange for the handler to bring his dog to the area and meet you after the heavy is hidden. Explain exactly how he should proceed, with the dog held on the full length of leash, on a course that will take him by the building about ten feet from the door that the heavy will use. So that the surprise will be as great to himself as to his dog, tell him nothing of what is to happen, except to start on a casual walk when he hears your signal and to hang on to the end of the leash no matter what happens.

Your own place of concealment, from where you will watch the action, should be located so that the dog won't be distracted by your airborne scent and thus confused in his reaction to the thug. Use a whistle signal to alert the heavy and start the handler on his walk. *There should be no further communication between any of you until the test is finished and the dog is taken back to his car.* Watch intently as the dog approaches the shed, because much of importance can happen in an instant. When the handler and dog reach a point about ten feet from the building, the heavy should jump out only a step from cover, let out a war whoop as he fires two shots into the air, and then duck back into concealment and slam the door. The handler should give his dog a bit of praise and take him back to his car. There should be no more and no less threat than I've outlined. You'll soon see the necessity for this rule.

Here is a practical way of grading your dog on the test. If he ignored the "thug" who was attacking his master, rule him out. He would be hopelessly insensitive to less pronounced situations. If he flung himself back away from the thug, showing that his one desire was to break the leash and run away, write him off as a bad risk. If he backed up, as though startled or confused, but stood still when the leash tightened, he's worth trying a bit further. If he didn't back up, but stood his ground defensively, if not aggressively, he is a good prospect. If he responded playfully, as though eager for a game, he's worth further consideration. He wasn't afraid of the threat, and with some dogs it's a very short distance psychologically from games for fun to games for keeps. If he lunged forward, or indicated in other ways that he was ready to fight the thug, gun and all, score him high—his kind are more rare than you would suppose.

It may appear to you that the foregoing method of testing a dog's courage is too severe. Experience will show you that such is not the case. While training and conditioning will sometimes seem to qualify an inferior dog, it is logical to bet your time and life on a dog that has shown the courage to face up to the unexpected threat of a man with a gun.

I am well aware that a dog for whom you may have quickly developed a fondness could have had an unfortunate puppyhood, and that I cannot say that he would not turn out right if given the "proper advantages," but neither can you say that he *would* turn out right with the "proper advantages." Experience has made me aware of something else. *In the area of working dogs, depend on what you see, not on what you would like to see.* So, again, no matter how many times you have to work at providing helpers and facilities to test a dog's courage before you get a good prospect, don't try shortcuts or settle for an inferior dog.

When you have a dog that has demonstrated courage, you'll want to know about those many other qualities of temperament. I feel that by commenting on some of these factors I may help you to determine which are necessary to your own situation, and thus let you know what you should watch for in your further experience with your prospect. Though the terms used are not fully comprehensive, they are practical for our purpose.

Alertness. Essential to any police dog.

Aggressiveness. For our purposes, this term refers to a dog's desire to work. The degree of aggressiveness required of a dog may vary from one situation to another. In a night-blackened industrial area, a dog would need a lot of aggressiveness to keep him ready and hoping. His counterpart who was keeping the peace on a hoodlum-infested subway could be a little less "ready and hoping" since there would be some preliminary action to cue him and his handler.

Loyalty. This quality is essential. Though loyalty to his master is not the fundamental motivation of a police dog, as you shall soon see, it does give him the close orientation to his master necessary to his training and use.

Emotional Stability. Another essential for all police dogs. It is this quality that gives the dog a calm, clear head when the chips are down and makes him act in a predictable manner.

Responsibility. A dog's sense of responsibility is one of the most interesting and beautiful things in the animal world. It is the foundation upon which many of the dog's good qualities are rooted. It fortifies and directs many of his motivations. The conscience which a dog irrefutably demonstrates is founded in responsibility. The concerned way in which a guide dog protects a blind person is due in a great part to his assumption of responsibility. In police work, responsibility causes a dog to do beneficial things which he could not be caused to do by his central motivation of "hunting."

Instead of using blunt, staged tests like that which qualified the dog in courage, you will learn more about his fitness in other areas of temperament by observations made during his training and in the environment that he will share with you. This means that you must have the dog in your keeping, with the expense of caring for him, even though the experience may prove that he's unsuited to your purpose. In fact, he may be with you a long time before he fails in training or in some other respect. However, as yet there is no other way to determine a dog's fitness for police work than to spend time on what appear to be the best candidates. Until such a time as purposeful breeding programs bring a change, most candidates will not be acceptable, and time and trial will be needed to show whether a dog has that "balance" of qualities which makes him a good dog for a certain situation.

Some faults of temperament are disagreeable but, when offset by virtues which a dog may possess, need not disqualify a dog for a certain situation. I know of such a dog which for several years has served a small-town police force very effectively. The dog's bad fault is that he is "geared," a definition for the emotional torque which keeps him continually panting, slobbering, and jumping around in his screened-off area of a moving police car. He can hardly relax. The town in which the dog practices his specialty is bounded on its south side by two major railroads and some industrial plants. Two busy highways run close to this industrial area, making it an almost ideal situation for local and migratory hoodlums to evade pursuers by abandoning hot cars and taking off on foot. By deed and reputation, the "geared" dog has made the footracers forsake this area for courses where the competition is slower. His hunting instinct and fighting ability make the dark a bad place to run. So effective is this dog in the area where he works that his disagreeable feature can be well overlooked.

The above example should indicate that you should not expect a dog to be perfect in all qualities of temperament, but should require all of the essentials and enough of the other qualities to make an effective balance for your needs.

7. THE RIGHT START

Before you bring the dog into your keeping, provide for his security, health and comfort. Chapter 1 in Section 2 should be read thoroughly. Regardless of the facilities and knowledge which you may now have, the section on *poison-proofing* is essential to a police dog's safety. Remember, the dog may have formed attachments that for a time would pull him over, or through, an adequate fence and back to his former home. So, if you must improvise, make certain that you come up with something as big, strong, and comfortable as the run shown opposite p. 3 in Section 2.

Be sure that when you're away from the dog no one else is caring for him or playing with him. You are not going to be the big influence in his life if someone else is filling his mind with irrelevant impressions. Obviously, this means no visits from those with whom he has been living. If he doesn't make the grade, they can have him back; if he makes it, they may as well make a clean break with him now.

During the first week of the dog's trial period, try to build a calm, pleasant relationship with him. Avoid characterizing yourself as a playmate, and make certain that no one puts balls, toys, or anything else in his run. The ready acceptance of foreign objects is not particularly desirable in a police dog. Feed him, water him, talk to him in a calm manner, and watch for what he will show you about himself, but don't romp with him.

By the end of the first week of just getting acquainted, it will be time to start your dog's obedience training. In the case of a soft dog in a new home, it would be well to wait a bit longer before starting his education, but remember, your dog is a good physical specimen and had enough moral fibre to face a man with a gun. He can make the quick adjustment to a new home and activities, and you need to find out more about him in the least possible time.

I was reluctant, for a time, to begin this book because I wanted no part of that absurdity which features formidable dogs being handled by incompetents who have no comprehension of effective obedience training and what it can do for a dog. Then it occurred to me that there was a gimmick that could be used to force those who handle police dogs to acquire any proficiency they might be lacking. Readers who appreciate the potential of good working dogs will delight in helping apply this squeeze. It is easily used, inexpensive, and will be quite effective.

All over the United States, obedience trials licensed by the American Kennel Club have generated enthusiasm for obedience training. Books on obedience and training classes have served to make this fine sport available to thousands. The handlers who participate range from 12 to 75 years old, and the dogs vary from the Toy breeds to Saint Bernards. Even the novice exercises require that a competing dog heel free, do a recall off-leash, and hold the sit-stay and down-stay with dozens of other dogs around. If a dog fails to respond when he is given one command, he will be disqualified for that exercise. The use of repeated commands on a single requirement would be considered utterly laughable.

How do these facts constitute a gimmick? It's quite simple. With a couple of phone calls to a dog kennel or a good pet shop, any lawyer, city official, or layman can get the name of the closest dog show superintendent who, in turn, can supply him with the names and addresses of those in his area who have big, strong dogs with obedience titles or passing scores in competition. The rest is easy.

Anyone who has reason to believe that a city-supported police dog is deficient in its obedience training could ask a city council, or in some cases a court, to compare the performance of the dog and its handler with the performance of one of the smaller or more elderly women who would be available to work her big dog. Comparison—the unanswerable argument! What a fine way for those with high standards of training to inspire all slovenly handlers of police dogs to get squared away—or else.

92

Thus inspired, turn to the obedience section. The material is presented exactly as it appears in a book which has been used by dog owners of varying ages and physical ability to train many kinds of dogs. It will show you just what is reasonable to expect of a child or an elderly person. It is equally reasonable to suppose that its use could help a person who is qualified for police work to achieve a good foundation of obedience. Regardless of how much training the dog had before you considered him, do not omit a single step of the lessons. You'll benefit in many ways by training and observing your prospect at each level of obedience.

8. PREPARATION FOR AGITATION

Though your obedience training is a dynamic program that will continue after the ten weeks basic instruction are finished, you should have enough feel and control of your dog after six weeks of work to begin his agitation.

The word *agitation,* commonly related to such varied things as washing machines and politics, achieves dignity when it refers to the art of instilling alertness, suspicion, ability, and infallible confidence into a dog. You will find it an interesting and satisfying experience, if properly done, and will see why it is called an art. You will learn about agitation by participating, so let's get started with a program which will give you a step-by-step understanding of the accomplishment.

The first and probably the most difficult problem in police work is to find a man capable of being the agitator. Don't turn automatically to the person who helped you with the gun test; be sure that he, or anyone else you select, appears to be qualified by ability, not by convenience.

Before you choose a person, I'd like to tell you something that may qualify my statement as to the importance and difficulty of finding a good agitator. As one of perhaps no more than four trainers in the world who have done "man-work" and have also worked with top actors in motion pictures, I say without reservation that a good agitator is a more convincing performer than the best screen player—and just as hard to find. Your police dog cannot possibly be trained without such a person, so find him you must.

Probably you will have to find a man who, though inexperienced, has the qualifications for an agitator, and learn the many techniques along with him. He must be a man who is well-coördinated and in good condition. Above all, he must be able to understand and remember instructions. The ability to "read" a dog through his expressions and actions is another essential. Don't begrudge the time it takes to find and instruct the right person. The amount will be repaid many times by having good help in your training program.

By the time you find your agitator, you should locate and equip a work area. Because of his previous experience in that place where you ran the "heavy" and gun tests, and the need for another kind of setup, it's advisable to find a different location, even if it's only a short distance away on the same property. As in the test, it should be a quiet place with a moody atmosphere so you can control the sights and sounds.

You will need a section of solid fence, or a building side, which you should equip with a reinforcing board, an eyebolt, a baby bumper spring, and a chain with swivels and snaps as shown in the illustration on the next page. If necessary, you can make your own "board," as we will call it, out of old two-by-twelves or other used planks, like the one shown on page 170. It would be equipped exactly like the building side in the opposite illustration. The board should be situated where there are several nearby places for the agitator to emerge from concealment and approach the board from various angles. When you have the board equipped, test the strength of your spring setup by throwing your weight against the chain a few times. If you feel it wouldn't take any number of your heaviest jerks, it probably would break under the repeated lunges of a heavy dog.

The agitator should be dressed in shabby, strange-appearing clothes and a hat that will help in the first task, which is to make the dog suspicious of him. The clothes should allow the man to move freely as he will need to be quite active at times. He should have a burlap sack to work with, and a few more for spares. The dog must have a heavy harness with a wide breast strap so that he's not constantly made uncomfortable, and thus discouraged, by his own favorable responses. It may be advisable to have a leather worker make you a harness; the store variety is not up to the stress of agitation. A good whistle is

This agitation rigging is attached to a plank which can be bolted to a fence or building.

another useful item for you to have. Most important of all is your "mental equipment." It's your unyielding determination to follow all instructions to the letter. Anything less than an all-out effort has no place in the agitation of a dog.

9. FIRST LEVEL OF AGITATION

You and the agitator should always travel to the work area separately, and meet in such a way that the dog will not see the man before the session. The man should conceal himself in the place from which he will begin his first "approach" and remain hidden until you signal him.

The dog should be wearing his harness when you bring him from the car to the area, but you will lead him at heel with the same leash and training collar that you use in obedience work. You will gain from making him heel properly in this new situation. When you reach the board, fasten the spring chain to his harness, double check the fastenings, then remove the training collar. Take a position about 20 feet to either side of the dog, and stand quietly while he investigates the spring and other strange things around him.

You and your agitator will do a better job on the training of your dog, and feel your accomplishments more fully, if you have definite objectives for each level of the work. The purposes of this first level are to make the dog suspicious of a man who appears and acts differently from the usual person, and to increase his confidence by making him feel superior to such a man. Put these objectives firmly in your mind while the dog settles a bit; then blow your whistle for the agitator.

At this moment, the agitator begins one of the most convincing acting jobs ever seen in or out of the theatre. He oozes from conceal-ment with his sack hanging limply, a flaccid extension of an arm that has neither strength nor bone. His features are equally as slack, and if he is salivating, the drool from his wide open mouth may glisten strangely on his chin. He should crab along sideways with one foot sliding experimentally ahead and the other foot forcing him weakly along. The angle of his body shows only craven cowardice, no boldness. It is plain that one firm look from the dog would cause him to scuttle in terror back to his hideout.

Because, as the gun test showed, your dog has more than the usual firmness, he may want to do more than look at this creep who for some reason is inching toward him. He may show resentment with a bark or growl—or more.

But whether the dog only stiffens with alertness, or lunges aggres-sively, the agitator's reflex—no, I don't mean reaction, which could cause a half-second delay—is the same. Instantly, the terror-stricken creep heads for his hiding place.

Show your pleasure with a mild bit of praise, and then give the dog a little time to mutter an accusation or to scratch around in claims of conquest; then blow the whistle again.

The dog may show his alertness to the creep's approach a bit earlier or more aggressively this time, but regardless of the moment or manner, the man should retreat instantly. Again, the wait for the dog to savor his victory; and then, again, the signal for the creepy approach and still another victory for the dog.

Five victories over the creep, who comes close enough to cause the dog to alert, is enough for the first agitation period. You gain by using the first hiding place and angle of approach for all five cycles. You should feel very pleased if the dog showed promise of developing alertness and suspicion at the time of this first session.

Possibly the dog, which may have been eager to clobber the heavy who threatened him during the gun test, will show disinterest in the inoffensive man who seems afraid to approach him. That disinterest will give the man a chance to get close enough for a period of plaguing and teasing the dog with the sack. There should be no strong bluster-ing in the use of the sack, and it should show no boldness on the part of the agitator. Rather, it is the action of a coward who keeps well out of reach while he teases a dog he fears.

If your dog stands, sits, or lies and squints his eyes against the annoyance, it may take a lot of teasing with the swishing sack across his face to irritate him. The agitator should be just as patient as he

At the first sign of the dog's suspicion, the agitator should retreat.

"Flanking" will sometimes arouse suspicion in a naive dog.

teases and nags away. If the dog simply turns his back, the sack snapped against his rear may make him feel that the creep is worth his attention. When the dog shows the slightest resentment to the teasing, his tormentor should retreat. Something will be gained from the dog's victory in driving the tormentor away. As in the case of the more suspicious dog which alerts quickly, he should have five of these victories.

The dog may convince you that he would stand any amount of teasing without resentment. Before you write him off as a bad prospect, his patience should get a final test. The agitator should approach in a casual manner, stop a short step away, and then set himself for a quick move—or two.

At a moment when the dog's attention is turned from him, he should lean in and sharply grab the web of loose skin that runs from the hind leg to the body at the bottom of the flank. The grab and jerk should be hard enough to pull the dog backwards and off balance, and far enough so that the man is out of range when he lets go. While this "flanking" cannot injure the dog, it generally stings one into a fighting mood. It's likely that no advice to retreat rapidly will be needed by the man. He should run all the way back to his place of concealment.

If the dog showed resentment, not cowardice, when he was grabbed, give him a word of praise. Wait a few minutes, then signal for another approach. This time when the man approaches, the dog may show that he's quite ready for any flanking movement. Remember—all the time the agitator is trying, though unsuccessfully, to slip up on the dog's rear, the dog is growing in suspicion; so no matter how impossible it appears, he should try five or six approaches, each of which will end when the dog so much as wheels to face him and stands his ground. This is one of those points where the agitator must read the dog perfectly so that he is certain to retreat the instant the dog shows the slightest resentment.

Keep in mind that this dog would not alert to a merely suspicious manner of approach, but needed actual physical contact, so it follows that he is alerting because of the threat, not because of inherent suspicion. This is why the man doesn't retreat at the sign of the dog's alerting, but keeps on coming until there is a definite show of resentment. Although in most programs of agitation it is better to postpone physical discomfort until aggressiveness has been increased to a point where it seems no discouragement could result, in the case of a dog who ignores the creepy approach and the teasing, the physical contact must be used as the only practical way to build in the suspicion he lacks.

Possibly your prospect seems to respond well to the creepy approach and teasing but after a few days ceases to alert. In such a case, have the apparently harmless agitator provide a surprise with the same "flanking" attack that was recommended for the non-suspicious dog. If the dog alerts readily, but then turns away in boredom, as though expecting no more than a creepy walk, the agitator can use a surprise to advantage. He should approach in the usual way, and stop an arm's length from the dog. When the dog's attention leaves him, he should whack him on the rear end with the sack; by the time the dog whirls, the man should be retreating.

On the next approach, the agitator might have to wait longer for an opportunity to sack the dog. This difficulty should increase with each whack the dog gets, thereby proving that he is growing in suspicion.

There are two precepts the agitator must carefully observe while working with the sack. He must show by instant retreat that there is neither time nor reason to fear him, and if the dog whirls and lunges at the sack, the man must be certain that he does not get his teeth in it. Later on, you will see why there is an exact moment when the dog should get "relief" on the sack. The usual five or six approaches, using the sack when necessary to revive alertness, should be sufficient for each day's session. Do not repeat the approaches so many times in a day that the dog loses the savor of the experience. As in all training, quit on a high point. One negative experience can cancel out several good ones.

When the session is finished, give the dog a bit of praise, and let him settle for a few minutes. The agitator should remain hidden while you use the training collar and leash to take the dog at heel from the area. If you are lucky enough to have a dog who doesn't want to settle, but would rather hunt out the varmint who's been plaguing him, you might question as to whether control at this fruitful time might not discourage him. Actually, he will experience less discouragement from being brought under control at the board than would be the case if you were to let him drag you triumphantly to the hideout and then have to pull him away from where he has "treed" the man.

If you spent time in the war-dog program, or have had similar experience, you may be wondering whether I know about such things as having the handler stand with a dog on the leash while the agitator makes noises and circles around the dog in concert with the handler's pats and encouragement to "Sic 'em!" Yes, I know about such things. I also know about such things as stimulating a dog's predatory instinct by working the dog along with another who is responsive to agitation.

I know a few other techniques which will sometimes pump the breath of life into an underpowered dog, but you might lose more than you would gain by using any of them now. Right from the start, we're going to try to build some qualities into your dog which cannot be instilled at those times when he's motivated by sound effects and mass hysteria. And—in police work—it's much more practical to make a good dog great than to make a poor dog fair, so waste no time in priming the pump of an inferior prospect.

During your agitation periods of the next ten days, your objectives will be (1) to increase the dog's suspicion, whether it is accomplished by a creepy walk, teasing with the sack, or flanking, and (2) to instill confidence by justifying the dog's opinion of the creep and making him constantly victorious over the man. If your prospect is so unresponsive during this period that he fails to grow more suspicious, even with repeated flankings, spend no more time on him. He could be one of the many who will fight courageously when forced to do so, but are otherwise generally indifferent to their surroundings and forget an experience so fast that they are not worth further consideration. It's a big mistake to try the second level of agitation with a dog that has not made the necessary gains in suspicion and confidence during the basic ten days.

10. SECOND LEVEL OF AGITATION

The fact that you have met with success in developing some degree of suspicion and perhaps an increase of confidence in your dog shows that you have a likely prospect and that you and your agitator have some capability. Don't let his early success make you overconfident, so that you'll be tempted to experiment with shortcuts. The first objective for the second level of agitation is to begin to teach him that there are times and places where he must be constantly alert. Second, we will show him that it is well to suspect people in certain situations even when they are acting in a normal manner, because they might suddenly begin to act abnormally. Third, we want to further increase his confidence by showing him how the man will run from his first firm look.

Begin work with the same setup used in previous sessions. For the first four approaches have the agitator proceed as before, which will result in routine victories for the dog. The fifth approach will be different. Now, instead of leaving the hideaway in a creepy manner, the man should step out with the sack hanging behind him from his belt, and his hands at his sides. He should move forward in a nonchalant, disinterested way, ignoring any alertness or aggressiveness in the dog. Though the stop near the dog is for the purpose of getting set for a surprise swing with the sack, it should be done so smoothly that the agitator doesn't appear to be seeing him. As he waits for his chance, the man's hand should sneak around to rest with a secure grip on the sack behind him.

If your agitator is both skillful and fortunate in his maneuvering, he may lull the dog's suspicion enough to get in a hard whack with the sack, and run away.

Have him remain hidden until the dog settles, then repeat the pattern of four creepy approaches where he retreats as soon as the dog alerts, followed by the casual approach where the agitator actually tries to work his way close enough to whack the dog, and stays close until after he's had his swing. This second round of victories, four where he has chased the man away by merely alerting, and one where he's driven off the treacherous creep after being surprised with the sack, is plenty for the day. As always, let the dog settle; then take him in a proper way from the area, while the man remains hidden.

It's quite likely that the dog won't be as lulled as he appears, and the man will have to shorten his swing to save the sack. If this is the case, the man should counter with a high swing to get the dog up on his hind legs, leaning against the pull of the chain, and then make a quick backhanded swipe that stings the dog while he is off balance. In either instance, the man must retreat so fast that there is literally no time to experience fear—only victory. Once more, though he feels the victory of driving the cowardly man away, the dog must also feel the frustration of not getting relief on the sack. However, if the dog outguesses the agitator and does grab the sack, the man should not jerk it from him. Though relief at this time is regrettable, the dog would be left with the loss of a battle, as well as the sack, if it were to be jerked from him. If he gets the sack, the heavy retreats without a tussle. Give the dog some praise while he chews and froths out his vengeance on the burlap. When he has been satiated to the point where he gives the sack only an occasional disdainful glance, use your training leash and collar to take him from the board and out of the area. He's had relief, and further agitation on this day would be an anti-climax.

It would be senseless to try to give an exact number of days that you should work with the pattern which has been presented for this second stage of agitation, but even the sharpest prospect should have at least ten daily sessions during which it is impossible for the agitator to surprise him with the sack, regardless of how hard the man might try. This fact would indicate that you have reached the objectives set for this level. He's learned that he must be constantly alert in the work area or the sack will surprise him. He has found that he's been justified in suspecting the man, regardless of appearances, because the man may look innocent one moment and hit him with the sack the next. The readiness of the man to run from him has steadily increased his confidence.

When you are aware that the dog has made the above gains, you can start the next level of agitation confidently. On the other hand, if your inventory doesn't show these gains, you had better be on the lookout for another prospect.

11. THIRD LEVEL OF AGITATION

While all sessions of agitation contribute to the dog's fund of suspicion and confidence, from now on the objectives of each level will be to make a definable, qualitative change in that fund. For example, until now the dog has been made more and more suspicious of an agitator who has increased his confidence by running from the dog's attention like a craven coward. Now you must fortify that confidence so that it holds against an agitator who is less cowardly and who threatens a bit before running.

Begin by equipping the agitator with a light, tough switch about three feet in length which he will carry along with the sack. The purpose of carrying the switch at this level is so that it becomes a familiar part of the man. Have him conceal himself in a different hideout from the one previously used so his approach will be from an unexpected direction. Approaching from the new angle, while the dog may be concentrating on the former hideout, the agitator should try his best to slip up close enough to sack the dog and retreat as usual. If he fails in his sneak approach, he should retreat as soon as the dog alerts. Now that the dog is aware of this new angle, the next few approaches will amount to nothing more than the routine retreats when the dog alerts.

Now comes the fifth approach and a big change. No quick victory this time. He should work vehemently, swinging and snapping the sack with one hand while the other is busy scratching and smacking the ground with the switch. Any babbling idiotic noises he makes can add to the beauty of the moment. Both the actions and the sounds should be offensive but should not be authoritative, lest they overpower the inexperienced dog. Again the need for perfect acting on the part of the agitator. If he can be so realistic in his maniacal harassing that his eyes water and his nose runs, so much the better. He works with perfect timing until the moment when his actions, sounds, and sack have the dog lunging at peak fury against the frustrating give and take of the spring—then he runs away.

Praise the dog, let him settle, then take him from the area so the agitator can move undetected from where he holed up to another hideout and a fresh angle of approach. When the man is hidden in the new spot, he should remain quiet while the dog is put back on the board; then he should try again to slip up on the dog when his attention is on the previous angle of approach.

Probably he'll never succeed in surprising the dog, but the honesty of his try will be felt. As before, this attempt should be followed by four approaches where the agitator retreats as soon as the dog alerts, which will probably be done when he first sights the man; that means they will not be time-consuming. Then there should be another donnybrook, with the sack, sounds, and switch used as before, and a retreat that is timed to the high point of the dog's frenzy. This will conclude two patterns of agitation, which are sufficient for a day. Obviously, if you are so unfortunate as to have the dog get the sack before the two patterns are finished, you must end the day's session at that point.

Ten days of two sessions each should be enough to lift the dog to a new stature. He will know by then that no matter how many times the man retreats on his alert, there will be a time when the maddening agitation will involve him physically. He will have learned that he can stop the most persistent teasing by attacking at full fury. His constant frustration from the give-and-take of the spring will have changed his desire to grab the sack into an obsession that is impenetrable by fear.

12. FOURTH LEVEL OF AGITATION

The fourth level of agitation will form one of the most important and interesting steps in the training of your police dog, and will draw heavily on the understanding and teamwork that you and your agitator have developed.

One objective of this level is to begin with the education of a second agitator. Choose him as carefully as you did the first. Have the first man take him to the work area and instruct him to stay concealed in a place where he can watch each detail of the procedure. Though much was gained by letting the dog's vehemence intensify through holding its focus on one person, we can now change the focus to any number of individuals while retaining its full intensity. Safety, as well as effectiveness, demands that a new man has plenty of time to observe and learn before he takes his turn; otherwise, the dog may "suck him in" close enough to bite him.

In order of occurrence, the second objective of this pattern is to insulate the dog against physical pain, one of the things he must face unflinchingly in his work as a police dog. Start the session by having the agitator make as many straight-in approaches as it takes to bring the dog to a real high, sack-hungry boiling point. When he feels that the dog is ready, he should change the switch to his more skillful hand while, until the right moment, the sack will be merely flailing out of reach.

When the dog has a grip on the sack, the agitator should release it and run.

Now the agitator begins the most critical few minutes in the training of the dog. He should move straight in as before, hissing, flailing the sack, and hitting the air and ground with his switch until the dog is lunging in fury; then, in one of those split seconds when the dog is reared against the pull of the chain, he should sting the dog sharply with the switch and in the same instant swish the sack against the side of the dog's head so he can grab it. When the dog has a grip, the man should release the sack and run for his hideout.

In this same moment, you are well on the way to the third objective of this session, which is to let the dog relieve his frustration so fully that he'll be eager for further combat. Probably you will now get a chilling demonstration of how formidable your dog can be as he shakes the sack like a rat, or stands on it while he chews it to pieces, which he may even swallow. Possibly he may drop the sack and show every indication of wanting to annihilate something more than burlap. Either way, you have won a big victory. He didn't back up from the sting of the switch. Praise him, give him plenty of time to work out his feelings on the sack or gloat over his victory. Then end the session by taking him from the area in the proper manner.

Ten daily sessions following the above format should change the dog's confidence in kind, as well as degree, to where he feels he can win over a bold man as easily as he can chase a coward. By now, the new agitator has had many opportunities to study the demands and risks of working against the dog and will be useful in the next stage of training.

13. FIFTH LEVEL OF AGITATION

In order of procedure, the objectives of this level of agitation are as follows: (1) to teach the dog that his suspicion and fury should not be reserved exclusively for the man whose appearance and actions have typed him as a heavy; (2) to provide experiences that will start developing the discrimination which a police dog needs; (3) to begin to focus the dog on the offensive hand; (4) to give the dog his first experience in transporting a prisoner. These objectives add up to a lot of important work—and a lot of satisfaction as you see the pattern of work accomplish each of them. Talk the whole thing over with your agitators before you start so that there will be direction to their efforts. This time, have *both* men conceal themselves in the work area before you put the dog on the board.

You have no doubt noticed how your dog has been taking your whistle signal to the agitator as a cue to alert. This time, when you're ready for the first approach, use a signal which will not be significant to the dog. If the agitator's hideout has a peephole, he can see your hand; if not, he can hear a cough or other non-significant sound.

The new man will make the approach while the other one remains concealed. He should be dressed as an average man, and there should be nothing in his hands, nor anything unusual about his attitude, appearance, or movements as he steps casually from concealment and walks along a course that takes him past the dog about five feet out of

*chain reach. Whether the dog's attitude shows aggressiveness or con-
fusion, the man should act completely disinterested in him, and continue walking until he no longer can be seen or scented by the dog.*
Your own attitude should match the agitator's, which is to say you will
show no interest in the man's passing nor what the dog thought of this
stranger. You should neither praise nor reprove him for anything he
might do. After a lapse of about three minutes for the dog to reflect on
these "strange happenings," the man should make the return trip,
again passing the dog without interest, and then disappear into his
original place of concealment. After another short lapse, the man
should repeat his casual walk and return. Again, neither you nor the
agitator will react to the other, nor to anything the dog does.

After five of these round trips, you'll probably notice a bit of
restraint in the dog's actions, and quite logically wonder if he should
not be praised for his discrimination. No. At this time and place, he
would associate praise with your encouragement of aggressiveness,
and would feel encouraged to go after the man.

Though this "walk-by" may seem to be a static, fruitless experience
to you, it is one of those times in dog training when the dog must draw
his own conclusions, uninfluenced by his trainer. Vague as those
experiences may appear, they leave a spot of indecision in your dog's
mind which your later disciplines can penetrate more easily than if
that mind were hardened by experience which showed only the need
for constant aggression. It will take roughly half an hour for the
agitator to make these five disinterested round trips. Then we'll call on
the more experienced man to begin focusing the dog on the offensive
hand.

To understand how necessary the aspect of the offensive hand is to
the safety of the officer-dog unit, let's take a look at the mechanics of
an armed assault on a policeman by a suspect. Regardless of the
weapon used, it is almost certain that the offensive hand will be either
pointing or in an otherwise noticeably peculiar relation to the body. If
the dog drives at this hand, he is certain to divert the attack from the
officer and probably avoid injury to himself; but if he is slow to
recognize the offensive hand he will forfeit the demoralizing speed
that gives him his big advantage over a man. Rarely will the dog's
opponent have the will or ability to fight with his weaponless free
hand after his offensive arm has been disabled.

A suitable protection for the agitator during this phase of his work
can be provided by wrapping three-inch wide strips of heavy innertube
rubber in a snug, overlapping spiral from elbow to wrist of his

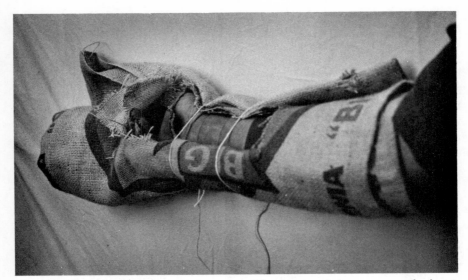

Carefully read the text on p. 115 so you will understand the purpose of what is shown here.

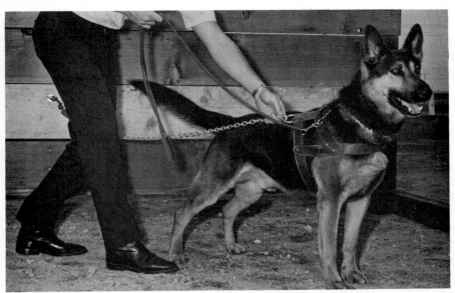

It will be easier and safer to take your dog from the board to start transporting if the leash is on before the agitator appears.

working arm. A heavy glove or gauntlet should cover the hand. The burlap sack should now be wrapped tightly over the innertube so that it extends like a long sleeve past the hand for about eight inches to make an "empty" section for the dog to grab. A few wraps of very light string will help hold the sack in place and make it more like a tube. Now the agitator's switch should be shoved into the tube so that his gloved hand can grasp it. Although you may already own one, we're not ready to change to a padded sleeve at this time.

When the agitator is prepared, bring the dog under full control from the car to the board. Fasten his harness ring to the chain, but do not remove the leash from his collar. Stand so the dog is on your left side in the heel position, and hold the leash at the hand loop so you can avoid interfering with any quick move he might make.

To the best of his ability, the first part of the agitator's approach should match the action and attitude of the five "disinterested round trips." He should minimize the threat of the sack and switch by holding his offensive hand down at his side or slightly behind him. When his casual walk brings him to a point opposite the board, he should stop and face the dog. Though the man continues to hide the sack as much as possible, the dog may notice that his position is a bit unnatural, which may arouse his suspicion. Whether he alerts or sees nothing peculiar about the person who has been "walking on by," you and the agitator should act in perfect coördination to each other. You encourage the dog with a good word, such as "Rrready!" The moment he hears the word, the man should move, switch held in front, toward the dog.

The sight of the familiar switch and sack will show the dog you were right about "ready." The man's next action is to move close to the dog's maximum reach, and then try his best to sting the dog with the switch. Then, though caution is called for, he must poke the sack close enough so that the dog can grab the protruding end and tear it from his hand. Instead of a retreat, the man's immobility tells the dog he is the victor.

Give the dog a pat, some praise, and all the time he wants to wool the sack or glower at the man. When the dog is calm but not indifferent, tell the man in a stern voice to turn around and with his hands at his side walk slowly toward his place of concealment. Tighten your grip on the hand-loop of the leash and, when the man is about ten feet from you, free the dog from the board and follow the suspect to his place of confinement.

If the dog wants to bring the sack along as a trophy, let him. Do not

"Clancy" of the Montclair, California Police Department, transports a "suspect" to confinement.

insist that he heel perfectly during this first experience in "transporting." In fact, it's a good sign if the dog should want to herd the man along in a business-like manner.

When the door closes behind your suspect, the training session is finished. Later in the program, you will see how this logical and satisfying culmination to an arrest pays off, and will wonder at some of the illogical practices where a dog is dragged away from his victory, or the suspect is permitted to simply walk away. How can dogs victimized by such methods be blamed for the dangerous disinterest they show after a suspect has been stopped?

At this point, you may be asking what could be gained by repeating the exact procedure of this lesson, since once fooled by the nice-appearing man it's unlikely that the dog would again wait for the stick to move offensively before he alerted. True enough, but, regardless of his suspicion, his discrimination will still be sharpened by the fact that the man sometimes walks on by without the stick and, too, proper focus will be made more certain with each victory over the offensive hand. Along with these benefits to the dog, the experience will give your new agitator the coördination his safety will demand when the dog has graduated from the board. This gives you plenty of reason to repeat each step of this last pattern daily for ten days.

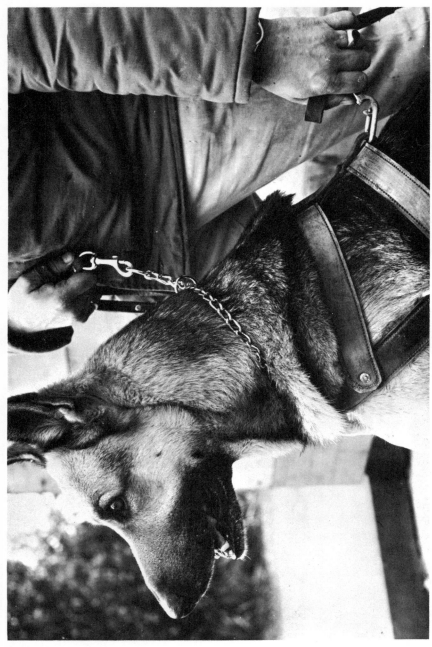

Double-rigging will provide added control when you work your dog off the agitation board.

14. SIXTH LEVEL OF AGITATION

You can prevent hazards and save yourself much difficulty by facing a moment of truth before you begin the next level of man-work. Carefully check the obedience section to make certain of what is required of your dog at this level of training. Remember, the requirements stated are no more than are expected of big dogs worked by old ladies and young children, so how can you reasonably demand less of your dog?

When you have worked him the number of days necessary to bring him to reliability, and you rarely have to make a correction, you will be ready for another essential step. Take your dog to the place where you know the foot traffic is the heaviest, such as a downtown street or a shopping center. Now work him on all of his on-leash exercises while hundreds of people pass by. This is valuable conditioning to help prepare both of you for later service on the street. It is here in a crowd where the stand for examination exercise will do the most to develop your dog's faculty for discrimination; however, be certain that the person who "goes over the dog" does not approach in the creepy way of the one who first agitated him. There are off-balance folk who seem to invite bites. For quite a period, we want it to be impossible for the dog to avoid a deserved correction, so until told differently, omit practicing the off-leash work in the crowded area.

After a few sessions of working in a crowd, you will understand why the environment means so much to your dog. Literally, and with no arrangement by you, he is passed by hundreds of people who turned out to be good guys. The more good guys he sees go by without giving him trouble, the more quickly he will recognize the man who is different and thrusts a weapon at him. *Often overlooked by trainers and dog owners is the fact that there can be no discrimination without comparison.*

When your dog will obey reliably in a crowded area with a manner that is very alert, but not trigger-happy, you are ready to start the next level of man-work. The first objective of this pattern is to adapt the attitudes and actions gained during the work on the board to another situation. The second is to begin a definite program of instilling some of the disciplines your police dog will need.

Your first concern should be that your equipment will provide an adequate margin of safety. Double-check the condition of your training collar, harness, and leash; then provide yourself with a second training leash.

When the agitators are hidden, bring the dog at heel to his usual position before the board, and stop so that his automatic-sit has him facing right for action. Give him a sit-stay command, and fasten your second leash to the ring of his harness. There are reasons in addition to safety why this double rigging is necessary. There will be times when you will need the harness to cushion the dog against what could be mistaken for a correction; and there will be times when you will need the collar to correct him effectively. Grip them, one in each hand, so you can handle them effectively, or together if safety demands.

Because the action when the dog is controlled by the leashes instead of the chain may be a bit unpredictable, it would be better for the experienced agitator to answer your first signal. The agitator, without the sack or stick, should leave concealment and start one of those casual walk-bys exactly like those used in the previous pattern. Because the physical limitations of your dog will not be as predictable as when he was on the chain, the man will feel a whole lot more "casual" if his course takes him about ten feet from the dog.

In obedience, you have learned the difference between training and restraining, so have some slack in your leash. Without any nervous movements which could influence the dog, set yourself so you could cope with any lunges or make a correction if your dog should break his sit-stay. *A hard stay in a definite position is the best way of telling your dog that the situation of the moment is not one in which you expect action.* Specifically, the sit-stay position is used to stabilize your dog because of the mechanical advantage it can give, as it uses both your back and arm muscles to jerk the dog back to position. Use that advantage if the dog breaks, and make that correction a good one. After the man disappears at the far end of his walk, take your dog off the stay in the usual way and give him lots of praise.

If you've been doing a sloppy job of obedience work, you may get a quick education as you wallow about trying to keep the dog from getting the "casual"—and he'd better be casual—man. Unfortunately, the person who tries to train a police dog without giving him a thorough foundation of obedience is generally too stupid to realize the harm he does when he is forced to introduce his first controls when the dog is lunging, in what he feels is the right attitude, toward the man. *This means that if your dog ignores your commands, you had better postpone further man-work until your fundamental obedience is up to par.*

After your dog has had his praise for a good job of holding, the man can make his return trip. Again, the dog should have an experience which shows him that there will be no assault when the man does not face him, and that obedience to the "stay" command will bring him praise. This casual round-trip experience should be repeated half a dozen times or more, if needed for the dog's comprehension, before we give him another picture of this same man. When the last casual trip has been made, punctuate the lesson by taking the dog back to the car and letting him "soak" for a few minutes, while you see that the agitator's arm is rigged with the rubber and sack as explained previously.

When the agitator is equipped and ready, bring the dog back to his position near the board, but instead of putting him on a sit-stay, give him an "O.K." release, which means that he can move around at will within the length of the leashes. The man should begin his approach as before, trying his best to conceal his rigged arm until he is opposite the dog. At this point, the man should stop and face the dog. *The fact that he wasn't told to stay, plus the man's preliminary actions, will give the discriminating dog just what he needs to warn him of trouble.*

Again, there is that need for perfect coördination between you and the agitator. Regardless of the dog's attitude, the man should move in with his offensive hand working to tag the dog's forelegs with his switch. When the dog focuses on the offensive hand, it must be the "empty" end of the sack that is in position for him to grab, not the switch. In this moment, the dog has won the battle. However, if he is able to grab the switch, it must not be pulled from him; he must be given the victory as though he had grabbed the sack. Watch, though, so a timid agitator doesn't "feed" him the switch instead of getting the arm out where it can be grabbed. In practical application, a dog is many times more effective when he grabs the wrist or arm than when he bites at a club, knife, or gun, so the agitator should work at teasing and stinging him until he focuses on the sack end as his only possible relief.

When you feel that the dog has had sufficient time to wool the sack or glower at the agitator, use your stern tone to order the man toward the place of confinement, and give the dog the experience of ending the capture by transporting his prisoner. Probably, if your dog is enthusiastic, the pull will be divided between the collar and harness as you let him crowd along possessively behind the man. When the man has been confined, praise your dog. Then remove the leash from the harness and take him at heel from the area with the other leash and training collar.

There will be some interesting changes as you start the next day's work. Choose a hideout different from those that have previously concealed the agitator, and instead of placing the dog in his familiar spot, move him about ten feet away from the board and put him on a sit-stay facing the new angle of approach. As before, one leash will be rigged to the collar and the other to the harness.

It should be very clear to you, as the agitator begins the first of his casual walk-bys, that you and your dog have accomplished a lot from the combination of the rigid exercise in crowds and the sit-stays. Experience has shown him that there are more times than not when even the agitator will not be offensive. In addition, his other experiences have shown him that anyone who appeared to be hiding something and then faced him tensely, holding an object in his hand, turned out to be an assailant.

Some of the failures in training dogs are brought about by those who neglect a facet of the work as being irrelevant to their main purpose, when in reality that work is essential to their success. For future encouragement, consider how the authority you established in your obedience training is being introduced into the area of man-work, not merely as a means of control but, even more importantly, to make that control seem like a very reasonable thing to the dog. Very soon you will see how the practice the dog gets in holding, as the man walks by, will help to make other controls easier for you and more reasonable for the dog. It is therefore necessary to practice until the dog is resigned to staying. You will gain by alternating agitators and hideouts during this "casual" period, as well as moving the action around to different parts of the area.

You may wonder why we don't use persons who have never offended the dog to provide the casual subject in the discrimination exercises, and use the agitators only when staging assaults. There are three good reasons.

1. The exceptional interest the dog shows in the two heavies will make him very attentive to their manner.
2. He needs to know that even those whom memory tells him to suspect must not be attacked without provocation.
3. An unlimited variety of passers-by are provided by the crowds where some of your obedience work is practiced, so the dog will have the opportunity to see an ample number of strangers.

When the dog's attitude makes you feel that he's had a good day's practice in studying the agitators at times when they are casual and unarmed, give him a chance to watch the signs that promise the sport of action. From the agitator's stop and turn and the other preliminaries that give the dog practice in reading the threat, through the victory and the transporting of the man, follow the pattern of the previous day. Though this exact repetition may bore you, the more times the dog is successful in interpreting each step of the format, the more his faculty of discrimination will be exercised and the more reliable it will become.

Another reason for exact repetition at this time is the fact that he may already be feeling a big change in working away from the board. Careful handling and lots of praise can do much to keep him from being disoriented or confused at this point. By the time he sees you close the door on his prisoner, he'll be convinced that human varmints mean sport no matter where you catch them. Ten daily sessions spent on this pattern are generally enough to give the dog the feel of working on the leashes instead of the chain, and in addition will develop the necessary coördination in the handler. When you've reached that objective, you will have taken a big step toward a level of man-work which can bring you some of the most satisfying experiences in the world of dogs.

15. TESTING FOR THE FIELD

The memory of some of the dogs I've trained tells me how much the effectiveness of this book depends on your sincerity and good judgment. Some of these dogs were so "varminty" that they responded to an agitator's first offensive move as though their full enthusiasm had been turned on by a valve. With others, who made equally good dogs in time, many periods of agitation were required to "break the taboo" against biting a man. With this variation in dogs, it is plain that you'll need something more than a record of the time you've spent to tell you if your dog is ready for the next level of work. Your good judgment and a few simple tests can answer that question.

First, in order of importance, there should be a test to see whether you and your dog have made adequate progress in your obedience. With no more than the material contained in the obedience section of this book, many women and children have qualified big, rugged dogs to pass tests as demanding as those that will be given your dog, so there is no room for compromise.

Choose for your testing area a busy street or a shopping center where your dog has never been. Arrange to have two persons, each with a dog on leash, at designated spots in the area. The tests will begin when you bring your dog at free-heel from confinement to your car. He should sit automatically, and not enter the car until you tell him, "In." When you arrive at the testing area, he should not leave the car, even though the door has been opened, until you call him out. He should travel reliably at free-heel on a course that takes him about a city-block-length among the pedestrians to a stop within five feet of one of the dogs that you have spotted. He should hold a sit-stay and a down-stay for one and three minutes, respectively, with people passing near him. This is no more than the time requirement for dogs in the novice obedience ring. After you have broken him off the down-stay, take him to within ten feet of where the second dog is planted and leave him on a sit-stay. He should hold while you walk 50 feet away from him, and then recall promptly and reliably on command. He should free-heel back to your car with you, sit automatically before the car door, and not enter until he is given the command.

During these simple tests, both you and your dog should have shown stability and smoothness. If you have seen dogs worked in the novice obedience ring, you know that any evidence of the dog's inattentiveness or the handler's lack of confidence, such as double commands, footstamps, and other extra sounds and signals, would disqualify a dog. Certainly there should be no lower standards for a police-dog prospect and his handler. If your dog fails any of these tests, review the work as it is presented in the obedience section until he can meet the requirements in a positive manner. Do not take the successful completion of this test as an indication that you have a thoroughly obedience-trained dog. Your success shows that you have made enough progress in the obedience factor to qualify for the next level of training.

A dog's motive for man-work is based on his hunting instinct and developed by experience that establishes man as his quarry. How true this is will be plain to you as soon as your dog is asked to begin finding his "varmints" instead of waiting for them to come to him. Before you begin the fun of man-hunting, you must determine whether your dog has enjoyed enough victories to whet his interest in human varmints. The test should be made in the general area where he has been agitated, but not in the exact locations where he has been threatened and attacked. We already know how he responds to a threat; now we want to know how he responds to an opportunity to hunt.

Select a part of the area where you and your dog can walk in a straight line for about 100 feet, and which would permit the agitator to be concealed 30 to 50 feet to one side of the course in such a way that he will become visible to the dog from a point midway along the course. If you have a choice, place the man to that side of the course

Make this test exactly as explained on page 127.

where the air currents will carry his scent toward the dog. For this test, do not rig the agitator's arm or do anything which will make him appear threatening when the dog sights him. However, a burlap sack and the switch should be placed on the ground behind him. Rig both your leashes in the usual way, then give your dog an enthusiastic "O.K.!" and influencing him as little as possible begin your stroll along the course. If he reaches a point where the air currents are favorable, your dog may alert on scent. Otherwise, as the dog comes into view, the agitator should cough loudly as a non-significant noise to attract the dog. We are not concerned with your dog's powers of detection during this test—only his attitude.

The dog must see nothing threatening when he gets his first sight of the man. You should have slack in your leashes and do nothing to encourage the dog at this time. Particularly if there is no help from the scent conditions, there may be a bit of indecision while your dog determines if this inoffensive character standing in this strange place is really the "varmint" he's been fighting recently. Then he'll probably move in for action or a closer look. With the first move the dog makes toward him, the man must whirl around, grab his sack and stick, and start backing away. Be sure to follow along swiftly and smoothly so nothing in your actions makes the dog think you don't want him to hunt. Check the dog's rush when he reaches a point where the man can swing at him with the sack.

After the dog grabs the sack, the man should drop his stick and stand motionless until you order him away. The dog should then transport him to confinement in the usual manner.

This short test showed a lot. Without being triggered by a threat, or encouraged by you, and when he had the opportunity to turn in another direction, your dog was motivated to hunt and fight the man as his quarry. Such a dog will enjoy police work. If your dog showed no motivation to "go in," your best course is to put him back on the board and increase the intensity of the teasing until he's convinced that in some situations there are human varmints who must be sought out and conquered before he must face their maddening harassment. If this does not bring his drive up to par, you will have to recognize that you have a dog that shows plenty of bravo when attacked but lacks the "varmintiness" needed for police work.

When you have a dog that has passed the tests for obedience and motivation, you are both qualified for some interesting work.

A good dog will succeed where a gun cannot be used.

16. FIELD TRAINING

As nearly as possible, the field training location should duplicate the areas where you plan on using your dog. Obviously, there are a number of unusual conditions that require special training and familiarization. For example, a dog used in Tucson, Arizona would hardly be confronted with the problem of pursuing a man through water, yet Yuma, at the state's southwest corner, is on the Colorado River and has miles of water and bottom land which can be used as an escape route to California and Mexico. A dog that may be a whiz in Tucson might therefore be of limited value in Yuma.

Consider all conditions your dog may have to face, and choose your training areas thoughtfully. Do not use the area where your dog will probably be on duty for your basic training in man-work. Such a mistake would make your dog trigger-happy. Like a young setter who streaks for the exact bit of cover where he has always found birds, and the hound who heads straight for the mud flat where there's generally a coon track, your dog would come to regard his own "beat" as top varmint cover and would travel about with a mighty short fuse. The dog won't lose anything in readiness by giving him lots of practice in obedience in his future work area and doing the man-work elsewhere. His targets will hide, run, or fight, so there will be plenty of signs, plus your encouragement, to tell him that a varmint may be in a crowd of innocent people. Later, if you feel he's a bit too slack, you can tighten him up by running him on a couple of problems in the duty area.

In the case of the car dog, which may be used in any part of your community, you should do your man-work in all possible situations. Your dog will soon come to take each exit from the car as the start of some action, but his hair-trigger will not be too much of a risk in these instances because, generally, when he leaves the car while on duty it is to go into a "hot-spot" and his "ready" appearance is an asset.

A good example of a place to stage the first lesson is an alley in a business district, although the same procedures and goals will apply regardless of where you make your first setup. The first objective is to give your dog an experience that will show him that varmints aren't all confined to the place where he began his hunting career. You should use very simple problems to gain this goal. You and your agitator should visit your new training area and become familiar with its characteristics before you set up your first problem. Determine which features of the alley would give the man the best concealment, combined with good footing and room to maneuver and run. Find out the daylight hours during which the alley is most deserted, and schedule your session for that time. You'll need good light for the coördination you must have.

The agitator should arrive for the training session ahead of you and park his car about 100 feet from the alley so that it can be used as a calaboose. For equipment, he will need only his switch and sack. He should walk back into the alley and conceal himself in one of the spots that you selected earlier. Though not essential, it will give the dog a bit of practice in using his nose if the problem is set with the wind blowing from the man to the dog. The man should be hidden and quiet by the time you drive up with the dog.

The dog should be wearing his harness and his training collar, to which a leash has been attached, so that you are prepared to make a correction if he starts to leave the car before he gets your command to "come." When he's out of the car, have him sit-stay while you fasten your second leash to his harness. You should continue to use this double rigging for safety, control, and the dog's comfort until told to do differently. Tell the dog "O.K.," and let him go out to the full length of the leashes as you start into the alley.

If the air movement is right, your dog may alert on scent from the man or his tracks. If so, praise him, and let him lead you toward the man. If scent conditions are unfavorable, he may start to walk on by the man's hideout, in which case the man should make a slight noise to attract his attention. This experience will show him that he can hunt varmints by listening as well as watching. Regardless of how he detects the man's presence, he'll probably show a moment's indecision after he has identified the varmint. Now, whether or not there is indecision, by slowly raising his sack for a swing, the man confirms that the dog really has found his first varmint in new cover. As the arm raises, give your dog the command to "Go!" and let the dog lunge toward the man. The varmint should scramble away just ahead of the lunge, with his sack swinging out behind him. You must use your two leashes skillfully to prevent the pursuing dog from grabbing the sack until after the man has run 15 or 20 feet. The agitator should resist just enough, as the sack is jerked from his hand, to give the dog the satisfaction of beating a weakening varmint. When the dog gets the sack away from him, the man should freeze, with his hands tight to his sides.

Now, even if the dog is still shaking the sack, order the agitator in stern tones to "Move!" Then transport him back to his own car. Lock the varmint up; take the dog back to your car and let him soak while you go back to the agitator and, with no possibility of the dog seeing you, set up another similar problem in the alley. You need not make a big move from the spot where you worked before—with an inexperienced police dog, as with a young bird dog, a lot of quick finds in easy cover can do much to build drive and intensity. Make a dog want to hunt and he will learn how to hunt.

Four or five problems, set up and handled in the above manner, will be enough for the day. Though there will be some variation in the geography of the problems, none should be made very difficult, for while they have some value in exercising the dog's powers of detection, the main objective is to use easy successes to build the dog's hunting interest into an obsession. Give the dog five such days of this work. By the end of this time, you will agree fully that the basic motivation of your police dog is not affection and concern for you, but a hunting desire which has become focused on men whom he will identify by their actions whenever you take him from home to field. But don't feel deflated—you will find that the affection and understanding the two of you share will make him an even better hunting dog.

Accustom your dog to all kinds of footing.

17. CONDITIONING TO OBSTACLES

Now that the dog's enthusiasm for man-hunting has become an obsession, it is time to accustom him to the many variations in physical conditions which he may meet in the course of duty. If he's had no experience around water, and might have to work in wet areas, introduce him to the element by calling him across a shallow creek while you hold the end of your slack longe line so that he can't run up and down the bank trying to find a drier route. Let him decide that water is the only route to you, but don't force him. He may soon develop such a familiarity with water and swimming that he will jump off a bank and swim to you.

Accustom your dog to all kinds of footing: high, strange-appearing, shaky, narrow, and noisy. Old-fashioned fire escapes, elevators, small boats, springy single-plank piers, and slippery tile floors are examples of places where your dog should gain experience. A great variety of noises and sensations will be provided by such places as cabinet shops, machine shops, airports, construction jobs, tunnels, and absolutely dark rooms. A week of this supplementary program should be ample to accustom the dog to nearly all situations and to reveal any exceptional conditions which may require additional work.

For your dog's confidence, as well as your own, have him work out a few man problems in some of the more unusual places. As your dog readily meets these new demands on his courage and stability, you'll come to appreciate what was accomplished by that early "threat and gun" test.

18. THE TRIGGER

The fact that you now have a dog dedicated to hunting and fighting human varmints in many kinds of physical situations has brought you a well-earned satisfaction—and a very obvious responsibility. This responsibility is that of understanding and controlling the "trigger" that launches the dog's attack. What signal to attack may be most safely used? Should it be words, the varmint's actions, either, or both? For example, one may well question that nice-sounding phrase, "attacks only on command," realizing that the handler of such a dog, if occupied with a group of hoodlums, would not be protected by his dog from a surprise attack from the rear. If, instead, you want your dog to act if he sees a varmint about to brain you from behind, you'll have to violate the "attacks only on command" precept.

Without doubt, you'll make the only logical choice, and are wishing that we'd get on with developing a dog that will protect you from the threats you may not observe, but will refrain from making unwarranted attacks. Let's start by considering what you've accomplished so far by means of experience and association in providing the dog with a signal.

Actually, since you have never set your dog on an inoffensive or immobile man, it is obvious that the release of "Get 'em!" or "Go!"— and it is a release, not a command—has always been accompanied by a varmint's provoking actions which are more stimulating than anything you might say. If a varmint does not act, you will find that your words will be no more than further encouragement to readiness. Your dog's background will cause him to withhold his attack until the man moves. Because of this, it can be well said that the signal to attack is a combination of words that "cocks the gun," and the trigger is pulled by the varmint's threatening action. However, experience has taught the dog from the first day on the board that he need not wait for a word signal before fighting a person who is starting to attack him or his master, a comfort to those on the "cop's side" in this game of cops and robbers.

Further protection for the innocent who might make sudden motions such as waving to a friend, or stepping forward with a friendly gesture, comes from the rigorous obedience work you've given your dog on streets among "good guys." He knows from the differences in the physical signs that no threat exists, and through those other mediums that dogs use (to the astonishment of humans), that none charges the atmosphere.

The above considerations emphasize the fact that a police dog must use initiative as well as discretion in deciding when to attack. This "when to attack," then, is a matter of the dog relying on his own judgment instead of being influenced solely by your controls. You can further develop his judgment in this area by supplying more experience with good guys and bad guys, and you can do much to increase his self-control with your supplementary obedience program. The answer to equipping the dog with a reliable "trigger" lies in giving him adequate experience of the kind that he's been getting, rather than any change in the method of training.

This shows how a hand can hold both the sleeve-grip and a weapon.

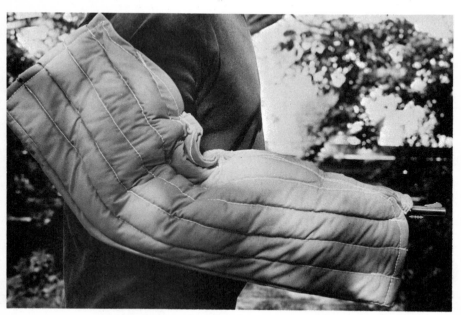

The canvas sleeve and weapon in profile.

19. SOLID ON THE ARM

Your next responsibility is to make certain that the dog attacks and holds the offensive part of the varmint's anatomy, which is to say that he should be "solid on the arm," for it is the arm that extends a gun or knife, raises a club, or throws out a hand to grab. Again, we have training that is not a matter of what you can teach the dog but what the dog can learn from the experience you will provide.

Because you started properly, you have already provided a good foundation of experience. Your dog's first focus was set back on the board when that maddening burlap sack was the only thing that the relief-hungry dog could grab. Later, he began to get an inkling that he could get in behind the switch, and lock on the sack, which would stop the stinging. From the work that followed, he learned that the handiest way to stop an attacking or a fleeing varmint was by a hold on the arm which each time extended either threateningly or protectingly out from the man. Further experience can teach him that it's not only inconvenient, but painful, to focus on anything else but the part that extends. Just as a tough old wild boar can quickly teach a green hound that "the right hold" can keep the dog from getting ripped open, a human varmint can teach your dog that the way to prevent pain is to get and keep that "right hold" on the arm.

The sacks you used during basic agitation, and which were later wrapped around the heavy's arm to start the dog focusing properly, served their purpose well. Now, so that your dog can be conditioned to lock and hang, your heavy will need a sleeve such as the one shown on page 136. It extends from just past the wearer's hand to his elbow, which it permits to work freely, and continues on, on the backside, in a way that shields the upper arm. The filler that protects against injury is a layer of kapok or hair. The cover, inside and out, is heavy canvas. It is quilted with longitudinal rows of stitches about two inches apart to prevent the padding from shifting. A hand-grip, made from a roll of the cover material, is sewn across the lower end so that the heavy can hold both his weapon and the sleeve firmly as he tussles with the dog. From the above description and the picture, an upholsterer can easily make a sleeve for you.

As you start this next level of training, remember that a mistake can rob you of all you have accomplished with your dog, so be certain that you and your helper proceed correctly.

Put the sleeve on the heavy's arm, and see that he has a good grip on a lath about three feet long. Position the man in a hideout which will permit good footwork and freedom of action. Before you bring the dog into the area, double check your equipment. The collar, harness, and both leashes should be used. This exercise to make a dog "solid on the arm" is not a problem in detection, so the man can scuff his foot or make another noise to cause an alert as you and your dog approach his hideout. The man should be in a fighting posture when he's discovered, with the lath poised to whack the dog on the side at the moment of the charge. *Your job is to slow the dog just enough, without discouraging him, to give the man time to finish his swing and square his arm to the dog's attack.*

If the dog should be surprised by the shape and texture of the new sleeve and pause, he should get another whack with the flat of the lath, and any other agitation necessary to fire him. When the dog is locked on the sleeve, the heavy should give him a short tussle, then release his grip on the sleeve and lath, and stand motionless. Praise the dog, and, if he wants to, let him shake the sleeve a bit. Transport the man to his car or other confinement. Take the dog from the area while the heavy sets himself up for another exercise.

Nothing will be lost by using the same hideout several consecutive times, even though the dog heads directly for that spot. However, the fact that he does make a beeline for the heavy will make it even more necessary for you to use great skill in slowing him a bit as the heavy gives ground, so that there will be time for two swings with the lath before the dog gets the arm. Also, the tussle should be a bit longer this time. Repeat these fighting-patterns five times daily for a few days, progressively lengthening the periods of action until your dog is standing up to several whacks with the lath before he gets to stop the blows by locking onto the arm and hanging for a tussle of a minute or more before the heavy releases the sleeve.

Occasionally, have the heavy change from lath to a gun, so that he can fire a couple of shots straight up as the dog starts his attack. Caution the man against firing in alignment with the dog, because the powder from a blank can discharge unpredictably. *Do not permit the heavy to grip the sleeve with one hand and the weapon with the other hand.* In actual combat, it is almost .always the weapon hand that is extended offensively, so condition the dog accordingly.

If you and your heavy are careful and skillful, a few days of work should convince your dog that he can drive right through any threat or physical discomfort and stop all the trouble by locking onto its source—the arm.

Instant and absolute control around livestock is a good fundamental step in teaching the "out."

20. "OUT"

When you have progressed to a point where your dog is attacking at the right time and is solid on the arm, you will come to the most exacting job in the training of a police dog: teaching the dog to release his hold and to stop any other action when he hears your command, which will be the word *out*. Until now, the fights have been resolved by the heavy stopping his resistance as the dog tears the sack or sleeve away from him. Such dismemberment would be a most impractical way to end combat with a suspect, deserving though he may be.

Once more, what you have accomplished will make a good foundation for what you must do. The alertness and instant response you've gained by doing intense obedience work in varied situations, particularly when you've used the throw chain and light line, will show you a new worth. We'll start building on these past accomplishments by working the dog in hundreds of situations which, though they may seem unrelated to the problem, will give him further practice in instant response.

Equipped with a throw-chain, and with your dog on a light line, give him an "O.K." release to go into a situation which will be sure to interest him very much. A corral with livestock, a pen of noisy pigs, or a similar environment should do for a starter. Try not to jingle your throw-chain or tighten the line, or do anything else that would lessen his involvement with temptation. Be behind him by the time he becomes more concerned with the distraction than with your presence. At the moment when he's most occupied, command *"out,"* in a positive tone. If he responds immediately to the word, give him praise; if not, use your throw-chain. It's an "out," not a recall, so it isn't necessary for him to come to you. If your tempting animal should start to run, the light line will squelch any thought the dog might have about chasing after it. Though they may be hearing it for the first time, most dogs will react to the guttural sound of "out," with a promptness that cannot be attained by "no-no," "naughty-naughty," or other such drivel. This is easily understood, since it's akin to the snarl a mother makes to a pup just before she clobbers him.

You may have to work for a long time before your dog will let his attention go from you to the next temptation, but work until you get a chance for another "out." As is mentioned on page 152 of the obedience section, even during those moments when the dog refuses to interest himself in the temptations you supply, you are gaining in another way by building self-control and attentiveness in him. *The more difficult it becomes to distract him, the more reliably he will "out" in the maximum distraction of combat.*

When you are sure that no available animals will pull his attention from you, set up situations where he will discover food or other good odors, and work for opportunities to get him to "out" when he is deeply occupied with smelling. One thing that makes an excellent distraction is a soft cotton cloth that has been wiped around in the scent dripped by a bitch in season. A kennel or a veterinary hospital can supply such a scent or, better still, use the bitch herself during her most attractive days. Don't feel, as some might, that the reproductive urge is such a strong motivation in a dog that such a temptation would be unfair. The predatory or fight instinct is stronger. If not muzzled and carefully handled, a dog and bitch from pit-fighting stock would try to kill each other rather than breed. Though the American Kennel Club tries to prevent such a situation, every dog show has a few females that provide attractive odors that are completely ignored by the great majority of the dogs competing in obedience. This should show you what is reasonable to expect from your dog. Later, out on the job, you won't want him to turn his attention from work to a passing female, so it is perfectly in order to teach him to "out" in the middle of such distraction now.

When you reach a point—and not before—where it seems that nothing living nor inanimate can make your dog ignore your "out" command, you will be qualified to try the dog on a man. Before you ever try an "out" command when he's in combat, you should work on stopping your dog when he's streaking toward a man who acts like a varmint, then surrenders before the dog reaches him. Again, we'll forego any practice in detection so that the setup can be simple and well coördinated, such as in the following example.

First, place one of the men known to the dog as a heavy in a situation that provides good footing and where he can suddenly confront the dog. For the purpose of quick identification, the man should wear the sleeve. There is good reason for wanting this prompt recognition. If you can control the dog when he is faced by a man he remembers fighting, you can control him more certainly against those he has no reason to hate. Only the chain collar and one leash should be on the dog as you bring him into the area. Unlike the harness, which he associates with agitation, his chain collar is associated with immediate response to you. Move toward the hideout with the dog at heel. The throw-chain should be held quiet but ready, so if you are right-handed and are holding the leash with your left hand, be certain to have the usual amount of slack in it.

Now comes another one of those moments when you and your heavy must do things exactly right. He should jump out when the dog is a few yards from him, and make a threatening gesture. At this moment, you should give the command, "Get 'em!" or "Go!" and move forward with the dog's lunge. The man should backpedal as though in retreat until the dog gets about ten feet from him, then stop and stand motionless with his hands at his sides. Your "out!" should be timed to the man's stop. Reward your dog with a mild word of praise if he responds to the command; use your throw-chain properly if he does not. With the dog at heel, take one step toward the suspect, then stop. Because the dog was at heel, he should sit automatically, so make any corrections necessary to enforce obedience.

Past situations that have developed into fights have been resolved by the dog's getting the sleeve and have ended by transporting the suspect to confinement, so if you order the man to walk, the dog's experience will tell him that the move is not an attempt by the man to run away. The dog will probably be less pressing than at the times when he was influenced by the harness and hot from a fight. Transport the man to confinement, and give the dog a ten-minute break in your car while you set up another simple problem, which you should handle exactly as you did this first one.

Repeat this format over and over the first day, using the same agitator, until the dog "outs" and starts to sit at the instant of the man's surrender and your command and seems determined not to give you a chance to use the throw-chain. At this stage of training you are not likely to diminish the dog's interest in his work by such a strong concentration of experience, and later there will be more fights to revive any lag in his enthusiasm.

For the next few days repeat the format outlined above. Do not do any man-work other than that used for teaching the "out." You will gain much by concentrating on the single aspect at this time. When your dog takes the suspect's surrender as a cue to stop his attack, and only one word is needed to prevent him from tightening the leash when his quarry stops, you can begin to teach him to "out" when surrender comes in the heat of battle.

Again, the simplest setups should be used so that all concerned can concentrate on the sole objective of teaching the dog to stop fighting when the varmint quits the battle. Give the agitator who has worked the most time to hide. Then equip the dog with the chain collar and leash and, with your throw-chain ready, head for the spot where the fight will take place. Give the command to attack as the heavy jumps out to threaten and, with a good grip on the leash, let the dog have plenty of slack to get the arm. After a short and not too violent tussle, the heavy should let the dog know by the only logical means that he has surrendered, which is to stop resisting the jerk of the dog, who has been conditioned by past success to wool the sleeve from the arm. *Although the man's arm should be as relaxed as possible, he should not release the sleeve.* Remember, this is an exercise in getting the dog off the man's arm, not getting the arm off the man. Although some regard the classic position of surrender as that of the hands raised over the head, this may be quite difficult for a man to assume when a 90-pound dog is hanging on his arm. (Humorously enough, the proponents of the upraised arms are fully aware that the least offensive way to address a strange dog is to stand a bit obliquely to him with hands hanging casually, not in a "hands-up" position.)

If your dog responds immediately, give him some sincere but quiet praise. Failure to respond should bring quick use of the chain and a leash correction that jerks the dog into a sit position. The heavy should walk in a subdued manner as you give him the order to move and transport him back to his car. Repeat this lesson enough times the first day to bring the dog to a point where he "outs" promptly on command.

The great deal of obedience you have given your dog, plus the experience of "outing" on the empty sleeve, leaves little chance that anything more than the throw-chain and a jerk will be needed to

144

enforce your "out" command, but if you have one of those exceptionally aggressive dogs that seem oblivious to the conventional corrections, you have no choice but to use a more drastic means. It is absolutely necessary that your dog release his hold under any condition when he hears your "out!" On page 53 of the obedience section you will find a detailed description of an implement used for correcting the fighter and indiscriminate biter. Read it carefully. The same corrective measures can be applied to the dog who has learned full well what "out" means but won't quit the joys of battle when he hears the word. *Do not substitute a lighter weight hose for the one described.*

Set up a situation in which your position will enable you to bring the hose down with a good clean chop midway across the top of the dog's muzzle should he fail to "out" immediately on command. The stroke should have the force you would use to drive a medium-sized nail. It is not pain that convinces the dog that he should have heeded your "out": it's the momentary numbness that deprives the dog of his faculties and stirs his deep instinct that tells him not to invite another correction that would leave him momentarily helpless. Your sit-and-stay commands should immediately follow this correction, and the lesson should be ended by transporting the suspect in the usual way.

There is another device that can be used for correcting a dog who understands the word *out* but does not respond satisfactorily. It is a low-voltage electrical shock applied with perfect timing. Its advantages and disadvantages can best be understood by comparing its use with the use of the hose.

The prototype of the devices I have used, but sparingly, was made in 1944 with a motorcycle battery and a Model T Ford coil which were fitted into a small army pack. Bell wire carried its six volts into a hand-held switch, and from there out to any ordinary chain collar on the dog's neck. With my thumb on the button, I could handily quicken a dog's responses. Now, with the fine small batteries and coils available, a compact unit can easily be made by any electrical shop. At least three brands of commercially made shocking units on the market sell, complete with wire and collar, for about $30. There are more sophisticated units made for frustrated houndmen who would want to correct a "trash-running" dog at distances up to a mile. These remote control devices cost approximately $300. Advertisements for both types of units can be found in all trailhound magazines.

As you reflect on the fact that touching a button can correct the dog on the end of a wire, or by remote control a mile away, you may wonder why these units aren't used exclusively for certain kinds of corrections. They have some disadvantages, the most harmful of which is that they will invite a button-balmy jackass to substitute meaningless discomfort for the fairness of adequate instruction and deserved correction. Another disagreeable feature is that an accidental pressure on the button can give a shock with ruinous timing. Further, in the case of a remote control unit, the signal from an electric garage door opener can activate the shock collar.

There are two definite "don'ts" to remember in using a shock device: (1) *Do not shock any dog with more than six volts, and* (2) *do not try to substitute a stock prod for one of the above-described units.* Decorum prevents me from telling you how I would like to dispose of those prods that get into the hands of dog trainers, but surely I may say that I would like the current turned on when I did it. You can see that in the hands of a good trainer, who will make certain that the dog will never get a shock before he understands what is required of him, such a correction is a most effective and humane way of enforcing obedience to the "out" when the dog is at a distance. The shock should be a matter of an instant, timed to the moment of the dog's refusal, and followed with the stabilizing "sit and stay," and the transporting of the suspect.

The weeks of experience you have had in training and handling your dog should qualify you to choose from the foregoing corrections the one that will be most suitable for him. If you choose wisely, a week of intense work should bring you to a level where you feel that your dog would "out" promptly under any condition when he is on leash. This means he is ready to be polished by the method of the gradually diminishing light line. It is important that you turn to page 155 of the obedience section and review that method. Its use has been proven infallible in straight obedience work, and it will be just as infallible in taking your dog to the point of "outing" reliably off leash.

21. FINAL POLISH

Strange Faces and Places

When you reach the level where your dog understands why and how he should attack, and he "outs" reliably off leash under any conditions, you can safely begin to give him experience in handling strange varmints who, like real lawbreakers, will not be wearing padded sleeves. Also, it will then be time to begin giving the dog practice in attacking and "outing" at longer distances from you.

The hardly noticeable protection that replaces the bulky sleeve can be made of a 6:00 or 6:50 tire with the bead cut off and its edges held together with wire or strong cord, as shown on the next page. Notice how the hand-hold is installed. This device is not only bite-proof, it is stiff enough to prevent sprains and fractures, and its diameter and firmness will condition the dog to hit with a wide-mouthed bite. Though it will bulge beneath a coat sleeve, this arm guard is not conspicuous to a dog.

As always, instruct a new heavy well before you let him work against your dog. *Be certain that your dog handles predictably at each level before going on to the next.* As in the case of the shorter distances, the light line joined to the collar by the tab will give you confidence in your ability to contact the dog in emergencies and, more important, is a constant reminder to him of the times when there was

Made from a tire, this protector can be covered by a coat sleeve.

something attached to his neck that was long enough and strong enough to stop him in his tracks. All other things relating to the attack, surrender, and "out" are the same as with the canvas sleeve.

Detection

Your dog will serve you much more often as an instrument of detection and a psychological deterrent to a suspect's resistance than as a weapon of attack, but keep in mind that both his ability for detection and the threat he poses spring from that varmintiness that you have developed in him. Because of this quality, he will show you an eagerness and sustained drive that can never be found in one of those dogs whose greatest satisfaction has been limited to barking at a suspect.

Sight is perhaps the least important of the senses your dog will use to detect things that you might not notice, although it is well to remember that some dogs are remarkably keen at seeing motion at night. Place no credit in the experiments that have been conducted with a few breeds and which have led some to believe that all dogs are similarly inferior in vision. Any dog man will tell you that their conclusions are only good for a laugh. Listen as a hound runs wide open through a brush patch on a black night and draw your own conclusions. Routine work with many opportunities to look at the actions of suspects will cause the dog to use his eyes to the greatest advantage.

A number of acceptable tests have established that the hearing of a dog is about seven times as keen as that of a man. Think what this can mean to you if your dog is given the experience that will attach significance to the slight sounds he hears so that he will want to investigate them. You can provide this experience at night by having a suspect conceal himself in a place unknown to you and the dog, but within the carrying distance of light sounds from where you will pass by. So that detection will be made through sound, not scent, the suspect should not be upwind from the dog. When you come along in the best beat-walking fashion, which is with the dog on an O.K. release a bit out in front of you on a slack leash, the suspect should bump something, slide his foot, or make another slight sound that is different from the other night noises.

Probably the dog will hear the sound before you do, so be ready to follow in any direction he might take you. The suspect's sound should

A good dog's powers of detection are greatly superior to those of a man.

be repeated intermittently so that the dog will get practice in orienting himself to a sound's source. He should take you to within a few feet of the suspect and then, since the man is standing inoffensively in the beam of your light, he should stop, because there is no reason to attack. Praise your dog sincerely, and with good reason—he just found a suspect you might have missed. Transport the man to end the session.

You might feel that it's a bit unrealistic to transport every suspect you encounter. On the contrary, there are at least two good reasons for the procedure. It keeps the dog attentive until he gets the definite release from alertness by seeing the job completed. Actually, you would transport nearly everyone you found hiding out on a night beat to a car, a call box, or at least to a lighted area for questioning.

Vary the nature of these sound setups until your dog has led you to investigate strange sounds that several different suspects have made in such places as old sheds, empty boxcars, stairways, and other hideouts that would be part of his work area. Let one in every half-dozen investigations result in a fight which the dog wins before "outing" and transporting the man. Later, when he enters service, he will need only an occasional "fight" to keep him checking out noises in a way that will be a comfort to you on black nights to come.

Sense of Smell

The sense of smell is the most important means of detection a dog can use to the benefit of man. It is also the sense that man does not possess to a practical working degree. Perhaps this disparity is the reason why a policeman will so often overlook the fact that there are situations where his dog must be used with a certain relationship to air movements if he is to get fullest benefits from those wonderful scenting powers. Examples of failure to use those powers fully are those instances in which a man and dog unit hunts a suspect in a deserted park, cemetery, or an orchard, and the dog's handler works down the middle or crisscrosses the area, disregarding a firm breeze that is carrying all scents to the downwind edge of the area. If you will keep in mind the existence of airborne scents, and run some daytime scent problems in which you correlate the effect of air movement on a piece of ribbon with the way the dog is working, you will soon learn much about scent work.

However, remember well a fact known to all who have lived with bird dogs and trail hounds: a scent can behave so unpredictably that

A dog's sense of smell can solve problems in heavy cover.

nobody can know positively the distance at which a dog should detect it. There are conditions which will make the finest setter bump a bird that is setting on what appears to be a perfect wind. When it comes to scent, your dog's judgment will always be better than your own. Be quick to move with your dog as he zigzags about in working out a scent pattern, so that a slacking leash encourages his investigation. If your work area includes parts that are seldom traveled, you will probably find that your dog will alert to a fresh track almost as intensely as he reacts to an airborne scent, and instinctively follow it. On both airborne and ground scents your dog's nose will prove to be a mighty valuable asset to you.

Manners on the Job

When you have polished your dog in the functions of detecting and handling suspects, turn your attention to another aspect of the police dog on the job: the relationship he has with you during the great preponderance of time when he is not engaged in working out a problem. Your dog should not make the hours when you are walking a beat an ordeal by taking your O.K. release from the heel position as a cue to strain on the leash. Each time he tries such a tactic, let out a bit more slack and catch him with a sharp right-about turn. He'll come to realize that even when you don't want him in a formal heel position you won't permit him to wear you both out by pulling on the leash.

At those times when your dog alerts on something, show encouragement by your willingness to follow at the pace he sets. If you encounter a suspect who would sooner bet on his speed than respond to your order to halt, take time to unsnap your dog's leash before you send him after the man. Although a desperate man may be lucky enough to gain advantage over the dog by grabbing a leash, he would need more than luck to grab a collar. If you feel you might be facing a desperate character who would try to get his fingers in the collar, you can play a real dirty trick on him by using a leather break-away collar that would not hold the weight of a fighting dog. This would con the man into grabbing for an apparent advantage and leave him holding a useless strap.

The dog that is part of a patrol-car operation should not be a squirrelly, frothing, noisy annoyance to the other occupants. You cannot instill quietness into your dog by trying to work him with one hand while you steer a car with the other. You can best make him regard his car as a place to be quiet by having him hold down-stays in his riding place while the car is parked, the doors wide open, and he is subjected to strong temptation from nearby dogs and other distractions. By the time he gets so solid that it seems no fair temptation can make him break, you'll find his attitude toward the "quiet place" will be stronger than the "motion-happiness" that makes him pace and whine. You may have to work very hard to bring about this change, because dogs that have the predatory drive for police work are quite often buzzed up by motion. Ideally, you will not put him on a stay as you drive about, unable to enforce your command, but the above process of associating the motionless car with temptation and correction can induce calmness to such a degree that it will carry over to when the car is in motion.

Your program of teaching the dog to stay when the car doors are open will pay off in another way. If you should rush from your car when a door or window is open, your dog will be more certain not to leave his place without your command, because he has had extra practice in holding while you make fast exits and leave the doors open.

Work just as diligently to make your dog come from the car on command as you do to make him stay. *To avoid confusion, work him on the recall with a light line until he will both stay and come reliably.* What a moment when a pack of troublemakers sees an able-looking dog come from a car on command and move eagerly up to a policeman they are surrounding! If you want him to appear ready, don't have him dragging his leash.

There might well come a night when you have the job of moving into the blackness toward some hard character who has nothing to lose by stopping you cold. Your footsteps will remind you that he can hear you coming and that you cannot hear him. These are the moments you will weigh against the hours of training and polishing you have given the dog who moves quietly near you. You'll feel that you made a good deal.

22. KEEP HIM SHARP

Congratulations! You've come a lot of hours and a lot of steps since that day when you first looked at what you hoped would have the makings of a police dog. Hard, intelligent work has brought him to the point of proven proficiency in detecting and apprehending suspects. You can greatly increase your chances of full satisfaction from the dog, and maintain his effectiveness, if you are as careful in your on-the-job handling as you were in your training, because whether it is done intentionally or carelessly, improper handling will adversely affect your dog.

The following example indicates just how unfair some of this poor handling can be. The victim was a very capable German Shepherd that served a wartime ordnance base. The dog's post included a road that divided a security area from several barracks occupied by the Women's Auxiliary Corps. After dark, there was no right, no reason, for anyone to cross the road. However, one major, a dedicated male, found reason to use the road as a secluded means of crossing from the ordnance area to the women's quarters. A civilian guard was regularly informed by the dog of these clandestine moves and, instead of challenging the officer's presence, responded to the dog's alert with an embarrassed "Shut up!" and nervous restraint with the leash. This example of stupidity may remind you to sympathize with your dog's viewpoint if he should alert on a councilman or your police chief.

Challenge the presence of everyone who appears to warrant questioning and, if they are cleared of suspicion, resolve the challenge by praising your dog for his alertness, and move on with him at heel.

You were advised not to run problems on your actual beat because the dog might become trigger-happy when he encountered someone in the place where he had fought a varmint. Omitting such practice makes it imperative that you prevent eager children, bubbling dowagers, and he-men who "know dogs" from forcing themselves onto him. Such sedation could lull him into feeling that his beat is part of a happy world where all evil is suspended. Regardless of how careful a handler is, it seems that the objective of holding a level will not prevent a dog's decline. The goal of improvement will best protect the quality of the dog's work and the status of the police dog in the community. Try to make your dog better.

Comparatively few of the individuals your dog encounters will be suspects who will give him exercise in fighting and breaking out on command, so about once a month you should run a few problems, more if needed, to keep him in good form.

Those responsible for the administration of the law force which you represent have a duty to see your dog work. In these demonstrations, do not be one of those patsies who let some antagonistic character set up a situation where the dog is made to match his senses against one or more men to whom the solution to an unrealistic problem is already known. Hold out for a difficult problem where there are many possible hiding places, and ask that the varmint be placed in a hideout which would be unpredictable to any of the participants; then, while your competition is guessing where the culprit might be, use your dog's senses to win out. *A varmint's breaking and running should be part of the problem.* Any official must admit to the logic of comparing a dog's speed with that of a man for the significance it might have to capturing a man in a crowded area where guns cannot be used. A short case of only a block is enough to leave the spectators feeling that a dog has certain advantages. If you can persuade the officials to use night problems, which are certainly the most realistic, for their observations, you will be doing a public service. Invitational demonstrations for the entertainment and education of non-official groups may not be a matter of necessity but, if carefully done, they will help to establish the police dog's prestige. Do not defeat your purpose by asking too much of the dog for the conditions that prevail. You can accomplish much by having your dog look good to a large group of spectators, so set up your problems in a way that will give them a look at all of the abilities he has, from detecting through capturing and transporting a suspect.

In the area of obedience, which makes the dog a safe and pleasant asset, there is often confusion brought about by meaningless commands, and disrespect caused by failure to make authoritative corrections results in an uncomfortable relationship between the handler and his dog.

Remember, the objective of merely maintaining a dog's level of obedience will not prevent decline. Instead, hold to the goal of constantly improving your dog's promptness and reliability as your best assurance that they will not diminish. This task can be made very enjoyable and profitable by polishing him up for competition in licensed obedience trials or, if he is not registered, in the very similar practice matches which are held in nearly all parts of the country. The experience will have great value to you and your dog, and you will find that the more your dog learns the more he is capable of learning.

When your dog is truly impressive in his response to your commands, *and not before,* obedience demonstrations before service clubs, school bodies, and other groups can help in another area of maintenance—the maintenance of his image.

It is my hope that your success in training your dog and maintaining his effectiveness will cause you to become so impressed with his potential that you will be challenged to make him into a worker that will truly demonstrate the worth of a police dog. A single dog trained to such a level can do much to promote high standards of police dog work that will help discourage lawbreaking. Your single dog can make me feel that this book was a very good thing for all concerned with it.

III. The Plant Security Dog

1. AN ALARM—AND MORE

The ways in which a good security dog can outperform the best electronic-alarm equipment and the senses of a human are interesting. For example, Macy's, one of New York's largest department stores, found that its conventional alarm systems provided no protection against thieves who entered with the shoppers and by closing time were hidden among the rugs or other merchandise. With their presence unknown to the security force, they had time to steal and conceal the loot on their persons, and hide out until they could exit with the next morning's shoppers, or in other convenient ways. Something better than electronic equipment and human faculties was introduced. A number of Doberman Pinschers did the job by being able to smell and hear with an efficiency that has not yet been duplicated by humans or electronics.

However, it was not the dog's ability to detect that did the most to eliminate the "night shoppers." The same thieves who would have had little fear of detection, relying on a court to accept such improvisations as "I fell asleep," "I was confused," "I fainted," or at the most to mete out a minimal sentence for trespassing, were discouraged by the thought that a dog might act without considering the legal complexities of treating a thief roughly. They did not want to test the truth of claims that the security guards "had excellent control of the dogs."

The value that dogs have to the security forces of stores and shops are demonstrated in greater measure in service to such plants as factories and industrial yards. Such areas are large, often poorly lighted, and generally the man who patrols them operates under conditions that afford perfect ambush. Moreover, they are likely to be situated in lonely areas where any alarm would bring a fruitlessly slow response. It is a fact that detection is no longer a strong deterrent to some trespassers, particularly to juveniles who feel it adds spice to the game. It is in such situations that a dog has the ability to confront intruders with something more than detection and the threat of arrest. His speed and fighting ability can make other places seem more attractive. If you will visualize the lonely job of a security guard in one of these isolated situations, it will be easy for you to appreciate the worth of a capable dog.

Valuable though he is when aided by a guard, a plant protection dog offers an even more impressive service when he acts alone. As is the case when he has a human helper, the dog offers more than detection and an alarm. Speed and fighting ability, and the certainty of attack, will make most intruders seek other areas.

Surely the foregoing statements of his usefulness indicate that time spent in selecting and developing a good security dog is an excellent investment.

2. WHAT HE IS

You must be sure that the objectives and training for a plant protection dog are compatible with your needs before you use the instructions presented in this section. Do this by comparing the function of the common watchdog with that of a plant protection dog. Because a watchdog on the farm or in the home is generally in the presence of someone who will answer his alarm, he can be useful whether or not he bites. Those he protects in turn protect him with their presence. In contrast, the plant protection dog is apt to be the only legitimate night occupant of a factory, store, or industrial yard. Probably no one will hear his alarm, so the only way he can protect himself and his property is by a prompt, all-out attack on anyone who enters his area without right. This means that he should attack the youth who crawls over the fence to retrieve a ball as well as a crook who may try to steal a truckload of tires. Only those responsible for his feeding and care should be able to safely enter his area. To start watering a dog down by "introducing" him to a stenographer, a maintenance man, and four other people is most inadvisable.

Trespassers who turn back from a dog do so from the absolute inevitability of attack, not from an alarm that no one is around to answer. The right of indiscriminate attack when a dog is on guard cannot be modified without lessening the dog's effectiveness. Anyone who says he wants a dog to work alone reliably, and then expects the

160

dog to welcome an employee who returns to get his forgotten tools, or a stockholder who wants to see the plant after dark, should not have a plant protection dog. The dog should have him. If the foregoing convinces you that you want a capable plant protection dog, the following instructions will take you to that goal.

3. FINDING A SECURITY DOG

The first step toward developing a plant dog is to recognize that such a dog must be motivated by something more than a sense of protectiveness. It is true that a watchdog in a small yard or in a house will oppose intrusion onto his property, but if that same dog were put in a ten-acre industrial yard he would probably feel that anyone rattling the fence at the far corner was really no concern of his. The motivation that sends a plant dog streaking toward a distant sound is the same quality that keeps a police dog primed for action.

He must be both a hunter and a fighter. Like the police dog, he must not retreat from the threat of club or gun. Because the two types of dogs have in common the need of hunting and fighting qualities, the processes of procuring, testing, and training a plant dog are, at certain levels, identical to those used for finding and developing a police dog. Read the material found in Part II, Chapters 4–6. When you have finished those pages, turn back to this section for answers to some questions that your study may have produced.

The first question that may have occurred to you as you read the above-mentioned chapters on screening and testing was why only purebred dogs were included on the "suitable" list when you might be able to find a big tough crossbred. The reason is that a greater percentage of these purebreds will possess predictable traits than would be found in crossbreds. Although, unlike the case of the police dog, the appearance of a plant protection dog need please only his owner, the reputation of breeds such as the German Shepherd or the Doberman Pinscher will help your cause. Further, the fact that many fear such dogs will sustain and even increase the dog's suspicion of those who show mistrust of him. So, unless you know of an outstanding crossbred, you are much better off to concentrate on a purebred.

If your watchdog's work area is to be in a store or shop where great speed will not be essential, as it is in the case of the dog who works outside, it will pay you to consider prospects in the Great Dane and St. Bernard breeds. Some of these dogs will agitate easily and are not often inclined to bother the stock and equipment left in their care. But consider only those who are exceptionally sound physically and mentally.

Another question that you may have is why you should spend time considering a lot of temperament traits when all you want is an indiscriminate biter who will not be exposed to the public. If you do not concern yourself with temperament, you may end up with a "mean dog" who appears formidable when he's on a chain or behind a fence but turns in panic when someone really moves in on him. More often than not the "mean" one is neurotic who blows up during a thunderstorm or in other noisy situations. If you find one that appears mean, and he does stand up to the gun and "heavy" test, give him a good try. If he won't stand his ground in the presence of his master, he's not likely to face up to a threat when he's alone.

Why choose a dog who looks like he could clear a six-foot fence when a less agile dog would be easier to confine? Great speed is one of the best assets of an attacking dog, and the appearance of agility helps to inspire fear. If your dog appears fast, it's a rare individual who will enter an area to find out how fast he is. As previously stated, in a store or other closely confining area, this speed is not so essential.

Naturally, if your dog is going to work outside in bad weather, a rough coat has advantages, while as long as the shedding of long hair is no problem any type of coat is suitable for the interior of a store or plant.

Time spent in doing a lot of looking for a dog that will pass your tests will be well repaid in a saving of training time.

163

4. START RIGHT

When you find a dog who appears to qualify, plan for his care and training before you take possession of him. *To house the dog in his future work area, where anyone would have the chance to befriend him and lessen his suspicion before he is trained, would be a costly mistake.* Wherever you house him, even if it's temporary, you must be certain that his accommodations are very secure as well as comfortable. Until you are his friend and master, your enclosure is the only thing that will keep him from heading back to his former home.

An example of a good portable facility which can be moved from one area to another is shown on page 2 in Section 2. You will find such facilities advertised in all leading dog magazines.

Your dog's effectiveness will be greatly influenced by his physical and mental condition, so it will pay you to study carefully the entire chapter on Care and Housing. *The part on poison-proofing may save his life.*

Do not permit anyone other than those one or two individuals who may share responsibility for the dog's care to contact him. Do not try to force yourself onto the dog. He'll come to feel that you "really belong" if you are the one who supplies his needs and cleans his run. If he's very aloof, casual acts such as sitting on a chair in his run while you actually interest yourself in reading a magazine will soon bring him around for a curious sniff at a guy who is so unconcerned with him. React to his advances with a mellow casualness that suggests such a relationship had been going on a lifetime. Soon you'll have the start of a friendship, and after one week can begin your obedience training.

You might be questioning why you should give your dog obedience training when he is to work in confinement and be unapproachable to people. Unapproachable as he should be in the area where he works, there will be times when you will have to take him other places, such as to a veterinarian's or to another place of confinement while work is being done in his home area. Obviously, as a dog who has been taught to bite in one situation, he will need obedience training to make him controllable in those areas where he dares not bite.

How much obedience training he'll need will depend much upon you and the dog. Don't worry that you will make him less effective as a protection dog by such training, for such will not be the case. At least eight weeks of training will be required to take him to a point where he can be handled easily when confronted with unfamiliar situations at a veterinarian's and elsewhere. You will gain such control over your dog if you follow the instructions given in the obedience section.

The "right start" with your dog should include a definite program of familiarizing him with the alternate handlers that were suggested on page 164. This can best be accomplished by having them work the dog correctly in his obedience exercises with the objective of being able to approach the dog and take control of him under all manner of conditions. Provide the district police and firemen with the phone numbers of these alternates, and post such information outside the plant premises for the most prompt and certain action in case of fire or other emergency.

5. BASIC AGITATION

You should be six weeks into your obedience program before you begin your dog's man-work. By such a time you will have sufficient feel and understanding of each other to communicate properly. Begin your work by carefully following the instructions for basic agitation, which are found in Chapters 8–12 of Part II. Choose and equip as illustrated a part of that area which your dog will later protect. If he is to work in a store or small shop, you may have to do some of your basic work elsewhere, but eventually he will have to have some on-the-spot training at his place of responsibility.

Again, do not house your dog nor install him in the work area until he shows you during his training periods there that he can no longer be approached by those other than yourself and one or two persons to whom you will accustom him.

After thoroughly completing the work required by the first four levels of agitation, your time can be most profitably used by concentrating on the training techniques that are especially intended for plant protection dogs.

6. PLANT AGITATION

That fourth level of agitation which let your dog satisfy himself on the hated sack should have left him looking for more combat. From now on, in his agitation we'll give him lots of practice in looking and listening for trouble—right in the area he will protect.

Each time a heavy attempts to enter your work area he will make distinctive noises which will come from definite directions. Both detection of and orientation to sounds are important to a dog if he is to make early and accurate alerts, and we can best keep his senses attuned by making him think that anyone he detects near his work area is certain to fight him, whether he comes over, under, or through the fence or door.

We'll start with the approach most commonly used, that of climbing over the fence. To save wear and tear on your agitator as well as your fence, you will need some sort of a scaling ladder. This piece of equipment should be a two-faced ladder of the type used by painters, and should be able to straddle your fence. The homemade ladder pictured opposite will serve nicely. The ladder will not only permit a man to enter easily—later he will need it to exit rapidly. Although the ladder will help the heavy to get across the wire with less sound than if he were scaling the bare fence, he can add a few natural noises by tapping the fence a bit on his way over.

The ladder should be positioned in a place where it can be seen by

167

The steps of this hinged scaling ladder are too steep for a dog to climb.

the dog when he is on the agitation board. Beginning with the sight of the man climbing the fence will give the dog the association with the sounds that such action produces. Everything necessary to the operation—board, ladder, and agitator—should be in place before you bring the dog into the area. Your second agitator, who watched the last level of work, should also be concealed in a place where he can watch this new action. When you've fastened the dog to the board, give him a few minutes to settle, then signal the varmint.

Your dog might be a bit puzzled by the unusual action of a man climbing over the fence, but by the time your heavy is walking toward him he'll recognize him as the "enemy." The dog's memory and the agitator's maniacal teasing should take him right back to that white-hot eagerness he felt before getting the sack at the last session. Finally, when he's throwing himself into the chain, the varmint should sting him with the switch, let him have the sack, and run for the fence.

You will do much to make your dog suspicious of unusual entrances by having the crook escape by the route he used to enter. Out of the area, the man should run from sight. Give the dog time for a few shakes of the sack, then signal for the agitator. This time the dog will probably alert as soon as he sights the man; however, the agitator should again make a bit of "natural" noise as he comes over the fence.

So that your dog doesn't become a sack-happy character who would shake and wool anything thrown to him while a thief walked off with the stock, we'll start teaching him to keep at least part of his mind on the heavy, even if he's still chewing the sack. This job rests with the agitator. As he starts flailing the ground with his switch, he should be alert for the frustrated dog to turn his attention back to the sack he had just been shaking. At this moment, the switch should sting the dog, and he should be able to grab another sack from heavy's hand. After a brief tussle, the heavy should scramble over the fence and out of sight.

A few times like this will start the dog thinking that it's better to tear something from the varmint than to chew on something already on the ground. After five days of having the agitator enter by the same route over the fence, your dog will be alerting on approach sounds that you cannot hear. It will then be time to begin moving your board to various parts of the work area. Generally, two days of agitation at a setup is enough to acquaint the dog with the sounds of approach for at least a hundred feet around the point of entry. *Each bit of ground and each part of the fence will have its own peculiar sound patterns, and the dog should become suspicious of them all.*

As you move your board around the area, have the heavy vary his mode of entrance occasionally by having him come in through a gate. If your fence stands over unpaved ground, the sight of a man digging under it will show the dog that even the man who comes in prone will stand up and fight him. Although it would be impractical to cut up fences during training periods, the agitator can tap and tug at the fence material, then enter and begin to agitate, which will show the dog that anyone who touches the fence in any way will be a person whom he should suspect. When you have worked the dog until he alerts reliably and resists all manner of approaches from all sides of his work area, he will be ready for advanced work in fighting.

This agitation board, made of heavy planks, can be moved from one part of an industrial plant to another.

170

7. FIGHTING

For a few moments try to think of yourself as a plant protection dog on duty. Unless you can do this, you cannot possibly appreciate why a certain type of fighter is best for the usual industrial building and yard situation. You couldn't do anything to hurt a trespasser who appeared behind a wire fence or atop a solid wall, but if you went too close to him there are things he could do to you. He could spear you with a sharp instrument, throw blinding material in your face, or clobber you with a rock, all without physical danger to himself. By staying back a bit until he is on your side of the fence, and then going for him, you would eliminate much of the threat to yourself, and be fighting on more equal terms. Your effectiveness would be greatly increased because rarely does a thief want to enter a place where a dog would have a fair chance to get at him. He knows that a dog wouldn't have to beat him in a fight in order to end his career. One bite can put quite a mark on a suspect, especially if it should require medical attention—and a dog, where he has room to match his speed against that of a human, has a good chance of getting more than one bite.

Now that you've considered plant protection from the dog's viewpoint, you are probably wondering how one goes about making a dog into a good fighter for such a purpose. First, we're going to call on something that Mother Nature puts into the dog family—a hunting ability that can be quickly shaped by experience. As the coyote learns

171

to wait until a careless rodent reaches a point where he can be cut off from his burrow, your dog must learn to wait until a man gets far enough inside the fence so that retreat can be cut off and the man can be made to fight where the odds favor speed. Just as the hungry coyote loses a meal when he rushes a rodent too soon, your dog must lose the chance for a good, satisfying fight when he moves in while the man is behind a fence or close to it. He must learn that his premature rush will end with the man on the wrong side of the fence.

So far, the dog has been on the board, back from the fence, and has had to wait for the fight to be brought to him. Each time he waited, he enjoyed a satisfying fight. He has developed the habit of waiting for the varmint to come to him. Now we must deepen that habit. Make a setup so the board is back about ten feet from a gate. As usual, have the agitator hide, fasten the dog to the board, and give him a few minutes to make him hungry for the trouble that always seems to come in such a situation. Then signal for the heavy.

The man should approach as quickly and quietly as possible and rush through the gate at the dog without a single pause. The fight must be brought to the dog so fast that there will be no reason for him to move toward the man. The dog must get the sack immediately—he should need no preliminary teasing by now to make him want relief. When the dog has his grip, the agitator should give him a short contest, and let him win. The man should run from the area as soon as the sack is torn from his hand. Give the dog a few minutes to soak in his victory, then repeat the formula of the man's quiet approach to the fence, his quick rush through the gate at the dog, the dog's victory, and the man's retreat. Work the dog five or six times in the above pattern for several training periods to convince him that, if he waits, the fight is sure to come to him.

Now, let's show him what will happen when he rushes in before the man reaches "the point of no return." Here's one good way of giving him an opportunity to make that mistake. The setup facing the gate will be the same, but the heavy's approach must be different—and perfect. This time the man should hesitate, not rush, as he opens the gate. If the dog stands watching the man for a few seconds, as though expecting him to rush, the man should reward him by rushing. *To make the dog wait more than a few seconds before rewarding him with a rush would be a big mistake*. When the dog has won a short tussle, the man should retreat.

It would be an even bigger mistake to reward the dog with a rush if he doesn't wait for the man to come to him, but lunges against the

172

chain before the man leaves the fence. In such a case, the man should go back through the gate and disappear. Through enough repetition of this experience, your dog will learn that he is sure to lose his quarry by making a move when the man is too close to the fence. To strengthen his pattern of waiting, the agitator should pause progressively longer at the gate, thus working to condition the dog to wait longer and longer for the man to come away from the fence. Eventually, the dog should be steady enough to wait while the man alternates between "sweet talk" and light teasing, which are always followed by the man taking the fight to the dog when he waits a bit, and foiling him by disappearing every time the dog tries to charge prematurely.

Wouldn't it be better to use a method that punishes the dog, not merely disappoints him if he rushes the fence? No. To use even a very effective method of physically correcting a dog that rushes past a point, such as a hot wire, would not be as good as developing a dog's craftiness in fighting. A dog inhibited by such mechanics could not match the intentness and concentration of a dog whose timing was controlled by his own cleverness.

When your dog does a good job of waiting for the man while on the board, you can start working toward the time when he will be unrestrained and alone. To protect the agitator, this must be done with caution. The procedure is to make setups all around the area, just as when you moved the board around; except that now, as the last step before complete freedom, your dog will be secured with a nylon cord of at least 500-pound test, which will be about 1/8" in diameter. The line should give the dog at least ten feet of slack, although more can be used if needed to reach back to good anchorage. See the example on page 174.

This line will have none of the weight or jingle of the chain, but it will deliver a solid, surprising jolt if the dog, encouraged by the "feel" of freedom, makes a premature lunge. As when he was on the chain, give the dog a victory when he waits, and deprive him of the satisfaction of a fight when he blunders. Again, it is better to develop the dog's natural tendencies than to train him to work a pattern with a handler or to use mechanical corrections, because when he's working alone all decisions will be his, and he can best meet the unpredictable problems by using his animal craftiness. Your line is merely a mechanical aid that will give his craftiness more opportunity to develop, and thus make him better at avoiding a thief's booby trap.

Reflect again on the fact that your dog will be alone in a situation where a thief could have hours to bluff him or sweet-talk him down.

A few surprises from this tied-off line will teach the dog to hold his rush until the man is close enough to trap.

Even though he has seen all types of approaches, suspicious, casual, and friendly, result in nothing but a fight and victory for himself, he can well use a bit more agitation. These heavies, both male and female, should be of various ages.

Instead of there being weight and tension to warn him that he's nearing the end of the line, he'll learn to gauge the distance he can move, and to hold his rush until the man gets close enough for him to grab. Work him on this exercise of gauging and waiting until it seems no teasing or talking could make him rush prematurely and blow the chance of getting the agitator.

8. TESTING FOR READINESS

There is one more thing you must do before trying your dog off the line. He should be tried against a variety of would-be intruders, both male and female. It is not feasible or necessary for you to train such helpers to do any agitation. They will not be exposed to the dangers of contact with the dog. They need only to make themselves seen or heard by the dog, and to retreat when he alerts. This will be enough to deepen his suspicion of all shapes and sizes of humans that may approach his area. When you are convinced that your dog is amply suspicious of all who try to approach him, he will be ready for a very interesting test.

Safety demands that before going to the process of testing and working your dog off the line, you should remember that he is not taught to "out" or stop attacking on command. There is good reason for this omission. The plant protection dog works in a unique situation. For him to be responsive to anyone's voice, even yours, during the heat of combat, could result in a moment of hesitation that could cost his life and your property. He is his own general when he's fighting alone and should be heedless to all shouts and commands. The only time he should quit fighting a trespasser is when you, or another familiar handler, take him out with a leash and a command, and even that shouldn't be too easy. As for him "holding a man at bay" until morning comes, forget it. The best way he can protect himself and your property is by the initiative of attack, not crouching like a sitting duck before one person while a second one gains an advantage. You can see where this inherent danger makes it necessary for you to proceed with the utmost caution in your off-the-line test.

You will need to test your dog under actual working conditions, when he is off the line and you are not right at hand, to prove that he does not construe your absence and his freedom from restraint as something that calls for a change from the suspicions and reactions of the training session. There are two contrivances that can be used in a limited way to protect a heavy during his fight with a plant protection dog. One is a muzzle that will protect the man from bites as the dog goes through the motions of fighting. The other is a padded suit, which is generally so grotesque and unrealistic that it allows only scant similarity to a human's appearance and movement. Obviously, the muzzle is the better choice. Have the dog wear the muzzle a few times before the test to make certain that it is secure and comfortable, and to accustom him to its feel. *Do not ever have him wear the muzzle when he is alone in the area.* He would know that you were subjecting him to a handicap in the very area which you have trained him to protect. I have actually heard of a few morons treating a dog in such a manner in an attempt to create a "bluff that would not get them into trouble." It's doubtful if such an unfortunate dog could be enough of a bluff to protect him against those who would revel in his helplessness. However, for the purpose of protecting those individuals who will help you test him, the muzzle will serve nicely.

To test your dog under actual working conditions, you will need a "thief" who is new to the dog, physically strong, and able to follow directions accurately. *Before you bring the dog into the area, the two of you should dry-walk the following instructions until there are no questions in your minds.* First, because more trespassers will come over the fence than through the gate, get set for that manner of entry. Put your scaling ladder where you can watch the action from a place of total concealment. In your dry-run, have your heavy rehearse his approach and retreat until he has the feel of the ladder and you have made sure that you can see all of his moves from your hideout. Set an exact time for his approach so that you will be alert at the moment of his entry. Muzzle your dog, and turn him loose in the area about half an hour before the approach time; then conceal yourself.

At the time set, the man should climb the fence and stop at the top until the dog moves into a position where you can see if the muzzle is in place. When you do not stop him, the man should start down the ladder, sweet-talking, bluffing, or doing anything he likes to get by the dog. Because your dog has been conditioned to "wait," he will probably let the man move out a ways from the fence before he makes his rush. However, the man should be set to foil a premature rush by retreating to the ladder at any time. *Without showing yourself, you should be ready for any emergency.* When contact is made, the man should let himself be borne back by the dog's attack, but should apply a couple of stinging cuts with the switch as he retreats to the ladder; then he should climb out and run away. Get to the dog in a hurry and put the leash on him so you can control his movements while you praise him and remove the muzzle.

You stood to gain in two ways by this test. If the dog attacked the man in the usual manner, it was a successful test under true working conditions, and the sting of the switch proved to the dog that he was right in his judgment. If the dog was confused by the change from the previous situations, where he was secured and you were close by, the fact that a stranger brought a fight to him was more evidence that, regardless of the situations, all intruders are enemies. Four or five such tests, changing trespassers, the places of approach, and the period of waiting, should give your dog a chance to prove he's ready to take his place on the job.

Protection Dogs for Stores and Vehicles

The same processes of basic agitation and on-the-job experience used to develop a dog for industrial yard service should be used to train one for work in a store, shop, or commercial vehicle. Because the area is less and the trespasser's access is limited to doors and windows, the problems of interior protection are generally fewer. However, care must be given to selecting a dog where physical and temperamental qualities are suited to the specific interior where he will work. As has been mentioned, such things as excessive shedding and destructive chewing would hardly be acceptable in a dog who guards a department store.

9. HE'S READY

Congratulations. You have brought your dog to a point where he would be quite a problem to any aspiring thief. Earlier, you looked at the problem of facing a heavy from the dog's perspective. Now, it will be very satisfying for you to look at some problems from the heavy's position. The dog you see is no "patsy" who crowds up against the fence where he could be clubbed or stabbed. He's had so much experience with "hot food" that you couldn't trap or poison him. Even your chances of hitting him with ammonia or projectiles are lessened by the distance he stays back from the fence. Whether he is barking or quiet, there is a look that shows you that he's not hanging back from fear—a look that tells you that once inside the fence you are going to have trouble. Your dog is ready to convince any prospective thief that he would encounter fewer problems elsewhere.

10. POSTING

A plant protection dog's greatest deterring force is his threat as a fighter but, if it is needed, he can be the keystone of an alarm system that will be effective even when the dog is alone—and more tamper-proof than a rigidly fixed, electronic-eye system. The following is an example of such a use which might be adapted to your situation.

The owner of a machine shop that was located in an outlying area was using a big German Shepherd for plant protection. He felt it best to use the dog inside the building for maximum protection of costly precision machines, which meant that the dog could do little to protect other things of value which were stored outside. This owner used ingenuity and a few simple materials to increase the dog's effectiveness. Inside each window at the exact level where the alerting dog placed his forepaws, the man installed a four-inch wide board. Each of these shelf-like boards was hinged on one end with the other end resting on a light coil spring, which kept the board's weight from bearing on a push button switch until such time as the additional force of the dog's paws made the board push the button. For as long as the dog looked out of a window, which was when anyone even walked near the property, a circuit of lights inside and outside the plant was charged. You can see how this sudden illumination could be quite discouraging to clandestine callers. The variety of things that can be done with such a dog-activated circuit is practically unlimited. It could ring bells, shoot a spotlight into the sky, or blow a horn.

Another example of an unusually effective way to use a dog has to do with the solving of a security problem in a rather large auto-wrecking yard that was plagued by more than average small parts thefts. The one dog, though excellent, could not protect the several acres against the teenagers, some of whom would hold the dog's attention at one end of the area while others raided the opposite end. The problem was solved not so much by the addition of a second dog, but in the manner he was posted. He was confined in a small enclosure in the middle of the area and was completely hidden from view by hundreds of car bodies. At the sound of the first dog's alert, the second dog's bark would echo through the corridors of junk. No one could tell exactly where the second dog was, and none of the brave *bandidos* wanted to be on the wrong side of the fence when he found out. You can see how this practice of posting one dog in concealment would be much more effective in a two-dog area than merely letting both dogs run in plain sight.

11. KEEP HIM WORKING

A plant dog, like other dogs that are motivated by a hunting instinct which was sharpened by agitation, must be protected against declining effectiveness. By the time he starts on his job, training experience has confirmed that all who approach his area will, indeed, turn out to be varmints whom he must fight. In all probability, much time will pass, and the dog may even see several meaningless approaches made to his area without his motivation being refueled by a fight. It is natural that such a total lack of reaffirming experiences could change the dog's attitude.

You can retain the effectiveness of your dog by giving him the right kind of experience once every three or four months. Start by anchoring the dog with your nylon cord as you did when you were teaching him to hang back from the fence and time his rushes. Have a skillful agitator, with a concealed switch and sack, make a stealthy approach and enter through the gate as though he has every right to be there. Without waiting for the dog to alert, the man should unlimber his sack and switch as he moves quickly to within the dog's range. By this time the dog is sure to be in action, and the agitator should sting him once with the switch, then let him grab the sack. When the dog has his grip, the man should run from the area. Give the dog at least half an hour to settle down. Then equip him with the muzzle you used in the latter stages of his training, double-checking it for security. Free the dog from the line so that he can run to any part of the area. Prepare to watch the proceedings from a nearby hideout, and when you are concealed, whistle for the agitator.

By now, the working patterns have probably been revived in the dog's mind and he will wait for the man to enter and get close enough to make a successful rush possible. The man should be borne back by the dog's attack, just as he did in the training sessions, and, holding the dog off as best he can, retreat from the area. Repeating this routine every three or four months will keep your dog convinced that eventually a varmint will enter his area and need to be fought.

Not so immediately apparent as the above results, but equally important to the overall effectiveness of your dog, are the benefits gained from providing your dog with the kind of care and personal interest that builds the emotional substance that all working dogs need. Section 2 can provide you with some helpful suggestions in such matters.

Thieves and vandals generally move along lines of least resistance and do not like being involved with dogs. The more capable your dog appears, the more certain they are to avoid him. This is another way of saying that time and money spent on good training, periodic reviews, and proper care will bring excellent returns.

IV. Military Dogs

1. THEY ARE NEEDED

"How would you take a sentry post covered by a man and dog?" This was the key question asked at the orientation meetings that introduced new students to the programs of the War Dog Reception and Training Centers during the last World War. When you consider that a great part of a sentry's purpose is fulfilled by detection and alarm, the significance of the question becomes very graphic. Should either the sentry or his dog alert and give alarm, the job is done. Such a post could only be neutralized if the man and dog were eliminated simultaneously. To attack one at a time would bring an alarm from the other. Though the movements of a man often follow a pattern, the actions of a dog are unpredictable, and neither bows and arrows nor guns could be expected to stop consciousness in an erratically moving dog concurrently with that of his master. A bark, or even a yelp of pain, would provide the alarm. The chance of jumping from ambush to club a dog is not worth considering. These foregoing facts occurred to the soldiers who listened to the above question, and no answers were forthcoming.

The question did more than instill confidence in the men whose lives could well depend on dogs. It gave sudden comprehension to those who doubted the value of dogs. Soon the keen senses and physical ability that made a good sentry-attack dog were employed in other military jobs. In vital defense plants, dogs increased several-fold the efficiency of the men they aided. In other cases they reduced security costs by replacing a man. They were used in enclosures to guard motor pools, and often were the sole guardians of warehouses, shops, and scores of other facilities. Prospects that were particularly impressive during basic training were placed in advanced classes for specialized military tactical work.

When the war was finished, the values that the dogs had demonstrated were generally forgotten, and only casually recalled at the time of the Korean conflict. Now, during the action in Vietnam, the uses of dogs are being "discovered" willy-nilly in a way that shows disregard of the fund of knowledge accumulated during World War II. I know of one trainer, with vast dog-training experience in this country and Europe, who probably contributed more than any other one man to the start of the K-9 Corps program. His advice could be of inestimable value, but it has not been sought. The same "oversight" applies in the cases of former Principle Trainers who might have shared their knowledge had it been requested. Oblivious to the wonderful results our scout dogs achieved in the South Pacific Theatre, the present Air Corps-administered facility has only recently "discovered" that dogs can save the lives of some of our men when included in patrol actions in Vietnam.

It is particularly in the areas of military use that are counterparts to police work and plant protection that knowledge has gone begging. In most situations the police dog that works for a civilian officer would do an equally good job for a military policeman, and there is no reason why the M.P. should be content with less. As a case in point, the author maintained a force of ten dogs that worked with civilian guards on an ordnance base; later, when security was taken over by the military, soldiers were familiarized with the dogs. All agreed that the extra finish on the dogs made them superior in all respects to the ordinary sentry-attack classification. Likewise, the dog that has been carefully trained to protect the yard of a trucking company will guard a motor pool.

The basic agitation that is common to these categories of dogs has another distinct value to the military. It creates the motivation fundamental to the training of a scout dog.

Consideration of the above similarity in requirements establishes that the advanced development of civilian training programs can provide some useful information for those working with military dogs.

2. SELECTION AND TRAINING

Military dogs of the kind motivated by agitation have exact counterparts among police dogs and plant protection dogs. The most widely used of the military dogs during World War II was the sentry dog, whose main purpose was to alert on smells and sounds that the human he accompanied could not sense; and the sentry attack-dog who, by reason of more agitation or greater aggressiveness, was eager to attack intruders who approached him.

Sentry Dogs

The instructions given in Part II, Chapters 1–14, plus the recommended obedience training, will provide a more thorough training course for both classifications of sentry dogs than that which the military is using at present. The author has seen some situations on military bases that required dogs of such finesse and polish that nothing less than full police training would suffice. The complete police dog section (Part II) will provide the instruction for choosing and training a dog of such capabilities.

The Scout Dog

The scout dog is that classification of military dog which is motivated by agitation to detect men. The distance at which a good scout dog can pinpoint a man makes for one of the most dramatic performances of a dog. The ability shown by scout dogs in the South Pacific during World War II was the substance of our jungle patrols by day and prevented infiltration of bivouac areas at night.

Because he must have a good nose in addition to a strong motivation, the selection of a scout dog candidate is more important than his training. The best trained, most strongly motivated dog cannot detect a man any farther than his nose will permit.

The following method has some value in determining a dog's scenting powers before you invest training time on him. The equipment you will use to make the test properly is the same as you will use in training and practice sessions, which means it will pay to get the best. A leather collar made of saddle skirting or other heavy material is essential. It should be two inches wide so that the pressure on a dog's neck when working will be comfortably distributed. It should be equipped with a heavy D-ring. A saddle-maker or a leather-worker can make you such a collar. You will need a web longe identical to the best quality "lunge lines" used for horses. It should be 35 feet long so that it will permit the dog to work an effective pattern. This non-kinking material is necessary to the handling of a scout dog, and is much better than a rope longe for any obedience training you might do.

At a time when there is a moderate breeze, have the dog's favorite person hide in tall grass or other cover. Hold the dog on the longe and leather collar, and starting at a point 100 yards downwind from the hidden person begin to quarter back and forth into the wind in casts that are 100 feet wide and not more than 50 feet deep. Keep moving slowly, giving the dog every opportunity to read the wind, until he shows you by his high-headed, eager attitude that he's on the "scent beam." By noting a bush or something else distinctive, mark the spot where the dog first reacted to the scent. Don't stop him, but retard him a little so exuberance won't pull him off the beam as he takes you to the person. Although you are testing, not training, he should be rewarded by letting him go to the man. Set up two more tests, moving the man about 75 feet to one side or another each time so that the dog must find him through scent, not memory. Each time, mark where the dog alerts so you can check the distances. A dog that shows he can scent a man who is 200 feet away on a breeze, though far from exceptional, may be worth trying.

As stated, this test will have some value in testing an untrained dog, but only in a rare case would one go out and seek a scout dog candidate from among untrained dogs. The general practice has been to make a selection from among those dogs that showed the best scenting powers during training or use as sentry dogs. In addition to proving they are trainable, the work that has been done on these favored candidates has made them want to hunt men, so further testing of their noses should be an easy matter. This is the way in which nearly all of the scout dog candidates trained so far have been selected. It will probably be the way you will find your prospects.

When a dog has been agitated to the point where he wants to hunt human varmints, particularly those hidden upwind from him, you can test his nose further by setting up problems where the agitator can be found only through powers of scent. Although your agitated prospect will be hunting a human varmint instead of scenting his master, you should handle your dog in the pattern of quartering recommended above for the testing of the untrained prospect. Each time the dog is rushing the last ten feet toward him, the agitator should jump up, stage a brief fight, and let the dog tear the sack from him as a running retreat takes him from the scene. The dog is slowed gently to a stop, and the exercise is terminated with enthusiastic praise.

Because there is no easy way for a human to reliably evaluate scenting conditions, you should make at least five of these tests on four different days before estimating the distance at which your dog can smell a man. In a total of 20 problems, a dog should score at least five hits at a distance of 100 yards to qualify as a prospect for scout work.

There is one thing that everyone who works a scout dog or an upland game dog should use at least once. This is some kind of a smoke pot which will help him learn the vagaries of the wind. On a day when there is a breeze, go alone with your smoke pot to an area that has a rolling terrain and some trees and bushes. Choose what would be a good place to hide an agitator, then move a couple of hundred feet downwind and face the spot. Now, as you stand there with the breeze square in your face, try to visualize what the air currents are doing. Next, start the smoke pot going and place it in what you thought would make a good agitator's spot. When the pot is putting out a good quantity of smoke, go back downwind to where you did your visualizing. Take a good long look. You may find you were wrong on the exact direction of the air movement. Certainly, you will be surprised by how the smoke splits and diffuses on the terrain and vegetation.

The smoke will do more than prove that you can be badly fooled by the wind. It will convince you that the key to your scout training will be to make your dog hunt men with such an intensity that he'll use his full ability to solve problems that you, with a human's limitation, could not even sense. *This means more agitation of the right kind.*

The best agitation that scout training can provide is that which comes as the culminating reward to each problem the dog solves. Let's study the example of a complete problem. Begin by surveying your work area so that you can hide the agitator in the spot that will permit your dog to make the longest possible approach to him from directly downwind. *Make sure your agitator goes to his hideout directly from the upwind side so that the dog will have to work an airborne scent, not a track.* A few minutes after the agitator is in place, bring the dog, equipped with the heavy leather collar and the longe line, to the bottom of the approach area, which should be several hundred yards downwind from the agitator. Your cue to the dog to start hunting will be simply to let out the full length of the longe and start moving slowly into the wind. Move forward in casts that are about 100 feet wide and 50 feet deep. This casting pattern seems to combine the best forward progress with reliable detection. However, as you go, keep alert to changes in the wind velocity that may indicate that you should vary your speed pattern or angle of approach.

When your dog hits, don't let him make a wild charge forward, which would be likely to spoil his reading of the beam. Move forward very slowly; his eagerness and instincts will then cause him to do some casting of his own, sometimes working as wide as the length of the line will permit. Naturally, if he takes all of the line to one side, you should move in that direction until he shows you that there is no reason to go farther. Then, as he gets closer to the agitator, and the scent strengthens, the casts will narrow and you'll know he is almost ready to make a rush. It's at this point that you can do something to increase his accuracy and your own ability to read him. Without a word, ease him to a stop so that he will be forced to take a reading on the scent while not running. When he moves out this time you can be quite sure that he'll be on the beam.

The agitator will see you and the dog before you see him, and should rise and set himself when the dogs gets to within 30 feet of him, so that you will be able to slow the dog's rush and coördinate the action before there is danger of a bite. The man should back away before the dog's rush, getting in one or two stinging cuts on the dog's side or front legs with his switch, and flicking the sack just out of his reach. This brief skirmish should end with a victory for the dog when he tears the sack from the man. The agitator should stand motionless while the dog wools the sack. The function of a scout dog is detection, and the fights are simply to add incentive, not to eliminate a man, so it's not a bad fault for him to be a bit sack-happy. Give the dog some praise, and then casually lead him away from the motionless agitator to where you can confine him while you set up another problem.

Use a lot of problems in a great variety of terrain to give both you and your dog practice in the fundamentals, ending each of them with the "running fight" that will keep him eager for the next hunt.

You have now reached a point in your training where you will acquire a new instructor. He will be your dog. "Learn by doing" is a phrase often heard. Hardly anywhere in the realm of human experience is its truth more clearly manifested than in scout dog training. Not only do trainers and dogs become familiar with the demands of their respective jobs through doing, but it is the way—and the only way—in which you can learn to read and evaluate each other's reactions to all aspects of a problem, such as wind, terrain, distractions, and so on. The dog half of the team often expresses his reactions so subtly that only the closest observation gained from many hours of experience will enable a handler to understand the significance of each move. It was this close affinity of man and dog, or merger of instincts, that was the outstanding attribute of some of the scout dog units that were so effective in the jungles of the South Pacific. One of the best of these dogs, a Giant Schnauzer, would indicate his first scent of man with no other sign than a quick raising and lowering of his ears. Each of the other dogs had a distinctive movement that meant something to his handler. By reading their dogs promptly, these men on many occasions saved themselves and the patrols they served. They had made this integration with their dogs in the only possible way: by hours of work in making their dogs want to hunt men, and a greater number of hours devoted to letting the dogs teach them how best to do that hunting.

It would require an extensive volume to cover all categories of military dogs that are used for a wide variety of purposes and trained in very dissimilar ways. Nevertheless, the inclusion in this book of the category of military dogs that is motivated by agitation is not to be taken as an incidental offshoot from the fund of material on their civilian counterparts. Dogs motivated by agitation are the ones most needed by the military, and the scout dog is needed most of all. It is the author's hope that the military will become more concerned with thoroughly researching the training and best use of these dogs. I believe that in many small unit operations the differences between no scout dogs, ordinary scout dogs, and the best possible scout dogs may be spelled out in blood. It could be in blood saved.

A Labrador Retriever scout dog helping seek out the enemy in Vietnam. Soldiers are of the Hawk Flight Squadron of 1st Air Cavalry Division, dropped by helicopter in areas of Viet Cong activity.

Section 2

CARE, HOUSING
AND
OBEDIENCE TRAINING

Runs like this, requiring no posts in the ground, are advertised in all dog magazines.

1. CARE AND HOUSING

Housing the Police Dog

You may be confused by the various opinions offered on the best way to house a police dog. In the past, the policy of complete isolation from anyone other than those he worked with was much used. Now many advocate that he should live in the house with a family in order that he may enjoy a fuller life and develop greater discrimination. Your own common sense and knowledge of your home environment will give you the answer as to what is best.

If your household is one to which a sound-sensitive dog could return after long hours on the job, eat his meal, and then get some hours of quiet privacy, he may not need other housing. On the other hand, if household activities were to constantly interrupt his rest, or if you have children with friends who may drop in unexpectedly, making unusual sounds and motions, your dog would be so busy discriminating between the sounds that he wouldn't get much rest.

If such is the case and you need an outside run, or would want one for part time confinement, you will find the one shown opposite worth considering. This run is made of pipe and chain link panels six feet high and ten feet long, which when joined together with fence fittings form a rigid structure that needs no posts in the ground. You can buy such panels and assemble the run yourself, and if necessary, it is easily dismantled for a move to another spot. Its top can be covered with light wire to stop a jumper; a wire or stones in the ground can foil a digger. You may find the local fence companies, particularly

3

those on the West Coast, surprised at the mention of these portable runs. However, such runs have been on the market for years.

These ten-by-ten runs have sufficient room for comfort and privacy. If you feel that your dog needs more exercise than he gets when confined and when he is working, you can give him a few minutes' liberty each day in a suitable area.

The world of people and dogs is filled with strange beliefs, but none more ridiculous than the common concept of what makes a suitable doghouse. Typically, one of the uninformed will point to a five-foot square house with a big door in its front and proudly call attention to its size, actually believing that an eighty-pound dog is fortunate to have such a monstrosity. No dog's body could heat such a building to a comfortable temperature in cold weather. A mighty big German Shepherd would have plenty of sleeping room in a square yard of floor space beneath a ceiling no more than 30 inches high. Obviously, in an extremely cold climate where a draft partition is needed, the "hall space" would be in addition to the sleeping area.

Feeding the Police Dog

Generally, it is better that advice on feeding come from a veterinarian, dog breeder, or other experienced person in the area where it is needed, because even in the case of nationally advertised brands, some dog foods and meats are more readily available than others in a particular locality. However, a police dog has some requirements aside from nutrition which may be overlooked by a feeding expert who is unfamiliar with the dog's work.

His confinement to a car or a downtown beat for long periods of time requires that your dog's diet be conducive to regular, predictable elimination and freedom from gaseousness. Further, he must be fed a kind and amount of food that will digest easily and not cause nausea when he is subjected to fast cornering and stop-and-go driving. These requirements can best be met by a basic diet of about 30 percent ground beef of the less expensive grades, so that it will contain the necessary fat, and 70 percent moist weight kibbled dog food.

Keep in mind that even the best brands of dog kibble vary in meeting the needs of a police dog. One brand, with national distribution, is outstanding nutritionally, but contains so much beet pulp and molasses that it produces twice the normal amount of fecal matter and is thus unsuitable for dogs that must be confined. Another brand,

4

widely available and good in most respects, is drenched with so much fish oil that it results in loose, unpredictable bowel movements. There will be some qualified person in your locality who can give you information on available kibbles that will meet your working dog's requirements.

Whether the meat should be lightly cooked or fed raw is a matter of whichever your dog digests better. Cooking a bit will provide some broth with which to mix the meat and meal to the consistency of a thick mush.

Gauge the amount your dog should be fed by building up to what he will eat with gusto and cutting back a bit when you have passed that point, or if his appetite threatens him with obesity. Feed him once a day; for the greatest alertness and comfort while he's working, the time of feeding should be a bit after he comes off duty. Wherever he might be fed, because of his poison-proofing your dog may be more at ease when eating from his own pan.

The manufacturers of the leading brands of dry dog food have done such a wonderful job that the country's most valuable dogs are fed on a diet such as above. It is debatable whether anything is gained by supplementing these fine products with vitamins. However, I am convinced that the addition of organically combined minerals can aid the dog's assimilation of his food and contribute to the good nerve sheathing that a hard-working dog needs. Such products, processed from sea kelp, have been used beneficially by many dog owners. Once a week, add a few big dog biscuits to your dog's regular diet, or give him a big beef bone, to clean his teeth.

When you find the diet that proves most suitable for your dog, keep him on it. To change because a dog goes off feed for a day or so will accomplish nothing. Neither canned foods nor their new dry substitutes feed your dog properly. Do not try to get by with them. The good diet you feed your dog will show in his top performance and health.

Housing the Plant Dog

The plant protection dog who guards such places as a store, machine shop, or any other area that has little or no yard space must necessarily be kenneled elsewhere. The fact that many of the best of such dogs are indiscriminate biters indicates that precautions are essential. The portable run described above is excellent, especially when its top is covered and either pavement, wire, or rocks in the ground would prevent any dog from digging out. A padlock is another good safety feature. Place the run where visitors cannot readily approach it and where the dog will have quiet and privacy.

In other types of plants, where there is considerable ground space, it might be possible to kennel the dog on the premises, providing that his run can be set up far enough from the day's activities to allow him the necessary rest and seclusion.

It is amazing how often owners who expect a dog to be alert and protective at night will make it impossible for him to get rest during the day by improvising a makeshift kennel facility in a noisy situation, thinking to save a few dollars. Check your own proposed location carefully to see whether it will provide the needed quiet. Don't kid yourself into believing that something inadequate will do; rather, spend a little money on a dog from whom you expect a lot.

The suggestions and precautions relative to the house or bed box for the police dog will apply to the housing of a plant protection dog.

In addition to the living accommodations dealt with above, the plant dog who works outside in extremely cold weather may need some shelter in his work area. This should not be so snug that it muffles sound and invites sleep, but only sufficient to offer shelter from the weather. If your plant dog has a suitable coat, such a shelter need be no more than a roof and windbreak. Place it in the most strategic part of the area.

Feeding the Plant Dog

The basic diet recommended for the police dog is well suited to plant dogs in nearly all situations, and is required by any dogs who ride as protectors of trucks and cars. Add from 10 percent to 20 percent ground suet to the ration of any dog who works in an industrial yard in extremely cold weather. If your dog works inside a building where he cannot relieve himself, feed him when he comes off duty. If he works outside, feed him about six hours before he goes on the job.

Housing the Personal Protection Dog

Generally, a personal protection dog will have the run of his property, sleeping in the house or another building. However, his adaptability shouldn't mean that his comfort should be overlooked. A wooden

6

bed box, placed in a strategic place, will give him the feeling of having something of his own and will make home all the more worth protecting.

If your dog needs to be confined at times in an area other than your yard, the portable run is especially suitable to the home situation because it can be moved about to accommodate changes in arrangements or landscaping. The other suggestions for housing police dogs apply nicely to the personal protection dog, except that if you have a small dog be sure that he's not provided with a house five times too big.

Feeding the Personal Protection Dog

There is a problem in feeding this type of dog that seldom affects the other kinds of working dogs. Living close to the kitchen, he may try to beg handouts. If he's successful, he's apt to become overweight, which will work against his health and effectiveness. Certainly, if he is fed a regular diet in his own pan and in a definite place, he will be less susceptible to bribery and poisoning. The basic diet recommended for police dogs is excellent for the personal dog. He should be fed at least six hours before you'll be depending on his alertness.

Grooming

You will probably develop such close familiarity with your dog that you will be quick to notice anything visibly wrong with him. However, some types of afflictions, such as parasites, the start of fungus infections, and, particularly, ear infections, should not be allowed to develop until they attract your attention. This is why thorough routine grooming and examination every two or three days is important to your dog's protection and comfort. A pet supply store can provide you with the proper equipment, insect repellents, ear lotion and other things needed to keep your dog well-groomed.

Poison Proofing

Police dogs and all types of guard dogs are among the most inviting targets to the dog poisoner. In addition to facing fiends who wish to cause suffering because of their sadistic nature, these working dogs represent barriers in the way of thieves and vandals who will profit by eliminating them.

Regardless of his motivation, you can foil any would-be poisoner by doing a thorough job of poison-proofing your dog. Obtain a battery-operated shocking device such as a stock-fence unit or an inexpensive substitute which an electrical shop can provide, neither of which supplies more than the six-volt output normal for such implements. Higher voltages would be useless and dangerous. Buy enough insulated light wire of the kind commonly called bell wire to reach from where you can place the unit out of the dog's sight and hearing to wherever you feel the dog might be exposed to poisoned food. Your unit is portable, so 100 feet of wire should be ample.

It will be easy for you to set up your unit and attach the wires. Check carefully to be certain that you've made a good ground connection to a pipe or a metal rod in the earth, and then run the lead wire to the point of the dog's first lesson. Remove the insulation from the last inch of the wire and shove the bared end into a choice piece of meat, raw or cooked, whichever might be the most appealing to your dog. Press the meat tightly against the ground or pavement so that when the current is on it will short out without arching or jumping a spark.

You can avoid looking foolish by making the following test. Turn the current on and come back; kneel down and place your ear close to the meat. Listen carefully. If you hear the slightest sparking, it means you have a bad contact with the earth, and you may be sure that as long as the sound occurs, your dog will refuse to sniff the meat, to say nothing of picking it up. Turn the current off while you press the meat tighter. Yes, I know—logically the meat would ground the current and you wouldn't be shocked unless you lifted it, but electricity can be so illogical. When you are certain all is ready, let the dog come into the area. Although it may take a bit of time, let him find the meat without help from you. When he does find it, the fact that it is in tight contact with the ground will prevent any indication that it is charged— until he has lifted it with his mouth.

The experience of having the shock take place in his mouth, instead of when he sniffed the meat, will be most memorable to the dog. It would probably be a waste of time to try another setup on the day of his first shock.

Regardless of how suspicious your dog has suddenly become of any food that isn't in his own feed pan, you must keep on challenging him with these "hot meat" setups in all places where food could be planted. Obviously it would be impractical to have anyone try to hand-feed a dog that has had agitation, but the more you can do to get an association of "hot meat" with varmints the less vulnerable he'll be. If he sees a stranger slide a piece of meat through a fence, and it turns out to be charged, he'll get that association. With work and ingenuity you can bring your dog to a point where he'll want to eat only out of his own pan. Test him every few months to see if he's forgotten his experience. If so, review the lessons.

To forestall any confusion, I would like to explain that the greater threat of poison to the working dog warrants the extra care required to arrange for the above-described experience, instead of using the simpler but somewhat less effective "spark to the nose" setup described on page 202 of this section.

Recreation

It is claimed that some animals are more intelligent than the dog but, by any standard of comparison, in emotional stature the dog is the closest creature to a good person. This means that a dog needs and deserves a pleasantly rounded life. True, working dogs enjoy opportunities for expression in the jobs for which they were found suited, but even the fullness of that gratification doesn't lessen an even deeper need. Above all other animals, the dog has a need to receive as well as give honest affection. He can stand much in the way of confinement and isolation without any adverse effects if his day is spiced by some period of companionship. In cases where his off-hours are spent in a home kennel, the dog can have some interesting breaks in the yard or house. Rides to and from the work area also help to round out his day.

The dog who is kenneled at the place where he works, with the exception of the home guard, doesn't have such pleasant occurrences to brighten his life unless a thoughtful owner arranges for them. Generally, an industrial yard has sufficient area to make the dog's exercise a simple matter, but twenty minutes of companionship in that same area during each day can make it seem like a more worthwhile place to the dog and give him more reason to protect it. *There should be no ball playing with any working dog. If he becomes ball-happy, he will be easy to distract from his job.*

9

An Emergency Handler

Aside from such association with humans incidental to his off-duty hours, there is something you should do for the dog's well-being and your own peace of mind. Bring the dog into close relationship with a capable adult member of the family, a friend, or an employee, so that he will become accustomed to the person's presence in many different situations, such as walking, riding, and visiting with you.

If the dog has had formal obedience training, as is certain to be the case with police and plant dogs, teach the person to handle him competently in all of the basic exercises. Be careful when you are instructing so that you do not confuse the dog by giving commands while the other person has the leash. When another is doing the handling, let the dog feel that he should obey that person without any voice from you. You are inviting trouble if you neglect this responsibility with a sloppy job of instruction. Your handler should be able to establish contact with your dog and bring him under control whether or not you are present. This work will pay off in security and convenience at times when you are away and your dog must be handled.

Instruction in obedience handling does not qualify its recipient to handle the dog on man-work.

Yes, I am familiar with the procedure of formally transferring the leash to an alternate handler and with it, supposedly, authority. When the substitute handler lacks the long hours of basic instructions needed to understand the principles of police work, the "turning over" can be ruinous to the dog. How can you pass on, in moments, what it took you hours and days to acquire? Think, and you'll realize the only way in which you can "turn over" the understanding and control of a dog is through a step-by-step program of instruction.

The Veterinarian

Introduce your dog to two veterinarians to double your chances of having one available at such times as he is needed. The best kind of introduction is that where you have the dog hold a stand-stay while the doctor goes through the motions of examining him. Because of his soundness of temperament and the conditioning he has received from the stand-for-examination exercise, your dog can be handled more easily than most dogs.

So that his first experience in being confined in a hospital is not when he is injured or sick, leave him at the veterinarian's overnight. Remember, you've made him suspicious of eating anything that is not served to him in the usual way, so arrange to leave his own feed pan at the hospital. *Point out to the doctor that there are some actions which the dog might misconstrue, such as someone hitting the front of a nearby run to quiet a noisy dog, or threatening moves of any kind.*

Many good dogs have been lost because laymen have tried to diagnose and treat an illness without the proper knowledge and equipment. In the case of a valuable police dog, which is generally supported by public funds, there is a definite responsibility to rely on the advice and care of the veterinary profession.

2. INTRODUCTION TO
OBEDIENCE TRAINING

The moral and legal responsibility to thoroughy obedience-train all police dogs as well as some types of personal guard dogs has been emphasized by facts stated in Section 1. That section provides exact instructions on how to prove to the satisfaction of a court whether or not a handler has sufficient control over his dog. The following obedience instructions have been included in response to these obligations. They present a method that has helped thousands to train their dogs to high standards of obedience in all conceivable situations. Among these thousands of owners are women and children with pets just as strong in body and will as your own dog, indicating that this method can help you meet your own responsibilities as well. Also, the widespread success of those less physically capable than yourself should remind you that your dog's obedience will inevitably be subjected to comparison.

The above-mentioned responsibilities are not the only reason why all working dogs should be obedience-trained. Regardless of his kind of work and his motivations, a dog that has been conditioned by such training is less confused by distractions. He focuses more quickly and accurately on the task at hand. It is therefore easy to understand why an obedience-trained dog, even one who has received no guard dog agitation, is generally a better watch dog after having been so trained. Such a dog has been closely oriented to his master and considers all situations in relation to him.

The step-by-step method of obedience training that follows does not lend itself to omissions. Complete each step in proper order. With your determination, the method will do more than help you shape your dog into a safe and effective worker. Happily, you will find that you and the dog will give something to each other that was not in the original job description.

Lesson I

FABLES AND FOIBLES

In the beginning, God created the Heaven and the Earth. Man, a bit later, created the fable that "the dog, when he understands, always wants to please."

The dog, the world's first opportunist, in some ways knowing more of man than man knew of him, sensed and endorsed this delightful state and was so constant and clever in his professions as to give man scant time to review the theory. Through generations the dog worked his wiles, sincere in his faith and devotion, but seeing no harm in throwing man an occasional herring, and in withholding respect from those loved ones whom he so easily bested in every battle of wits. So effective has been this strategy that in this day of communication, many books have catered profitably to those who believe they can train a dog while they hold him accountable only for those actions they approve, and write off the transgressions with, "He didn't understand —he really wants to please."

Offended? You feel a deriding finger is being pointed at the sentiment so many nice people have shared!

Let's check the "please" theory against the demonstrations of a large group of dogs. An obedience class will do nicely.

Here, from the sidelines of the brightly lighted tennis court that serves as a training area, we see a colorful pattern of thirty dogs and their handlers. It is the third lesson for the class, being preceded by a "debunking" night without dogs, and one other lesson with the dogs in a group. Standing in the center of the class, the instructor reviews the assignment that terminated the previous week's lesson, reminding the handlers that there had been time during the past week for all dogs to learn the actions of heeling and sitting at the handler's left side, in response to a single command, and that the period of instruction in these exercises is finished and that in all failures to respond promptly, corrections are justified.

We move closer as the class dresses into two long lines of handlers and dogs that face each other across a path four feet in width. The instructor tells the class that if obedience is needed most at moments of distraction or emergency, it would be stupid for a member to alibi a dog's misconduct with "he's so excited" when the animal is in tempting proximity to other dogs.

You notice four figures, apparently one male and three female, standing aloof from the other spectators. It is inevitable that you notice them. They're different. They're "wincers."

Your attention goes back to the instructor as he designates the first handler to heel his dog between the lines, emphasizing the difference between "restraining" and "training." The instructor points out that a dog's respect of slack in the leash proves that the handler has instilled the quality of attentiveness, as surely as a taut, restraining, cuing leash indicates a lack of effective training.

A man with a big fawn Boxer steps from a line and faces down the pathway. Before signaling the start, the instructor cautions the handler against the cruelties of light, nagging, unauthoritative corrections that, by their ineffectiveness, condition the dog, physically and mentally, to greater resistance.

"Mike, heel." Without a glance at his dog or a movement of the hand that holds the leash, Mike's handler moves forward in the detached, uncompromising manner of a wave sliding back to sea.

Mike, seemingly more concerned with the uncommunicative handler than with the dogs, inches away and walks attentively at the handler's left side as though charmed by the belly of slack in the leash.

A gyrating pup sees Mike approaching and stamps an invitation. Mike grows even more attentive to his handler. He is inches from the pup. A halt is called.

"Mike, sit."

Mike does.

The instructor signals Mike back to his place, then turns and points toward a dog at the far end of the other line.

"Faust, heel."

No glance down nor invitational tug accompanies the command as

14

a slender young woman steps out, makes a square turn, and moves smartly down between the lines. The big German Shepherd, ignoring the insults and advances of his classmates, does not challenge the slack in the leash as he focuses intently on his non-communicative handler.

"Faust, sit."

Faust does—a foot from a lunging Collie.

Six more times the instructor chooses a handler and dog to walk between the lines. Six more times we see the willing start, the dog's respect of the slack, and the prompt sit. Murmurs from the spectators tell you they share your approval of the performance.

The instructor nods toward the far end of the lines. "The brindle Boxer."

A man's voice asks, rather than commands, "Hans—heel?"

The dog that lunges out in front of the man resembles the first Boxer only in breed. In distracting situations where Mike had been attentive, Hans is heedless. Jerking his restraining, over-balanced handler with him, he jumps at each dog that comes into his wild-eyed focus. Action by the offended handlers of the other dogs prevents a dangerous and disagreeable "Donnybrook." Progress on the path between the lines is made possible only by the fact that the frustrated Hans seeks fresh opportunities in that direction. Hans is uninfluenced and even contemptuous of his master's puny restraining.

The instructor seems more concerned with studying the faces of the surrounding people than with the situation that threatens injury to one or more dogs. He appears unaware of a Great Dane's willingness to accept Hans's challenge. But when Hans is within one lunge of the rumbling Dane, the instructor raises his voice above the Boxer's air-starved gasps and growls, "Stop and sit him."

All observers turn the resentment they felt toward Hans full on the man who made such an unreasonable request.

Futilely, Hans's suffering handler strives with the big Boxer. "Hans, sit—sit. Sit, boy—sit."

Hans, delayed by the man's panicky efforts, rears up and mouths at his hands.

"Would you like to pet or praise him?" the instructor asks.

A snicker comes from the sidelines.

"Or," the instructor asks, holding out a small box, "would you like to offer him a tid-bit?"

Anger rumbles from the spectators. Obviously, Hans intends closing his mouth on something more satisfying than a piece of liver.

"Or would you like some help?" The man nods.

15

Turk and Duke, of Disney's *The Swiss Family Robinson*, strike out for the shore.

16

The instructor slips his thumb into the hand loop and deliberately drops the full six feet of slack into the leash. The dog, preparing to hurl himself at the Dane, is not aware that the instructor has done a quiet right-about turn and has gone, unannounced, in the opposite direction. Quite impersonally but very, very swiftly, the instructor travels four feet before Hans's unhampered lunge carries him to within a foot of the Dane.

It is inevitable that the leash finally tightens and, because of principles of inertia and momentum as old as creation, it is just as inevitable that Hans's flight change to the direction the man has already gone. Thwarted as to direction but not in purpose, Hans, the opportunist, shoots past the handler in the direction of a Poodle. Even as the dog passes, going north, another stealthy right-about sends the handler southward. Again, the impersonal force of momentum has its way.

Frustrated and furious, Hans turns his attention toward this handler who refuses to communicate his intentions. He rears against the handler, mouthing his protests at the man's arm.

"Hans, sit."

His command unheeded, the handler makes a correction with such force and in such manner that Hans sits from physical necessity.

"Oh—my."

The protest is snuffed out by the vehemence with which the watchers whirl and stare at the four "wincers." The idea that anyone would consider an emphatic correction to be cruel or undeserved when needed to save the dog from future injury, seems to nauseate the other spectators. Seeing themselves the only kindly people present, the four fly away like frightened crows, in the direction of some picnic tables. The other spectators turn back to the business at hand.

"Hans, heel."

Before the Boxer has time for appraisal, the handler starts back toward the Dane. Hans stiffens, then his attention flashes to the handler as though recalling that no communication will foretell a change of direction. Apparently there is only one way of knowing what this man will do—and that way is by watching him. You can't learn his intentions by listening, as there is no talking; and you can't know by feeling, since there is nothing to feel through a slack leash; and when the leash tightens, it is too late. He's already done it. You can't outwit a handler you can't outguess.

They are close to the Dane when the man makes the next right-about turn. Hans sweeps around to the man's left side before the leash has begun to tighten, and walks attentively, regarding the nearby dogs as so many booby traps.

The dog sits promptly on command when the instructor stops in front of the bewildered owner.

If the attentiveness and conduct of the dogs that preceded Hans was commendable, the seven that succeeded him were as impressive by contrast. Whether pugnaciously regarding their classmates as smorgasbord, or political in their attempts to exchange greetings, or merely over-exuberant, they demonstrated equal ability to disturb the peace. Their handlers were strikingly alike in their fault of constant communication, of giving the dogs the initiative, and of keeping themselves off-balance.

The nervous shuffling and stifled groans which the watchers accorded inept handling and lost opportunities, subsided. The contrast between good and bad handling seemed too emphatic to result from chance. The ease with which each struggling handler, when he followed the instructor's suggestions, eliminated inattentiveness and brought his dog under control, suggested that something other than dog training was taking place. The pattern seemed preconceived.

It was.

From the moment the handlers and dogs had moved from their cars to the training area, until the lines were formed, the instructor had been studying and classifying the people and their dogs, working to prepare the format he would use to prove his point—that intelligent dogs rarely want to please people whom they do not respect.

Because you, in influencing your dog to be happy, composed, and well-behaved in public places, must do some of your final polishing in distracting situations open to scrutiny, it is inevitable that you be bothered by overly sensitive spectators. It is important that you be equipped to deal with these eyebrow archers—and deal with them you must, lest you be confused by their protests and weakened in your purpose of thoroughly training your dog. The supersensitive observers are "kindly" people, most of whom take after a "kindly" parent or an aunt "who had a dog that was almost human and understood every word that was said without being trained." They range over most of the civilized world; generally one or more will be found close to where dogs are being worked. They often operate individually, but inflict their greatest cruelties when amalgamated into societies. They easily recognize each other by their smiles, which are as dried syrup on yesterday's pancakes. Their most noticeable habits are wincing when dogs are effectually corrected and smiling approvingly at each other

18

when a dozen ineffective corrections seem only to fire a dog's maniacal attempts to hurl his anatomy within reach of another dog that could maim him in one brief skirmish. Their common calls are: "I couldn't-do-that—I couldn't-do-that," and "Oh myyy—oh myyy." They have no mating call. This is easily understood.

When bothered by such critical observations, you will find the most effective counterirritant to be a proffered leash and a loud invitation such as: "Here—show me!" If the dog appears a bit formidable, the "wincer" is certain to hurry away.

Better still, let's use the initiative of a good general and hit the source of the misinformation which they would use to discredit your efforts. Take a look at some of the things that have been written in books and magazines—a really good look. This experience not only will prepare you for evaluating the comments and suggestions that come from the sidelines, but also will give you the confidence of action necessary for training a dog. The only equipment necessary for this analysis is an adequate public library, a telephone, and a twelve-inch ruler.

"But," you ask, "are you implying that writers and publishers of these books and articles have no facts to justify the opinions they express?"

Who, me? I'm implying nothing. Just grab your ruler and come on.

Here in a quiet corner of the library, from among volumes on the care and training of dogs, we take a book written by one of the most prominent men in the dog publishing field. Leaf past the pages where the author deals with dogs fighting each other, which fault he attributes to lack of confidence, making no distinction between the small dog who pipes his challenge from the sanctuary of his mistress's arms and the warrior who would smash his battle-scarred head through a window to engage an enemy. Next, dealing with contacts between the dog and cat, the author informs you, again without exceptions, that the biggest of dogs would be disillusioned were he to challenge a cat, and would surely be vanquished.

Now to a telephone. A call to a veterinarian of any experience will provide information that he has treated cats that have been rescued from dogs. A call to your local police station will reveal that the department has been involved in situations where a preying dog has harassed the cats of a neighborhood. So it seems that in spite of accounts of lucky cats who have jumped on the backs of the right dogs, it is universally known that there are dogs that hunt and dispatch cats for amusement, whether those cats are tough old "toms" or females rising in the indignation of motherhood.

"Everyone knows that some dogs kill cats. So what?" you ask.

Everyone except the man whose book is intended to advise you on training your dog!

Beginning with paragraph three of column two on page 133 of the November 1946 issue of *Better Homes and Gardens,* we have a priceless gem for your scrapbook. Mr. F. W. S., the discouraged owner of a "tugger," writes: "My wife and I would be very grateful if you will tell us how to break our Doberman Pinscher of pulling and jerking on the leash when walking. Giving a quick yank on his leash is just so much water off a duck's back."

Here is the "expert's" answer:

"The answer is heeling. This means to walk along by the side of the master in an orderly manner. This is taught by forcibly and firmly holding the dog in position, at the side of the thigh while walking.

"Specifically, the method is to take a firm hold of the dog's collar with the right hand, holding the end of the leash in the left hand. Hold the dog close-hauled against the right thigh, as you walk, not allowing the slightest give. Each time the dog tries to bolt, pull him firmly into position and hold him there, to impart to your dog your own firmness. Keep walking, holding the dog against your leg.

"Practice this heeling exercise ten minutes at a time, two or three times a day. It will gradually soak in—and the first thing you know, you'll have a well-behaved dog that heels as he should and walks down the street at your side without a leash. Don't forget to associate the word heel closely with the training, so that at its command, he'll quickly assume his proper position."

"But," you protest, "he's got the dog on the wrong side—he knows nothing about dogs."

You're right, both times. Now place one end of the ruler on the floor and you'll discover another thing he knows nothing about. People. Since the collar on the neck of a Dachshund, a Scotty, or a Yorkshire Terrier would rarely be a foot above the ground, holding the end of your ruler on the floor for fifteen minutes will give you a sample of the backache you would get if you tried to train a dog in the scuttling manner the "expert" recommends.

Recently, a pup beguiled people from the cover of a picture magazine. The accompanying copy told of a "tid-bit training technique," and decried punishment, claiming it caused inhibitions. Tragically, millions of readers will fail to see the difference between this popping of biscuits into "rote happy" situation workers and the training of dogs in conduct that is favorable even during moments of distraction or emergency—possibly when the dog is not even hungry!

A dog with a liking for leg-of-mailman will indulge his tastes, oblivious to the tid-bits that shower as manna from heaven. He'll probably end up as an incorrigible offender—another victim of the "have a cookie" or "shame-shame" shammers.

Magazines have dignified the prattle of "dog psychologists" who would rob the dog of a birthright that he has in common with all of God's creatures: the right to the consequences of his own action.

There will always be more emphasis and clarity to be had in the contrast between punishment and reward than from the technique of "only good," and if they obey, "still more good." And there is more meaning and awareness of living in a life that knows the consequences of both favorable and unfavorable action. So let's not deprive the dog of his privilege of experiencing the consequences of right and wrong, or, more definitely, punishment as well as praise.

Consideration of the above examples, and recollection of other things you have read, convince you that there are ideas expressed in books and periodicals not only infeasible but fantastic.

Confused?

You needn't be. Faithfully follow the instruction this book gives as a step-by-step progression to its first week's objectives and you'll be convinced that your dog is a thinking animal that learns by reasoning from the situations you provide.

You'll understand, too, why he doesn't always "want to please" the characters who belittle him with the belief that his proper conduct will be dictated by previous patterns through which he has been bribed or coaxed.

Dedicate your efforts to a fair trial of this book's instructions for one week and, instead of being confused, you will have acquired the mental equipment to correctly and confidently begin the training of your dog.

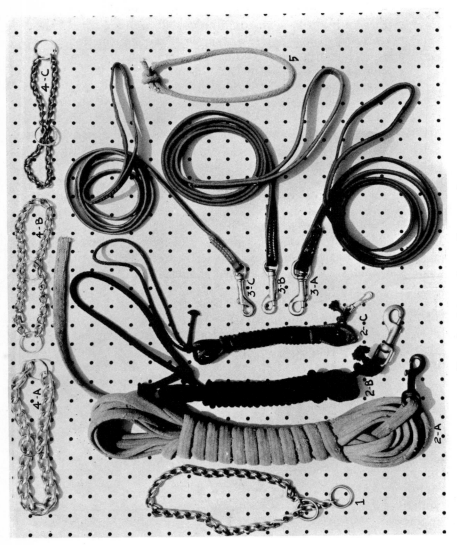

Have the right equipment for your dog.

Lesson II

CORRECT EQUIPMENT

No professional trainer would handicap himself with a short leash, or one made of chain, plastics, or other slippery material; nor would he attempt to use an improper training collar. It must be equally important for a non-professional to obtain the correct equipment, such as pictured and described in the following text. Remember—it will be impossible to employ some of the most effective and labor-saving techniques if you are not properly equipped.

Do not substitute.

ARTICLE 1. Collar. First in order of illustration is the article known as the "chain training collar" or "choke-chain." It is the most widely used of the two types practical for training. Its use is allowed in the exhibition rings of shows licensed or sanctioned by The American Kennel Club, which would permit its suggestion of authority to be present in all training and handling situations. This is certainly a most important reason for its selection. It is the type I use and recommend as being the most suitable for the methods of training and handling detailed in this book.

If your dog is larger than a Toy breed, avoid collars made of the fine, or jeweler-link material. Buy a collar of the heaviest links, preferably rectangular in shape, obtainable in the length you need. Make certain you are not sold one of the recent imports, which are made of inferior metal.

To determine the correct length, remember that, when made into a noose, your chain training collar should slide comfortably over the dog's head, yet not slip up on the dog's ears when his neck is bent toward the ground.

The second type of training collar is not shown, but is easily described as a band of interlocking, light steel sections that have short, blunt ends which bear on the neck of the dog. A loop of small-link chain passes through rings on the ends of this band, causing constriction and release as the handler tightens or slackens the leash.

Some experienced trainers use this type collar to advantage in field work and other specialized training. The advocates of this implement claim that, because of the limited constriction and wide bearing surface, together with the shortness of the stubs, there is the least possible chance of injuring a dog with this collar. An analysis by engineers and veterinarians would support their contention, despite the views of those supersensitive individuals who regard this collar as a torturous device. It is not cruel.

The American Kennel Club ruled it from use in the shows it governs, probably because its appearance caused the public to confuse it with a spiked collar. If the public once viewed the real spiked collar—a band of heavy leather, equipped with a row of sharpened bolts pointing inward, and with unlimited constriction—it would no longer regard the stubs of the commercial collar as "spikes." Whether or not the prejudice is justified, the fact that the implement is not acceptable for exhibition is a point against its use in training. There is an advantage in having the same authoritative equipment that is used in training, also present during exhibition.

The most important reason for rejecting this type collar is the curse of its "springy-clingy" feel. It is regarded by many top trainers as a clumsy implement, particularly when making a split-second change in the angle of correction.

Leather slip or choke collars do not function efficiently, and the conventional, buckle-on leather collar recommended for tying a dog, is useless for training. It would have to be fastened very tightly to prevent any possibility of slipping during moments of resistance or excitement, and, since its pressure is constant, the dog would be equally uncomfortable during his calm, obedient moments.

ARTICLE 2. The second figure is the longe. Do not dismiss it as "just another line" to be used in rote teaching. Its length of fifteen feet or more will enable you, if you are slow, speedily to debunk some

24

old fallacies and to learn one of the most important fundamentals of dog training.

Example A is a cavalry type longe, made of five-eighths inch webbing. It is suitable for dogs ranging in size from the very largest (it will hold a horse), down through the small but sturdy breeds such as the Beagle and Cocker. This web longe offers the advantages of a comfortable hand purchase and freedom from tangling. Unfortunately, it is very difficult to find in some districts.

Example B shows the second-best type longe for dogs of the aforementioned size. It is sash cord, one-quarter inch in diameter. Do not confuse this material with variety-counter clothesline that lacks the strength and the authoritative feel. Sash cord is sold at most hardware stores.

Example C illustrates a line of the Venetian-blind type for dogs ranging in weight from the twenty-pound class down through the smallest Toys. However, some of the Terriers that would fall into this weight class would, by reason of superior muscle tone, be too strong for the lightest cord. Be sure, for your effectiveness and comfort, to get a line of sufficient weight and strength.

ARTICLE 3. The leash shown in this illustration is the type necessary for effective training. After a week of experience with the longe, referred to above, you will be sold on the element of surprise afforded by lots of slack, and you will be relieved to know that you will be changing to a leash that is not less than five and a half feet in length. Because good training leashes are cut from the tapering back of a cowhide, they will vary in length from five and one-half to more than six feet.

Strength alone is not the reason for demanding top quality in your leash. The good, authoritative feel contributes to confident handling.

Example A is adequate for the largest of dogs and is suitable for dogs as small as the Beagle and Cocker class. This leash is five-eighths of an inch in width. It has a hand loop sewn and riveted into one end and a bridle snap is fastened to the other in the same substantial manner. A bridle snap, equipped with the necessary swivel, can be obtained at a hardware store, should you be unable to get suitable equipment at your pet shop.

Example B shows the size leash for dogs from the Beagle and Cocker class down to the Toys. It must be just as long, but is three-eighths of an inch in width, and the snap is a size smaller.

Example C pictures a leash as long as the others shown, but it is only a quarter inch in width. While the snap is much lighter than the others, it is very strong, and is equipped with a swivel. This leash is intended for dogs of the Toy size.

If your pet shop has nothing but slippery, improperly tanned, belly leather leashes for sale, or unsuitable contraptions made of chain or plastic, take this description to a shoe repairman or any leather worker, and have him make you a suitable leash.

ARTICLE 4. A necessary quality of the throw-chain or chainette is the "feel" or balance that assures accuracy in throwing. That's why it must be of sufficient weight and must be linked with rings in the manner shown.

The chain pictured in *Example A* is made of a sixteen-inch length of steel links that weighs about eight ounces. It should be doubled and the ends joined with a ring of any practical type, "S-ring," key ring, etc. Another ring links the middle to add compactness. This weight will serve for the largest dogs, and is not too heavy for such dogs as the Cocker and Beagle.

The lighter chain, shown in *Example B,* is made from a sixteen-inch length of links about the weight of that used in a heavy choke collar. It weighs about four and one-half ounces when equipped with rings in the same manner as the larger chain described above.

The lightest of the three throw-chains is made of material of the weight of a medium weight training collar. It is for the most delicate of the Toys. It is equipped with rings in the same way as were the larger sizes, and should be just as long. Remember—the smaller the target, the more important a wide spread of the chain.

The throw-chain will not hurt your dog, so make sure you get one that is heavy enough to handle properly.

If not available at your pet shop, these chains can be cut and made up by any hardware clerk.

Do not try to use the chain before you are completely informed of the psychology that is fundamental to its fullest effectiveness. To use the chain prematurely or improperly can make the attainment of absolute off-leash control more difficult.

26

ARTICLE 5. The tab is one of the most interesting pieces of equipment you will use. It is also one of the simplest and least costly. Get about twenty-one inches of exactly the same material which you selected as being suitable for your longe. When joined with a square knot as shown, your tab's length should provide a good hand-hold, six or eight inches long, which can be easily attached to the collar.

Any further equipment can be easily described and obtained when the need occurs.

The running part of the collar should
go through a ring and over the neck.

LESSON III

THE FOUNDATION

All is in readiness: you've got the mental equipment to start training a dog and to deal with those who would confuse you; your dog is at least six months of age (the old bromide to "wait till he's a year old" [and the house has been destroyed] has been debunked). So regardless of breed, there is no reason to delay training.

Your new "store-bought" equipment is all laid out invitingly like the gear of a Tenderfoot Scout on Christmas morning. Like a Scout, you're hurtin' to start. Good. Enthusiasm enhances the capabilities of dog as well as handler, so we won't pull the universal blunder of snatching the dog from the freedom of a big back yard or field, and introducing him to training by yakking, "Heel, heel, heel," from the other end of a short leash, thus emphasizing that, by contrast to his former state, he's being greatly restricted.

Think, and you will realize the advantage of making contrast, the factor that flavors a thing good or bad, work for you. Restrict the dog's liberty for at least two hours before each training period by penning him in his run, a garage, or a porch, or by tying him with a six-foot chain, and, by contrast, the long longe with which you'll start his training will signify a reprieve from prison. Cold mathematics substantiates that a dog is permitted a greater area of liberty by the longe than he enjoyed during his period of confinement. Your dog will come to recognize this fact. Why shouldn't you?

The tolerant smile on your face reveals that you find the facts on "the use of contrast" reasonable but not necessary to your situation

—"My dog already knows how to heel and sit. There would be no reason to confine my dog and start again on the long line, would there?"

Yes—particularly if you are one of the "oral dysentery" school, conditioned to reeling along beside a gasping, straining dog that is and always will be heedless of your efforts to influence him with insipid, neck-strengthening tugs and the babbling of "heel-heel-heel."

If another dog owner and you were to begin simultaneously the training of two animals of similar nature, and he followed the method of this book religiously, while you by-passed some elements as being unnecessary, a comparison of progress after five weeks would bring you shame. You bought the book. Give it a chance. Do what it says. And, for reasons of the dog's comfort during the period of restriction and training, refrain from feeding him for at least three hours before confinement, and withhold food until he's settled from the stimulus of his training lessons.

Two hours pass. If the area of your dog's confinement was suitably small, and uninviting, he'll be ready for a change of scenery, and you'll be ready for the first lesson. Make a loop in the training collar and place it on the dog in the manner illustrated on page 28. Attach the snap of the fifteen-foot longe to the correct ring of the collar. If the longe is accidentally attached to the wrong ring, or equally bad, to both rings, the collar will be locked open, probably to slide up on the dog's skull or off his head, in either instance setting a precedent that induces insecurity and collar fighting.

Remember, I said "accidentally attached to the wrong ring," trusting that you are not one of those "odd-balls" who believe they are doing a kindness in locking a dog's collar so that it cannot tighten. Their "kindness" is best defined by their dog's pitiful lack of confidence or disagreeable behavior in unfamiliar surroundings.

Should your dog at first fight a correctly attached collar, he will do so unsuccessfully and will shortly recognize the futility of steer-like bucking and bracing or shrieking hysteria that is as phony as a lead quarter. Be fair to your dog—attach the collar correctly.

If your dog has reached a trainable age without being introduced to some sort of collar, he will probably be equally unfamiliar with any kind of absolute control, so don't feel remorseful, thinking that a pre-training ritual of "line dragging" would have made things easier. He would still have been unprepared for your assertion of will power.

With one possible exception, you will need no other equipment for a week. You may need some tape to seal your mouth, if habit would cause you to cluck, chortle, or worse—to say, "Heel-heel-heel." For a definite period, we are not the least interested in teaching your dog to "heel-heel-heel" nor to "sit-sit-sit." We are fundamentally concerned with instilling and developing the quality that is the prerequisite of a good student—attentiveness.

Regardless of your problem—fence jumping, laundry chewing, etc.—the solving will be easier if we lay the proper foundation. The most fundamental thing is attentiveness.

We are going to teach your dog to be attentive.

Oh—but we are!

Get a grip on the hand loop of your longe and we'll leave the place of confinement. There is a ninety percent probability that your dog will leave the area ahead of you and will hit the end of the line before he remembers that his freedom has a "string attached." In the smaller percentage of times, some dogs, timid or questioning the new equipment and situation, will be more dubious than appreciative of their release from boring confinement. They may freeze and regard the "goings-on" a bit suspiciously. Regardless of your dog's attitude toward his increased freedom, your action will be the same: start walking toward the area where you plan to begin your training.

Resolve to head for a tree, a stone, or anything that marks a definite spot in the area, preferably not more than fifty feet distant, and to keep going until you arrive. It is important for both you and the dog to feel you have a purpose in your movement. Aimless floating can destroy confidence.

Quit that—don't look back to see whether the dog is aware of your going, whether he has thrown a foot over the line, or whether he is sniffing or looking in another direction. Don't cluck, chortle, or ask him if you can leave—just leave. Most important, give no silly little invitational tugs that are no more than requests for the dog's permission to move; and refrain from argumentative arm jerks that will change your reasonable decision to walk into an emotion-charged bone of contention as to whether you have a right to move without the dog's approval. The longe locked in your hands, ignoring the dog, just walk.

Shocked at your demonstration of will power, your dog may react in any one or a combination of many ways. He may brace like a comic donkey; try the line with shark-like rushes; follow meekly along; or snap at the line in a foam-flecked frenzy, accompanying himself with a screaming score that would convince an observer that his tail is fastened to the ground.

For you, embarrassed or apologetic, to relent and console him because you think he might hurt himself or because you are unnerved by an observer's raised eyebrows, would be a cruelty. This is not opinion. The author of this book has access to facts on the correction of hysteria, fear biting, and other manifestations of emotional instability that would amaze psychiatrists.

Regardless of gymnastics or sound effects, go until you reach the tree or other avowed objective, then stop.

If it is difficult to resist looking at your dog's face at the moment you stop, occupy yourself with watching the antics of a bird or with studying cloud formations. The dog cannot out-maneuver you emotionally if you don't favor him with your attention. And if he is not occupied with emotional wrestling, he will be more apt to appreciate how favorably his present situation compares with his preliminary confinement.

Whether he immediately begins to enjoy the freedom provided by the long line or whether he elects to play the role of martyr, sulking or cringing, he has his opportunity for a "break." After a few minutes, start to walk again without any invitational glances, chortles, or tugs. As before, head for a definite objective, so you and your dog will both feel you know where you are going. Again, aimless wandering and indecision are not convincing to animals.

Even if your dog is one that really flipped the first time the line tightened, you may find his opposition a bit less violent now. Or, as he realizes that to surrender would be to face a future where you walk and do other things without first asking his permission, there may be a new crescendo of opposition, physically and vocally. Possibly, because of advantages of temperament or previous experience, he may walk companionably along beside you. But though he plows a furrow with his fanny or saunters at your side, do not permit him the victory of stopping you before you reach your objective.

Here, at your second marker, you pause for another breather; then, regardless of the dog's reaction, start toward another objective. You arrive, repeat the short break period, and whether the dog's reaction is good, bad or indifferent, head down the last side of the square and back to the first corner of your training area.

You've spent ten or twelve minutes moving in a square, triangle, straight line or whatever pattern your training area offers, with trees or other markers about fifty feet apart. You feel that the period was impersonal and formless—that it would have seemed much more reasonable and definite to have communicated your desires with voice or a short leash. What, in comparison to the more immediately apparent responses to a direct approach, can this method of starting provide? This: for your dog to comprehend that he can only be aware of your actions by watching you is much more important than rapidly learning a few exercises that he will perform abstractedly as you pressure or coax him. By the end of the fourth day's training, you will be convinced of this fact. After a few weeks' work, your confident handling and your dog's remarkably attentive performance will attest to the significance of the method we'll follow.

Back at the starting point, pause, and when you have recovered enough breath to start walking, repeat the pattern of stops and starts. If he was uncooperative, your dog may now be a bit less violent in his opposition, or, sensing his tyranny challenged, may scream to the heavens that he can stand no more and that these are his farewell shrieks to an unheeding, heartless world.

After about twenty minutes of walking (or at least thirty minutes, if your schedule says you must do all your training in one period), we'll taper off in the manner that will end all of our training sessions. A correct ending to a training period is as vital as a proper beginning.

Don't jab yourself into a state of induced enthusiasm and hilarity, hoping it will be contagious; don't jump idiotically about as you strip the collar from the dog, and with playful slaps, encourage him to buzz the entire yard in a wild celebration of freedom. This propensity for making all activities fun, or a game, has done much to confuse kids and to cause mental nausea among working dogs. By repeatedly suggesting to the dog that he's had a bad time and its finish should be celebrated, you will teach him to regard the removal of leash or line as a cue to end his concentration abruptly and dash wildly about. Make this mistake, and thirteen weeks from now, the earliest date when it would be advisable to start your free-heeling, your dog may have the bad habit of bolting from you when the leash is removed. Thousands of dogs have been taught to bolt, bow, and whirl away because their screeching, grabbing handlers had been advised to end training periods with horseplay.

This bolting problem can be avoided. Release your grip on the line at the end of your training session and let the dog drag the line where he will for about twenty minutes.

Why?

Because the line dragging from the dog's collar prevents the situation where the dog recognized the existence of control from changing to a debacle where an over-exuberant dog would mow a cyclonic path through people and shrubs.

Oh—so you've got a dog that would scamper wildly, line or no line, probably carrying part of the longe in his mouth. Did you forget? The line is fifteen feet long and after you've grabbed its end, with gloved hand, of course, during one of the dog's wild dashes, he'll learn abruptly that the freedom permitted by the dragging longe should be leisurely enjoyed as a demi-tasse, not gulped as a dusty trail herder's beer. If you are slow-footed, tie another line to the longe before you start the dog's after-training break; the second line must be long enough so, though flat-footed you may be, your agile friend cannot out-maneuver you.

After you've abruptly ended a few of your dog's rushes, you will find him reluctant to chance another dash. A truth rocks you. He is not always sure of where the other end of the line is, so he has no way of gauging his chances of out-maneuvering you. Why, not even an Einstein could figure his chances of outfooting you without knowing the exact position of the end of that long line! You anticipate the future possibilities! And you thought the line would mean physically "horsing" the dog to you and, by rote, teaching him to come on command! Instead, you find its significance to be psychological, part of a situation you can always control by surreptitiously adding sufficient line and encouraging a wild rush. Read and digest this paragraph a few hundred times. It can change your life—and your dog's life. Remember—not even an Einstein could compute his chances.

When your dog has demonstrated that he has the capacity for living at a normal emotional level, take him, again without coaxing, back to his customary place in the house, pen, or yard, and remove the longe. If he should flare up in another celebration, don't be concerned. With that dragging line you've already laid the groundwork for a future booby trap and correction. You've done a good job of starting. Now with the dog off the line, it is important that you respect his right to some privacy. Let him alone. Make sure that everyone else ignores him for an hour or so. The essence of a training session will be more thoroughly assimilated and retained by the dog if there is no aftermath of sloppy commiseration to wash it from his mind.

Now, without being physically occupied with the training, let's review what we've done and why we've done it.

For two hours before the session, your dog was confined to an area that permitted less movement than that afforded by the long longe. Though some dogs may be slow to appreciate the fact, common sense suggests that eventually all must see that contrast favors the longe.

You were careful not to communicate your intentions to the dog by voice or tugs and so he has learned that if he is to be forewarned of your movements, he must watch you. Recognition of this fact will do more to aid the shaping of your dog's character than any number of responses to repeated communications. This necessity for consistently non-communicative handling will emphasize the need for a *single* handler during the period of training. Later, when the dog is trained, others can handle the dog—if they do so correctly.

For your assurance, let's justify your firm assertion of your right to walk, should panic or shrieking cause observers to label you "beast." Reflect on the following truths, and you'll continue reassured. While it is not suggested as the most satisfactory method of confining a dog, tying is sometimes necessary. This is definitely true at bench shows where hundreds of dogs of many breeds and ages are restricted to compartments, or benches, by means of short "bench chains." And bird dog trainers often tie the rest of their dogs to stakes and posts, while they work one or two dogs.

Now concentrate. Can you imagine a person to be more unyielding than heavy dog-show benching or a tree that anchors a bird dog? Hardly. Yet, you will never see a dog that, finding his lamentations of no avail, develops a complex regarding benching or trees. Nor are his yelps evidence that he is being abused. Many children "cry out in pain" for reasons other than physical discomfort. To charge that a person was cruel because his child wailed from a spanking, or a promise of one, would be ridiculous; yet some people seem to feel that the "crying out" of a dog is always reason for imprisoning its master. With population growth putting a premium on dogs' good behavior, training activity in public places will increase and overly sensitive observers must accept facts or they'll wear out the dial fingers reporting "brutes."

Convinced that you are right—that it is not unreasonable for you to place the dog in a situation where he must recognize physical laws —you will begin your second period of training with the great asset of confidence. If you divide each day's training into two sections, your second period should duplicate, from start to finish, the procedure of the first. The second day's lesson, whether single or divided, follows the same non-communicative, start-stop pattern of the first day. Don't vary your technique, even though your actions seem ridiculous as your dog appears to walk along burping with boredom. And if he jerks, lunges, or pulls, gather strength from the knowledge that, though old habits of the tugging leash and constant talking have naturally made him heedless, he will surely change on the blessed fourth day of training. So, long session or two shorter ones, stick to the pattern, preventing after-class hilarity by keeping the dog guessing with the dragging line.

The third day, as you take him from his place of confinement, you may see progress in his more willing responses to your unannounced starts. But, should he still oppose you, you will know in your heart that you have given him actual reason to regard the line and collar favorably, and have asked only that he recognize the emotionless law of physics that says when he is attached to another object that moves, he must also move in the same direction. So, on this third day of training, work as before, patient and expansive in the knowledge that tomorrow will see your emancipation—a wrong will be righted.

This is it. The fourth day of training. The day of the change. Oh—but we do mean your dog—the one that pulls and lunges. He'll change if you will memorize these instructions and plan carefully. Confine your dog in his pre-lesson place. List all of the temptations or distractions available to the environment of your training area that you feel would be most certain to cause your dog to ignore you, and to lunge or pull. Be it the appearance of a carefully planted dog; the invitation of an open door or yard gate; or a little girl on noisy roller skates, select the one most likely to distract, and we'll begin our set-up. Let's say, of a thousand things, your dog would be most tempted by an open gate. Motivated by a background of competing with those who have screamed, "Watch the dog," as they dashed to head him off, and conditioned by straining against the short leashes held by people who chirped, "No-no-no," the gate-bolter will furnish action.

Open wide the favorite gate. Prop it lest a roguish wind spoil your moment. Carefully note the time to the minute. Now, equipped with the longe, bring the dog from confinement and approach the open gate as head-on as the layout of your area permits. To best milk the situation, break the slack-line rule and hold the dog close as you approach the gate—just so he'll be confident that there'll be only a repetition of the silly remonstrating that he has so long ignored. Let him be on either side of you. You're not heeling, you're hoping—that he'll spot the open gate. If your dog fails to see the invitation, stop at least twenty feet from the gate until he alerts to his opportunity. Lock both hands tightly in the loop of the longe, and offer him Godspeed and the full fifteen feet of slack. As he moves toward the gate, hold your line-grabbing hands to your chest like a ball-hugging halfback and drive hard in the opposite direction. You should be going at least eight miles per hour to ensure follow-through for the dog's abrupt stop and complete reversal. And there is a reversal, unless you mush out and slow down. Let the unchallengeable force of your momentum carry the dog at least eight feet in your direction so that the lesson has the maximum significance as well as impact.

While your puller or lunger is still re-organizing, move toward him to provide slack for a repeat performance. The more slack you get into the line before he again heads for temptation, the greater time you will have to gain momentum on your reverse, and the more emphatic will be the surprise.

About the fourth time you sell him on the idea that slack means clearance through the gate, you may feel like you've "lost a fish" as you discover the dog has decided to play it the smart way—your way —and be headed your way long before the line could tighten. Now as he stands watching, more concerned with you than the gate, you may be red-faced, but not from exertion. You'll burn as a glance at the clock shows that three minutes of surprise and momentum have produced a significant result, while previous communication had merely shown your bright dog that it was unnecessary for him to pay attention. You ask, "Why do they tell you those things?"

You'll learn later.

If you are one whose knowledge of physics is so slight that you would construe the above technique as too severe to attempt, or, if because of your ignorance you were tentative—thus ineffective—in your handling, read and test the following theory until the truth has made you confident. You will find the example is of additional value in assuring others of the fairness of your actions.

By noose or knot, secure one end of your longe to your wrist. Now fasten the other end to the rear bumper of a friend's car. Arrange with the friend to start the car as slowly as possible in the lowest gear, which will be far less than walking speed. The line tightens and you are eased forward, irresistibly, but without discomfort. Even if you were lying down, the take-up on the line would be so slow as to permit a gradual application of stress to your bone and tissue, and there would be no injury to the arm. But suppose it was suggested to you that, before the line tightened, you turn and run in the opposite direction.

"Why," you maintain, "only a fool would do that—it would be as though the line were tied to a tree. Jerking against something immovable!"

Right—only a fool!

Now compare the imaginary situation to your dog's experience on the non-communicative line. He, by reason of his superior speed, could adjust to the direction of your greatest velocity and your irresistible momentum as easily as you could adjust to the power and direction of a slow-moving car.

Of course, if he were inattentive!

It hits you now! Only the foolish or inattentive dog could possibly feel discomfort from this method—and he would bring it on himself. You just went impersonally and very, very rapidly the other way.

If the incontestability of the foregoing facts has blasted the "yak-yak—tug-tug" theory from your mind, fill part of the void with another truth. Have someone loop one end of your longe around your neck and then have him fasten the line to a tree or post behind you. Do not peek or ask him how much slack there is in the line. No—I won't tell you to run. A brief thought is enough to convince you that the inability to prepare for the exact moment of the jerk is more of a remedy for heedlessness than the actual physical discomfort of the jerk.

Now consider the three ways by which a leashed dog might be informed of a handler's change of direction: hearing, should your voice or foot sounds tell him of your turning; feeling, should you be so foolish as to communicate your intentions through a taut, restraining line or by little tugs; seeing, which is the only sense that is dependent on a dog's attentiveness. He can feel you with his back turned. He can hear you yelling with no effort on his part. But, by all that's holy, he cannot see you unless he focuses his eyes in your direction.

There it is.

If the line is so slack he cannot feel you, and if, with closed mouth and sneaking feet, you prevent him from hearing you, he can only be forewarned of your change of direction and momentum by seeing you. Not theory, not opinion, but physical fact says he must focus his attention on you or be surprised by the consequences of the inevitable.

By recognizing and consistently using the combination of surprise and momentum, a handler can obtain a dog's attention; by repetition a handler can progressively increase a dog's attentiveness, thus building a foundation for favorable and permanent change of character.

Back to your gate, and then to the other temptations on the list. Repeat the distractions and right-about turns until your dog regards

38

each temptation with suspicion. Tempt him; repeat the right-about turns emphatically and, though your dog be knot-headed, he will soon regard the temptations with suspicion instead of anticipation. You'll be wailing, "He won't take his eyes off me." Here is a danger point—a sign that you do not realize that each time your dog turns from temptation without challenging the line, he is growing in capacity and character and is being properly prepared for the off-leash work of the fourteenth week. So tempt and turn until you are positive that he takes the strongest distraction as a cue to watch you. Then, hopeless as it seems, try your best to get him to fall for these same temptations, until he's convinced he guessed right—that they were traps and he sure won by watching you. Rack your brain for new distractions and repeat them, until, when he is on the line, your dog regards all stimulating situations—the squawking run of a cull chicken, a cat held at an open gate, food tossed by a stranger—as something you have caused and something of which he must beware.

During the training periods of the next four days, increase the appeal of the temptations until experience proves to your dog that the greater the distraction, the more certain you are to control the situation.

Though thrilled by your dog's response, restrain yourself. Enthusiasm and praise at this point can do more harm than good. Between your temptations, stop and let the dog have a quiet break of a minute or two without distractions. Even during the break periods your changing dog may choose to keep an eye on you. Don't let it bother you, and disregard any characters who say you'll "break his spirit" or "destroy his initiative." Rigid discipline and elementary schooling didn't stifle the initiative of H. G. Wells or Douglas MacArthur.

The attentiveness you've instilled during the first week of training will do more than simplify the job of teaching the exercises detailed in the following chapters. It will make the learning and performance of those exercises more meaningful and dedicated than the senseless mechanics that are grooved by repetition or performed for a tid-bit while most of the dog's mind is far away.

Most important, we are laying the foundation for dependability and control during times of distraction, when it is most needed. Right? Or are you content to be one of those persons who stand red-faced in an aura of nervous perspiration, tangling your fingers in the collar of a dog who is "really very smart, but gets so excited"?

The choice is yours.

Here is the correct leash grip and starting position.

LESSON IV

HEELING

If you have acknowledged that obedience is most needed during times of greatest excitement or in emergencies, you have used the first week's work with the long line to demand your dog's respect and attentiveness, and have laid a substantial foundation for the subsequent lesson of heeling. Because we must be certain that each new lesson has a proper foundation, we are going to follow the procedure of testing the dog before starting a new exercise. The first test is easy.

Stand with the dog beside you close to the wall of a building at a point about four feet back from the corner. As you hold the dog on a slack line, arrange to have someone appear from around the corner, leading or carrying a distraction of some sort. Whether the temptation is a cat, rabbit, monkey, or a bouncing ball, it should come as a complete surprise to your dog. The instant your dog sights the distraction, quietly trot in the opposite direction. If the line tightens before the dog notices your movement, it proves he's not attentive enough for you to start the lesson of heeling on a six-foot training leash.

To start the leash work before you have absolute attentiveness under all conditions will result in a very useless substitute for obedience. Let's go back and see where you got lost.

It may be that you "goldbricked" in your training—too little work, or too little initiative in supplying distractions. The remedy for this condition is a resolution to devote sufficient time to the preliminary line work so as to ensure the proper foundation.

Possibly you suffered a mental block on the right-about turns and failed to get underway before the dog tightened the line. It sometimes takes another person's observation to detect this fault. If your observer says that your actions were inhibited or tentative, turn back to the affidavit presented on page 11, Section 1. If you failed in your application of these undeniable principles because of a compromising or inhibited attitude, mislabeling your infirmities "kindness," the affidavit will prove you at odds with one of the most extensive and productive training programs in the world.

The degree to which a handler's inhibited thought waves and insecure actions adversely affect an animal has long been known to experienced trainers and now has been rendered indisputable by evidence produced by scientists using electro-encephalograph equipment. So, if you have presented an abstract, indefinite character to your dog—change.

Or it could be that you were guilty of one of the cruelest and most harmful of all handling faults—inconsistency. Be honest. Did you handle the dog effectively during formal training periods and then between times permit the dog to tighten the line as one of you took the other for a walk, or worse, let him run uninfluenced toward distractions? There is nothing unreasonable about asking a dog to consider his environment in relation to his master. To assure yourself of the fairness of consistently requiring the dog to think of you first during times of distraction, consider the situation of the wonderful dog who guides a blind person. You may be certain that his trainer, probably licensed by the state, was positive that the dog couldn't be distracted from his task by any stray dog or cat that happened along.

Certainly, a dog achieves his greatest stature and security when he considers the world in relation to a confident master. Comparison will direct pity to the lot of the poor dog whose capabilities are unrealized by a master who can give him only the kind of affection accorded to teddy bears.

Whatever mistakes you made, if any, in your foundation work with the line, correct them and bear down until, regardless of the "distraction at the corner," your dog thinks only of you. Then you will be ready for the first lesson with the training leash.

AS BEFORE EVERY TRAINING SESSION, WE WILL CONFINE THE DOG FOR TWO HOURS SO THAT, BY CONTRAST, THE OPPORTUNITY TO "DO SOMETHING" WILL APPEAR MORE INVITING TO HIM. FOR HIS OWN COMFORT, WITHHOLD FOOD FOR THREE HOURS PRIOR TO THE ACTIVITY.

It's probably with a bit of apprehension that you lay aside the longe and take up the leash. You recall your satisfaction at learning that the longe, with its fifteen feet of length, gave you a combination of surprise and momentum with which no obstinate dog could cope. You hope that the six-foot training leash will not mean forsaking that combination. It won't. The transition to the leash will be a continuation of those infallible right-about turns, with two important differences. With reduced length giving less time in which to turn and build up momentum, the demands on coordination and technique will be greater than when you worked with the longe. And now we are not merely interested in making the dog go attentively in our direction, but will also start to shape the pattern of heeling correctly.

And what is meant by heeling "correctly"?

Convenience, and oftentimes necessity, in the use of police dogs, military dogs, and other working dogs, has established the heel position of the dog at the left side of the handler. If you have driven a car, flown a plane, or milked a cow, you have learned to accept the conventional patterns of left and right, so if, erringly, you have encouraged your dog to travel on the wrong side or behind you—change.

Careful observation has found the ideal heel position to be that where the dog travels about a foot to the left of the handler with his head parallel to the person's body.

When your dog conforms to this ideal, he will be out from underfoot as you move ahead or turn toward him, and yet he will be within your forward vision. If you should turn right or right-about, he'll be up at your side instead of tripping someone who might be walking close behind. More importantly, being required to hold a proper heel position, your dog's attentiveness must necessarily be constant, which would not be true if he were permitted to slop around in a slap-happy "kind of heeling" attitude.

THIS PRINCIPLE OF INCREASING THE DOG'S CAPACITY FOR ATTENTIVENESS BY HOLDING HIM RESPONSIBLE FOR ACCURACY WILL BE EMPLOYED THROUGHOUT THE ENTIRE COURSE OF TRAINING.

That's the "what" and "why" of the correct heel position.

Here's how we teach it, regardless of your dog's reluctance or resistance.

Because we want to retain the advantages of surprise and momentum, it is important that the collar be on correctly so that the chain feeds from the leash through the ring and over the dog's neck when he is on your left side. (See description on page 30.)

Equally important, your leash should be held in the most effective way. The proper leash grip is shown in the illustration on page 40. See how the right thumb is inserted in the loop of the leash, and the exact manner in which the hand holds the leash so that the slack angles across the handler's knee when the dog is brought into the heel position at the left side. Suppose a dog—big, strong, and wild—decides to lunge toward a point of temptation. By simply opening and closing his hand, as he makes a right-about turn, the trainer can release the full six feet of slack and still retain an unbreakable grip. From the illustration, you can see that the handler's thumb absolutely prevents the leash from being torn out of the grasp. After the impact of a right-about has convinced the dog that attentiveness is as much required on the leash as it was on the line and he has decided that the only protection against surprise is a position parallel to the trainer, the left hand can be used to place the loop of slack back in the handler's right hand so that it is correctly held and ready for the dog's next attempt to pull or lunge.

Now you have all the reasons that anyone could want for holding the leash correctly. Let's get started.

By the most convenient means, bring the dog into the starting position, which is as shown in the illustration on page 40. Then start. With your leash hand held firmly against your stomach, give one command, prefaced by the dog's name; for example: "Joe, heel." Step right out into the leash with the left leg and keep on walking. Be sure not to show inferiority by giving little invitational tugs, nor by looking at the dog as though asking permission.

In the name of the science of physics, I ask: how is it possible for a dog to move forward at the handler's left side, if the handler stands looking at him?

In all the world there is no more graphic tableau of stupidity than a handler who commands a dog to heel and then makes response impossible by standing motionless, staring at the dog. Embarrassing, eh?

Make sure that your command is really a command, not a request, and that it is simultaneous with your first step. Again, he cannot learn to start on command if you stand there looking at him after you've told him to heel. You're moving, so keep your mouth shut and don't look back. No second commands, no invitational tugs; lock your leash hand to your body, keep your left hand off the leash, and walk. Yakking, backward glances, and coaxing gestures would merely postpone the lesson that your dog must ultimately learn—THAT HE MUST SOMETIMES DO THINGS THAT HE DOESN'T WANT TO DO.

44

When the dog begins to forge ahead—

Open and close your hand as you make a very emphatic right-about turn—

And drive hard in the opposite direction.

So, if you love your dog, let him learn this inescapable fact early and in the simplest way. Whether it goes against your teddy bear instincts or not, it's the truth.

Since your leash hand was locked uncommunicatingly at your belt line as you walked forward, it could never be said that you jerked the dog on the start. He merely had to recognize the physical fact of your going and he would then experience no discomfort whatsoever.

The results you obtained with your right-abouts on the long line, and which were proven when you gave the dog his pre-heeling test at the corner of the house, make it unlikely that your dog would try to pull or lunge ahead as you walk along.

But let's hope that he does. It will give us the opportunity to set him right back on the foundation of respect and attentiveness that you built with the longe line.

When he's moved his eyeballs far enough ahead of you so he's no longer aware of your action, merely open and close your hand as you make a very, very emphatic right-about. Because you are holding the leash properly, you have provided the slack for a jolting surprise without the possibilities of forewarning the dog or losing your grip. If he tried to switch directions, you would catch him flat-footed with another right-about. A few of these maneuvers will convince him that it's better to keep his eyes back in a position where they can see what you're doing.

Remember—you can make these corrective turns whenever the dog is tempted to forge ahead—immediately upon starting, or after you've walked away.

Again—and emphatically: there is absolutely no reason to restrain him, since no dog, worked by a handler who is familiar with the inviolate effectiveness of the properly executed right-about turn, can possibly pull on the leash. If you wonder why I am so certain of this when I haven't even seen your dog, review the affidavit on page 11. It is quite probable that a few of the dogs represented by the number on that page were as wild as your dog. If you can't keep that left hand from sneaking out and sabotaging your chances, lock it to your left side with a belt. Our job is not to restrain him, but to provide the inevitable consequence of trying to pull.

So keep moving along, administering one of the right-abouts whenever your dog tries to forge ahead. Because he has only six feet of slack at the time of your turn, instead of the longer length as when on the line, your dog will be forced to respond more promptly. Within a matter of minutes, his responses will be so rapid that it will be difficult to surprise him. Mechanically, then, you are forcing him to work in closer proximity to you. The very fact that he is making surprise difficult is proof that he is growing in attentiveness.

Let's reward that attitude with a word of praise, calmly spoken lest it be taken as a cue to hilarity and the thin thread of attentiveness be broken. Then go right back to walking, heading toward any temptations your situation might provide. Continue to head him toward those temptations, showing him with your turns and praise that forging, pulling, and lunging belong to the dim past. *Continue to work him until it seems that no available distraction can affect him. For it is now—after the pattern of response has been set—that repeated familiar experience can make attentiveness a predominant and enduring quality of your dog's character.*

"Well," you say, "it's certain that the right-about can convince a dog that he'd better stay back where he can watch you. But there are other things he could do to sidetrack your program of heeling. Things that the right-about couldn't handle."

You're right—there are. Since it is the opinion of all concerned with the publishing of this book that it is the owner of the most troublesome dog who needs our help, we are going to show you how to stop every stratagem the dog might throw at you.

This will be done without the conventional, spineless deference to those kind folks who cannot bear to see the dog suffer even slight discomfort in training.

Readiness makes confidence, so if you know, even before they start, where to find the solutions to any anti-heeling programs that the dog might dream up, you will be greatly aided. So let's leave the subject of "heeling correctly" for a short time and acquire some of that confidence.

WALKING ON THE WRONG SIDE

Whether old habits, confusion, or cussedness prompts your dog to walk on the right side, the need for staying back where his eyes will warn him against the right-abouts makes it almost certain that he won't move to the wrong side by crossing in front of you. Instead, he may test the "out of sight, out of harm" theory by slinking around behind you. Keep right on walking and, at the moment when the tightening of the leash shows that he's getting well around, lock your hand hard against your body and make a sharp right-about.

48

This time, instead of catching him flat-footed out in front of you, your turn will head you around right into him. As you turn, without releasing an inch of slack, the leash naturally wraps around your legs, causing the collar to restrict the dog's freedom of movement as well as his breathing. Hobbled though you may be by the wrapping leash, move right into him with sliding steps. This will further emphasize the awful predicament caused by his movement toward the wrong side. He may immediately retrace his path back to your left side. If so, make sure your voice and a pat with the left hand tell him that he's back to "pleasant haven."

Twenty percent of the offending dogs learn from the consequences of their first transgression never to circle behind to the handler's wrong side. If your dog is one of this percentage, he is certainly deserving of some warm praise.

However, if he panics and struggles the wrong way, so that the leash tightens, keep shuffling into him. Even if you are hog-tied by the leash, try to stay erect until a chance lunge in the right direction lessens the pressure on the dog's neck and shows him that he picked the right route back. Be quick in praising him for the correct response. If he continues to gasp, jump, and jerk the wrong way, keep moving into him. He's going to try to get out of your way and, eventually, that "try" is going to be in the right direction, resulting in the slackening of pressure and the consequent praise that will point "the way."

The experiences evidenced on page 11 include many examples of handlers with dogs that tried this maneuvering to the wrong side, so I am aware that the leash wound around your legs can trip you and force you to start over.

I AM AWARE OF SOMETHING ELSE—AND I WANT TO MAKE YOU AWARE OF IT: it has been a careful observation that three-fourths of the drifters from the left to the wrong side have been successfully corrected by four applications of this "winching" right-about and properly administered praise. And—dwell on this—of the 11,500 dogs trained in my obedience classes, I have seen only one or two that would move intentionally to the wrong side after the first week of work on the heeling exercise; and even these were corrected with a bit more work.

On the strength of this record, I will state that the efficiency of the above method and the dogs' receptivity have been adequately demonstrated and that any prolonged difficulty you might have reflects your lack of concentration or determination. Just let your dog know that each time he drifts behind to the wrong side, he'll cause a right-about in his direction and the only way he'll ever get out of his restricted mess is to slide back the way he came.

PERHAPS YOU WOULD LIKE TO KNOW WHY WE DON'T RESTRAIN HIM OR JUST REPEAT THE HEEL COMMAND AND PULL HIM BACK INTO POSITION. THAT'S EASY—WE DON'T WANT TO DEPRIVE HIM OF HIS RIGHT TO LEARN BY MAKING A MISTAKE AND EXPERIENCING ITS LOGICAL CONSEQUENCES, TOGETHER WITH THE SATISFACTION OF THE PRAISE THAT REWARDS HIS CORRECTION OF THE MISTAKE.

REFUSING TO MOVE

Your foundation work with the long line has made it highly improbable that your dog will hesitate to follow you on leash. However, if this new situation, where you are starting abruptly and with the command "Heel," should find your dog trying to halt the operation by the friction of his hindquarters on the ground, you can bet that his "confusion" is phony.

The subject of "the dog who just won't walk on a leash" is most amusing. Like every professional trainer, I have been brought dogs who were "impossible to leash-break." Due to no exceptional ability of mine, but, rather to the unyielding application of physical necessity, all of them have been trained to lead without difficulty.

REMEMBER—COAXING MIGHT HASTEN A FALSE PROGRESS, BUT IT WILL ALSO POSTPONE, TO A LESS FAVORABLE TIME, THE LESSON THAT THERE ARE THINGS THE DOG MUST DO, WHETHER HE WANTS TO OR NOT.

So don't kid yourself, nor let the dog kid you. Walk. He'll come with you, if only to be near his head.

THE LEASH GRABBER

It could be that your dog moves willingly, even exuberantly, when you give the heel command, but grabs hold of your leash and tries to shake or carry it. There is a never-failing remedy for this evil. Lock both hands onto the leash, for maximum traction, and lift straight up. If the correction is effectively administered, the dog should go up like a rocket and descend like a parachute. A dog's second attempt to latch onto the leash is positive evidence that you were guilty of that greatest of all physical and psychological cruelties, under-correction. (If you are the timid type, turn back to page 12 and read paragraph number twelve of the affidavit.) You can only agree that the cruelest correction is the ineffective correction, because it does nothing but encourage the dog to further resistance.

If your dog is one of those individuals who can give an exhibition of pseudo-panic or hysteria when faced with a person who will not compromise, you may find that, rather than recognize the rights of others, he'll resist by hooking his feet over the leash, biting at any part of you or the leash that he swings within range of, thus testing your will and your back. So, stiffen both and win out.

"Clear off the ground?" you ask.

Yup. Until he longs so fervently for mother earth that he'd hardly invite another "lifting" by grabbing the leash again.

WALKING WITH ONE FOOT FOULING THE LEASH

If your dog tries to foul the leash with one foot as he walks along, the correction is the same as though he were grabbing it with his mouth. And, as in other instances, any of the dog's decisions to contest your will by locking both feet over the leash, must be thwarted quickly and permanently.

Since you undoubtedly stopped for your correction, a new start with another heel command will be required.

THE PROTEST BITER

Possibly the heel command is the first one you've enforced, and so it brings out a character streak you didn't know your dog had. It may reveal itself as he crowds in and mouths or gnaws at you in response to your heeling action. However "gently" he might "mouth," you may be sure of one thing: to let him interfere with or stop your actions on this first attempt is to encourage future protests that will increase in number and decrease in "gentleness."

When he moves in to protest, shift to a short, firm grip on the leash and give him a jerk that bounces him right out of the mouthing mood. Simultaneously, tell him "out" in a heavy, disapproving tone.

This is not merely the rather impersonal "lifting" that results from his pawing or chewing the leash. It's a jerk that tells him very personally never to try those protests again.

Probably because, emphatically spoken, its guttural sounds are closer to the scolding of a mother dog, the word "out" is much more effective than "stop it" or "no." It is used almost universally in attack work and other situations where immediate response is imperative. However, if your dog responds to "no," or some other command to stop his action, continue to use the familiar word.

REGARDLESS OF HOW YOU TELL HIM TO STOP, TELL HIM ONCE, AND THEN TAKE STEPS TO SEE THAT HE DOES.

THE REAL "HOOD"

If your dog is a real "hood" who would regard the foregoing types of protest as "kid stuff" and would express his resentment of your efforts by biting, your problem is difficult—and pressing.

Professional trainers often get these extreme problems. Nearly always the "protest biter" is the handiwork of a person who, by avoiding situations that the dog might resent, has nurtured the seeds of rebellion and then cultivated the resultant growth with undercorrection. When these people reap their inevitable and oftentimes painful harvest, they are ready to avail themselves of the help of "the cruel trainer" whose advice they may have once rejected because it was incompatible with the sugary droolings of mealy-mouthed columnists, breed-ring biddies, and dog psychologists who, by the broken skins and broken hearts their misinformation causes, can be proven guilty of the greatest act of cruelty to animals since the dawn of time.

With more genuine compassion for the biting dog than would ever be demonstrated by those who are "too kind" to make a correction and certainly with more disregard for his own safety, the professional trainer feels morally obligated to perform a "major operation."

Since we are presently concerned with the dog that bites in resentment of the demands of training, we will set our example in that situation. (In a later chapter we will deal with the much easier problem of the dog that bites someone other than his master.)

First, the trainer makes certain that the collar and leash are more than adequate for any jerk or strain that the dog's most frantic actions could cause. Then he starts to work the dog deliberately and fairly to the point where the dog makes his grab. Before the teeth have reached their target, the dog, weight permitting, is jerked from the ground. As in coping with some of the afore-mentioned problems, the dog is suspended in mid-air. HOWEVER, TO LET THE BITING DOG RECOVER HIS FOOTING WHILE HE STILL HAD STRENGTH TO RENEW THE ATTACK WOULD BE A CRUELTY.

The only justifiable course is to hold him suspended until he has neither the strength nor inclination to renew the fight.

When finally it is obvious that he is physically incapable of expressing his resentment and is lowered to the ground, he will probably stagger loop-legged for a few steps, vomit once or twice, and roll over on his side.

The sight of a dog lying, thick-tongued, on his side, is not pleasant, but do not let it alarm you. I have dealt with hundreds of these "protest biters" and can say, under oath, that even the ones who would appear to be lying most supinely on the threshold of death will get up and walk when a new heel command follows a few minutes of breath-catching, much to the embarrassment of the owners whose cries of remorse were intended to follow all the way to the Promised Land. Again, I can claim under oath that I have never seen a dog which required even the maximum suspension, that was physically affected in such a way that he was unable to continue his training within a few minutes of the correction. None have ever been injured physically. Nearly all have been helped mentally.

And if the dog is too big and formidable for anyone to hang up? Then the operation must be carefully planned. This is how the professional trainer might "convert" such a dog, while protecting his own person from injury or even permanent disablement.

He would equip himself with a piece of rubber hose about sixteen inches in length and one and a half inches in diameter. An adequate scrap of used washing machine hose from a repair shop or the dump is as good as a new piece. Into this hose he would slide an equal length of wooden dowling, obtainable at most hardware and cabinet shops. Before working with the formidable dog, he would put this "tranquilizer" into his pocket or under his belt, in a quick-draw position; or, if he felt the dog was one which would explode immediately, he would hold the hose in the "ready" position behind his own right ear, above the dog's view but ready for action.

Naturally, to slow the motion of his target, he would have to use a left-handed, close-to-the-collar grip instead of the regular leash hold.

As well as he can with the awkward left-hand grip, the trainer works at the heel exercises until the dog shows the first sign of resentment. At this moment (not after the situation has developed into a seething, biting, leash-climbing struggle) the trainer's left hand steers the dog's attempt to one side as a right-hand, chopping stroke brings the hose across the animal's muzzle between the eyes and the nose.

If the correction was humane (forceful enough to be effective), the "biting idea" was jarred from the dog's mind and replaced with the conviction that attack was not worth the numbing and inevitable consequences. Inevitable and numbing because a competent trainer, familiar with the problem, would be keenly aware of the cruelties of threatening or under-correcting such a dog. His approach would express a finality that would end the problem with the first correction. Unfortunately, that "finality" is not possessed by many of the people who have to deal with the biting dog. In fact, a master's lack of absolute finality in dealing with the first puppy tantrum is generally the thing that influences the dog to make a career of rebellion.

The experienced trainer knows that a "major operation" which, by a fair request, challenges a dog to rebel and then convinces him of the trainer's authority is the only way to make a permanent impression on one of these more dangerous biters. This is in contrast to those unfortunate instances where a dog's physical opposition to his master's reasonable demands is met with a lack of decisiveness commonly mislabeled "love and understanding."

Here, by back pedaling or coaxing compromise, the "understanding" one puts ointment on a psychological sore, hoping that it will heal from the top down. By following the dog's dictates, such as: not asking him to heel, not touching him when he's excited, not walking into the room where he is eating, the family is permitted to co-exist in the house with their "pet," who just needs "love and understanding." Sooner or later, some lax member of the family or an uninformed stranger, will touch the dog's right foot, pet him when he's lying down, or break some rule, and a disastrous flare-up will occur before sufficient quantities of "love and understanding" can be applied.

Far better for the security of the dog as well as his master, when a "major operation" achieves a permanent understanding.

Possibly you might find the process of "absolute finality" incompatible with the sugary droolings of those who prattle that "doggies always want to please," and wonder how anyone dares to write such heresy.

Such truths are better written than spoken. Printed statements cannot be successfully misquoted. For example, *the "major operation" is advised in the specific case of the dog who regards the reasonable demands of elementary obedience as sufficient reason to attack his master.*

It is emphasized that the corrections must be made by an effective handler and, in the case where the dog is struck, the recommended course of action is definite in describing the procedure of a professional trainer. To all sensible persons, the handler's justification and method will be acceptable.

However, if you require so much as ten seconds to decide whether it is better to let your dog continue his biting, to always bow to his will, or to make the effective correction, be certain that the above procedure is not for you. Ten seconds' indecision would indicate you lack the clarity and decisiveness to put your point across.

When all of the dog's diversionary tactics (which may range from sliding around to the wrong side, through biting) have been countered, we can get back to the enjoyable process of teaching the dog the proper heel position.

As has been proven, the surprise of slack combined with the force of momentum will force a dog to pay constant attention lest he be caught with a jolting right-about. Since he can only be aware of his non-communicative handler by watching, he does not dare venture ahead to where the handler's crafty right-about catches him unaware. In concrete figures, this means that no properly worked dog dares to let his head get over two feet ahead of the handler. Caution: never confuse this natural limitation of distance, that comes from a dog's inability to see behind him, with any suggestion to restrain him with a taut leash. Understand that your task is to supply such strong temptations that he is encouraged to forge ahead of you, uninfluenced by the leash, until that split second when the slack is taken up by the jolting power of the right-about.

When you reach the point where it seems that no temptation is sufficient to interrupt his attentiveness, don't stop. Now make sure your leash is properly held, so as to assure the most effective grip and release of slack, and continue to work your dog in the most tempting situations. When you reach the level where nothing can interrupt his attentiveness, you are taking him past another "point of contention." Continue to work him and to praise him for "not contending" until his attentiveness and cooperation become a way of life. There will be a new feel to the dog's performance that shows that you have not only taught him to walk on a loose leash at your left side, but proves you've also added something to his character.

And when should this change come about?

The left turn is made sharply into the dog.

Here's a very definite answer to that question. The author's obedience classes are begun with a first night attended by the handlers only—no dogs. The techniques of combining surprise and momentum while using the longe line are outlined exactly as set forth in the previous chapter, entitled "The Foundation." At the next lesson, which follows the week of foundation work at home, the dogs are brought to class on the six-foot training leash.

After brief instruction on the necessity for the proper leash grip, each handler, in turn, is required to go toward the temptations offered by the opposing line of dogs and to employ the right-about the instant his dog is distracted. Most dogs, having been permanently impressed by their experience with the line, will regard the temptation of the strange animals as so many booby traps and refuse to be enticed into forging ahead. Of the four percent that will fall for the trap, only one out of four can be tempted after being caught with two about-turns, and rarely will this remaining one challenge the slack after the third correction.

All this evidence means that, after the first five minutes on the leash, your dog should stop his attempts to pull or lunge, regardless of the distractions you supply.

"But," you say, "the fact that he can get a couple of feet ahead and still be informed of your about-turns is bad—if you turned left, you'd bump into him."

You're right! And that's just what we're going to do—turn left and bump into him. But in such a manner that he'll not be anxious for a repeat performance. Here is the exact technique, as is emphasized on page 56.

Give your heel command and start. Having been previously discouraged from forging heedlessly out in front, your dog's technique will be to ease forward, but not so far as to be unable to watch for your about-turns. In one coordinated motion, as he starts to ease past you, take up the slack with the left hand and, pivoting on the right foot, turn into him in such a way that your turning step will convincingly thrust, not experimentally probe, your knee or leg into the dog, preferably between his shoulder and his nose.

Understand—the carefully timed moment of leash restraint was to prevent the dog from dodging the left turn and not to prevent him from pulling. Lest indecision influence you to a watered-down effort that results in under-correction and cruel ineffectiveness, let's visualize an interesting situation. Imagine a dog at liberty in a yard which contains a large tree. It is obvious that were the dog to charge the tree, heedlessly or intentionally, he would be jolted with such force that, unless idiotic or irrational, he would not again hurl himself into a tree. Proof of this is made by each hunting dog that avoids trees as he runs through the woods. Yet the dog's spirit is not broken though the trees are most unyielding and uncompromising. Absolute decisiveness on your first and subsequent left turns will lessen your task of teaching your dog an attentive, accurate heel position. You will gain in his respect, which would not be true if you were to cheapen yourself as his master by changing your God-given right to turn left into an emotional bone of contention. Convince him that circumstances, or inclination, might cause you to head into him at any time and that he'll be more comfortable if he's out of the way. Then get your left hand back off the leash until his "easing forward" tells you that it's time for another left turn. Repeat these properly timed and executed turns until your dog is concerned with keeping all of his anatomy back out of the path of those knee-thrusting left turns.

When you reach the point where he's holding a position that will not interfere with your left turns, you can use a little variation that will make him even more pace conscious. Increase your speed to a fast walk; then, as the exhilaration of your faster gait causes the dog to relax his attentiveness, suddenly slow up and make a left turn. Repeat the formula of speed up, slow down, and left turn until he takes all your walking speeds as a cue to expect the unexpected. So important is the dog's stability when his handler is moving fast that The American Kennel Club has included response to a change of gait in its heeling tests for the dogs entered in its obedience trials. It is felt that even a novice dog should run beside his handler without flipping his lid, though the handler be running across an inviting lawn.

The reason? Did you ever have an unstable dog take your mad dash through traffic as an invitation to play games?

So when your slow-downs find the dog anticipating a left turn, reverse the formula. From a standing start, a slow walk or a fast walk, break into a trot, without invitation or warning, and on about the fifth or sixth running step, make a quick left turn. At this speed, you may have difficulty making an effective turn—you may even take a header over the dog—but keep working. Whether you catch him with your knee or fall on him, keep working until he takes your bouncy trot as just another cue to beware.

In turn, he's been made suspicious of your normal, purposeful, training walk and your speed-ups, slow-downs, and runs. Now, as you saunter along, try to convince him that you are much too relaxed to

58

do the unexpected, and as he eases ahead, use a left turn to show him he was wrong. As you vary the formulas outlined above, as needed, your dog will come to regard all of your walking speeds as a reminder that a left turn may come at any time.

In each formula, inaccuracy has brought consequences that have made the dog suspicious of the handler's rather dramatized moves, and once the suspicion is created, the consequences and suspicion have been transferred to every-day "non-cuing" actions.

IN OTHER WORDS, THE DOG HAS COME TO TAKE THE VERY ABSENCE OF A CUE AS A CUE IN ITSELF.

Now as he makes an effort to cooperate, praise him with an enthusiastic pat or word, but not in a manner that he would mistake for release, or an invitation to play. If he were influenced in such a way and then corrected for his reasonable mistake, he would be miserably confused.

Keep sharply in mind the difference between the fairness and necessity of correcting a dog for being influenced by the legitimate distractions provided as part of his training environment and the unfairness of purposefully inviting him to play and then correcting him when he accepts your invitation. To demand that at his master's command he disregard all outside distractions, will build confidence and give control that protects the dog; on the other hand, to direct a personal, emotional appeal and then correct the dog for responding, will destroy confidence and make the dog miserable.

Another question that is certain to come to your mind is that of when to correct the dog if he is distracted by another member of the family. Here's a safe rule. It is proper for the handler to make a correction when the dog is distracted by family activities that are not addressed directly to him, regardless of how tempting those activities might be. It would be unfair for a member of your family to make a deliberate, emotional appeal to the dog which would result in the dog's being corrected for responding. A simple example of fair action would be that of correcting a dog that is distracted by a member of the family who might be rolling on the floor, bouncing a ball, or jumping up and down, so long as the distracting person does not direct his own emotions toward the dog.

Now that you are equipped to correct the dog that tries to go ahead of the proper heel position by pulling or by easing, we will consider the remaining two ways in which a dog might break the heel position.

He might lag behind, or he might veer sideways away from you with the intention of tightening the leash, thereby preventing you

Use a long-reaching step on the right turn.

from surprising him with a sudden movement. We correct these tactics with the last of our training turns—the right turn.

As you can see from the illustration on page 60, the handler pivots on the left foot as he takes a very long and emphatic step to the right. This is a natural and easy technique to master because the speed of your step causes your weight to take up the slack in the leash with a surprising, irresistible jolt. The dog soon learns to hold a position close in to the handler's side, whether walking straightaway or making a turn.

There you have the technique for teaching your dog to heel attentively in the proper position. Of equal importance, you have the six ways to correct a dog that would try to stop his master's reasonable actions.

If you make the turns in an effective manner and at the exact time needed, rewarding cooperation with sincere praise, you'll find your dog responding with the first lesson on the leash. Work until you reach this high point of attentiveness, then snap the long line to your dog's collar and remove the leash. Release him from command with the word "okay," and let him drag the line around while the two of you enjoy a twenty-minute break before returning to your separate, everyday affairs. Be careful not to remove the leash before the line is attached or the dog might cavort wildly away from you, thus setting a very bad precedent.

For reasons given in the preceding chapter, it is most important that you always end your lessons in the above manner.

Before the leash work of the third day is finished, your dog will be getting "mighty hard to fool." After five days of using the turn technique, he will be going along at your side, quite concerned with what you might do next, convinced that the praise he gets from attentiveness is much more desirable than the booby traps of turns that result from his lack of concentration. It may seem as he goes along, attentive to your moves and oblivious to distractions, that it might be time to add another exercise to the pattern of his training.

Let's find out.

Remember to keep your thumb pointed toward you as you push him to the ground.

LESSON V

SITTING

You will see why the following test is one of the most important you will ever give your dog.

Without making any preliminary turns or corrections, bring your dog, at heel, directly to a new temptation, such as a different gate, an open car door, or a cat in a cage. When you reach the point of temptation, stop. If your dog stops and stands as though wondering what you are going to do next, you've got the foundation for the next exercise. And what is more, you are getting the authentic kind of obedience where the dog responds reliably without any preliminary warm-up or steadying.

Is this tremendous attentiveness and reliability good?

I'll answer that by asking you a question: is it good to stop an excited dog from running in front of a truck?

It may be that, until now, your training lessons have featured a period of laxity between your first command and the time when you warmed up to the "finality" necessary to get response. Again, if obedience is to have practical value, your dog must be taught to respect the command that starts your training lesson, as well as those that come after he's been working awhile.

If your dog doesn't have that quality of immediate response without a warm-up, here's how you can instill it. Many times a day, bring him, at heel, directly from confinement to a new temptation and correct any inattentiveness with the methods previously outlined. Work for a few minutes only; then put him back in his place of confinement until he gets "good and eager" again. Probably a day or two of your demanding response at a high point of excitement will bring your dog to the level where he'll pass the test given above and be ready for work on the sit.

Of the many ways in which a dog can demonstrate his contempt for a deficient master, the "sit exercise" is one of the most expressive. By simply waiting for the second, third, or fourth command, or a number of nagging tugs before sitting, he can show his disdain. To add emphasis, he can sit sideways, his eyes and mind focused on something more interesting than his master, who by now is happily misconstruing his action as obedience.

Such response to a sit command is similar to the action of a child who, when told to sit on a chair, flops down on the floor. To say that the child's response denoted respect and the exercise of good qualities of character is ridiculous. To construe a dog's delayed, inaccurate response to command as character-forming obedience is laughable.

As our training progresses to the teaching of other exercises, you will see many reasons, in addition to character building, why your dog should concentrate on sitting accurately. So let's assure accuracy by starting correctly. Even though your dog may have already learned to sit properly and promptly, follow the procedure of teaching the sit as though he had never heard the word. You will gain much and lose nothing.

Since, when you stop with your dog at heel, he stops and regards you expectantly, as was shown by the test, you will find it easy to introduce him to the sit position with the technique shown on page 62.

Here we go. As you walk along with dog at heel and prepare to stop, adjust the amount of slack so that when you stop you can raise your leash hand to apply enough tension to encourage the dog to face in the direction that he's been walking. Now stop. Drop your left hand down across the dog's loin as pictured. Make sure your thumb is pointing toward you. If your thumb is pointing away from you, there will be a tendency to twist your body toward the dog, thus making it impossible for the dog to sit in proper alignment with you. The first job of the left hand is to help keep the dog's head and body in line with the direction that he's been traveling. When he's facing correctly, give him one command to sit, which should consist of his name and the word of command. For example: "Joe, sit."

Immediately, while you hold tension on the leash to prevent his front end from moving out of line, let your weight bear down on your

64

left hand as it closes, forcing thumb and fingers into the loin muscles. As the dog's rear goes down, you may find it necessary to take a short step backward in order to keep your hand in place. The squeezing seems to release the muscle tension, and certainly gives a more "unslippable" grip as the left hand pushes the dog's rear to a sit.

The instant he reaches the sit position, praise him and let the left hand work at patting him. And what stops him from standing up? Nothing. Why hold him there? This is not a sit-stay. We're teaching the dog the action of going from a standing to a sitting position and then praising him for that action. So praise him enthusiastically, but not with such excitement as to cause him to regard the sit lessons as invitations to excitement and horseplay.

Now give a heel command and, whether the dog is still sitting or has stood, immediately start walking. Go right back into the routine of varying your speed and correcting any inattentiveness and poor position with the proper turn, and rewarding cooperation with praise.

Work at heeling until the dog has given you his fullest attention, regardless of your varied speeds and sideline distractions, then stop and repeat the sit exercises. Immediately after praising him for the action of sitting, give a heel command and work for another minute or so on the heeling exercise, or longer if your dog should decide to argue any points of position or attention. Make it a rule never to follow the advice of a dog who opposes you on a point, believing he can switch you to another activity that he likes better. This is common practice with those dogs that have had long experience in training people and are not about to let the humans take over. So don't interrupt to repeat the sit exercise if the dog is inaccurate or inattentive in his heeling. Wait until he is again seeing things your way, then repeat the sit exercise.

If your dog's heeling was sufficiently reliable when you started to teach the sit exercise, things are going along smoothly and you are finding opportunity to place him in the sit position from twenty to thirty times during the first period of instruction. Probably by the end of the period, he'll be dropping his rear before you can apply the squeeze and pressure. This shows you that the command, the placing, and the praise are starting to add up. But don't gamble.

Keep right on placing him each time you stop and give the sit command, even though it seems that he could write his own book about the exercise. To gamble on his taking the position without being placed is to risk failure of response before you are prepared to correct him for disobedience. So, whether you work one or two periods a day, continue the heeling and placing until you are informed of the proper procedure for correction.

And what about the tough dog that doesn't want to be placed?

Although most "boils of rebellion" are brought to a head and lanced during the long line and heeling exercises, there is an occasional dog that fights the idea of being commanded and placed. Many times this opposition comes from dogs of extreme sizes: tiny dogs that have never been placed in any situation other than mother's arms and have insulated themselves from reason and reality with a baby status which they protect with phony hysteria and screams—huge dogs, well qualified to resist and conditioned to do so by a master who was told by the dog's breeder to refrain from training until the "bones were properly formed."

Regardless of the dog's size or his temperament, one thing is certain. There is no such thing as "taking it easy," because you are already trying to place the dog with the maximum gentleness. What would be more gentle than the way we introduced him to the sit?

If he tries, or threatens, to stop you by biting, you'll have to end the argument with the methods used for handling such problems, given on page 52 in "Lesson IV."

If you are one of those owners who awaited the "forming of the bones," you may be surprised to find that the dog's muscle and will power also did some "forming" and that your dog is amused by your attempts to push his rear down; or he may just sidestep from under your hand. It is always disagreeable to make a dog uncomfortable when introducing him to a new command, but it is sometimes necessary. Certainly, less harm will result from getting squared away than from trying to pussyfoot around the reality that a dog must eventually face.

So stop with your dog's left side close to a fence or a building. As you place him in the sit, his side-stepping will be limited to a few inches. And if he's so strong you just can't push him down? Keep him boxed in between you and the fence, put a lot of downward pressure on the rear and sufficient upward pressure on the leash to make his breathing quite a chore. Don't ease up until he weakens and sits. Then be prompt in slackening the leash and praising him. Heel him off and do a turn to which he's particularly responsive so that you can praise him for even more success.

This gimmick of backwashing the success from an exercise that a dog does willingly to an exercise that he does reluctantly, or is just learning, is surprisingly effective. Be ever alert for situations where

66

it might be used to sweeten a dog's attitude toward exercises that he regards distastefully.

If your dog should resort to panic or hysteria, handle him in the manner described in the preceding lesson for dealing with the "protest biter." I say "resort" because it's a voluntary defense that has always stopped "the master" in the past and which will only be permanently ended when sufficient firmness convinces the dog that "the jig is up." I have never seen a case of even the most convulsive panic that couldn't be cured. Rather, it has been proven that a dog of such inclination as to need the "major operation" is always helped by it and, once the carbuncle is lanced, the dog is always happier.

One word of caution: to approach the problem tentatively, as though the dog's spirit will be broken or his head will come off, is to make success impossible. Recognize the fairness of your objective and win it.

After two sessions of work on the sit, you will notice that your dog occasionally drops into the position before you put pressure on his rear —possibly upon being told. This is true, even if your dog is one of that small percentage which is at first resentful of the exercise. Nevertheless, continue to follow through with the mechanics of placing each time you stop, for to risk failure of response before it is time to correct the dog for not obeying your single command is to do damage. So *for at least the first four days* stick to the placing, or—if he is beating you to the position—keep trying. Along about the fifth day you may feel that it's ridiculous to try. He seems to melt from under your hand and into the proper position before you can apply any pressure. This proves that he knows what is wanted when you stop and say, "Sit."

You have proven that your dog is ready to be taught that he must sit immediately without any cue except the one command to sit. Remember—*one* command.

Here's how to teach him to respond immediately to the one command: a few feet before you make your next stop, shorten your leash so that there is about six inches of slack between you and the dog and see that the slack stays there until the moment of correction. This will prevent the evil of prayerful little tugs and will eliminate the need for any preliminary take-up. Now, being very careful to hold that six inches of slack, lock your left hand on the leash, tightly against the right hand, as shown in the illustration on page 70. Study the procedure until you are certain of the amount of slack, the hand position, and the angle of correction.

When you've memorized these things, make a stop with your dog at heel. After you've stopped completely, give the command—he can't sit if you give the command before you stop. Give one firm sit-command. Don't tug, stomp, burp, twist, or shuffle your feet. Just that one command.

If your dog obeys the one command, praise him, change back to the one-hand grip and, with the proper slack for heeling, continue on your way.

And if he doesn't sit? It has been proven that he knows what is expected, so his failure to respond must be treated as disobedience. Without preliminary, jerk straight up with such force and manner as to convince your dog that prompt obedience is the only practical course.

If your dog is large in relation to yourself, you can gain additional authority by jumping straight up at the time of correction, thus adding the power of your back and legs to your correction.

This technique of exploding the combined power of your arms, back, and legs in a surprise jerk, is necessary if you are to be certain of making a humane correction. (Any weak or ineffective correction must, by its very nature, be cruel, since it does nothing but condition the dog to further resistance.)

If you should have one of the wonderful Toy breeds, don't follow the insipid pattern of trying experimental little tugs. The sit-correction for a tiny dog must travel upward at greater than average velocity or the dog will learn to "yo-yo," skillfully riding each tug without the thought behind the leash ever reaching his rear end. Being aware of the potential of many of these small breeds, I am greatly sympathetic to their hard lot of being "beaten with words" and nudged into neurosis.

The following statement is for your assurance that, regardless of his size, you are not apt to injure your dog even though he is so insensitive to touch as to require a correction that jerks him high off the ground.

According to the records of the Southern California Obedience Council, dogs have been trained in classes conducted by member clubs. It follows that there was the usual percentage of problem dogs which required all-out corrections. It should reassure you to know that there were no injuries resulting from the corrections. In view of this record, if you are inhibited in your handling, don't represent your weakness as some sort of kindness.

So, correct emphatically when the dog fails to respond immediately to the one command. Praise emphatically when he cooperates. By

68

being emphatic in both correction and praise, you create a contrast between your show of pleasure and displeasure that gives the dog an effective picture of what you want. On the other hand, wavering corrections and watery praise dilute into indefinable slop.

If you have done even a reasonably good job, the end of the first period of correction should find your dog sitting on a single command each time you stop. Much can be accomplished by ending the training period at a point where the dog is cooperating smoothly in the heel and sit exercises. This point, where the dog has been taken "past contention," is a good time to praise him and let him relax by dragging the long line around for the usual twenty minutes while he makes the transition from being under command back to his ordinary home routine.

Make certain that you attach the line before you unsnap the leash, lest you permit the dog to spring away from the controlled situation to wild celebration, thus causing him to regard each future removal of the leash as a cue to buzz wildly out of control.

In thinking over your success in enforcing the sit, you may recall several instances in which the dog sat so promptly upon stopping that you had no time to give the command.

The sixth day of work on the sit exercise will follow the procedures begun on the fifth day, of enforcing your dog's obedience to a single command. The noticeable difference will be that now, on about half of the stops, the dog seems to be sitting before the command. Good. You will soon see that you have developed an exercise which, when combined with a bit of ingenuity, can become a tremendous force for adding good qualities to the character of your dog.

One good correction will do the job
where many tentative ones fail.

LESSON VI

THE AUTOMATIC SIT

The test of readiness for the automatic sit is simply a repetition of the work of the fifth and sixth days of sitting on command. Your dog may give you the opportunity for a correction during the early part of the review, but soon he'll be showing the same response that you noticed before the finish of the previous lesson—sometimes sitting as you stop and before the command is spoken. When, about half the time, his action is ahead of your command, you will know that he is taking your sudden stops as cues to sit. This response to a stop while at heel is called the automatic sit. A polling of scores of my obedience classes has shown that more than eighty percent of the enrolled dogs learn to sit automatically from the pattern of work even before specific effort is made by the handlers.

Since he learned the exercise so easily, it is obviously fair to begin correcting him if he fails to sit automatically when you stop. The correction is exactly the same as that used when the dog fails to sit on command. In fact, the only difference betweeen the sit on command and the automatic sit is that on the latter there can be no cue except the fact that you've stopped. No voice. No foot scuffling or stomping. No side-steps over to the dog. Only the stop and, if the dog fails to obey, the correction. If he sits automatically, praise.

As you start working on your pattern of precise heeling and prompt automatic sits, have someone observe your handling and inform you of any of the above-mentioned cues that you might be giving unconsciously. You will see very soon why this is a good idea.

After a correction or two it will probably seem certain that your dog is going to sit each time you stop. When you get to the point where he sits ten times in a row without a correction, you are ready to use the exercise to do some "character shaping." Head out of your regular training pattern toward a spot that will furnish great temptation for your dog. A good example would be any door or gate through which your dog is anxious to pass.

When you stop at this temptation, perhaps your dog may just stand beside you, considering the possibility that you might not expect him to sit when he's "so excited."

Let your correction be so authoritative as to convince him that if his mind turns at a point of temptation, it had better be toward you.

Now, take one of the most important steps in your character-shaping program. Correct him with such authority that he will remember the point of temptation not as an invitation fulfilled, nor as a bone of contention, but rather as a situation that you had well in hand.

This, indeed, will be a big step toward the most important objective of this book. Here is that objective defined: THAT YOUR DOG BE SO TRAINED THAT HE WILL REGARD ALL TEMPTATIONS, DISTRACTIONS AND EMERGENCIES IN RELATION TO YOU, HIS MASTER.

The correction made, give him a heel command and go back the way you came; do a right-about and stop at the point of temptation again. Praise him if he sits. Correct him if he doesn't. Repeat the formula. Bring him back to the temptation again and again until he is completely past the point of contention and then keep on repeating the formula until you would bet everything you own that your dog will sit automatically without any cue.

Above all, make sure that you are giving no cue on the automatic sit. No word. No tug. No foot stomp.

At the time when it seems to be a senseless procedure to subject him further to the same temptation, you can revive your interest with this truth—each time your dog is praised for his almost certain obedience, appreciation for a better, more attentive and respectful way of life is being more deeply instilled in him.

A great majority of those who train a dog do not realize the effectiveness of this formula of using the automatic sit in combination with temptations as a way of changing and developing a dog's character. They grow impatient with repeating a procedure that the dog accepts so willingly, and they want to take the next step before their unfortunate dogs have the qualities of character that make for easy, pleasant learning.

Perhaps you are wondering why the automatic sit is the best exercise to do this important job. It is the only exercise, until you reach the stage of advanced training, where the dog is cued solely by his own attentiveness. By not cuing or doing his worrying for him, you are giving him the responsibility of deciding whether or not to be attentive.

REMEMBER THIS—THE DECISION TO "DO RIGHT" THAT MOST HELPS A DOG'S CHARACTER IS THE DECISION THAT HE MAKES HIMSELF.

For this reason, it is good that The American Kennel Club has kept the automatic sit as part of its novice routine, against the wishes of the poorly informed who condemn it.

When your dog seems to be enjoying the appreciation of his response to the by-now-familiar situation, you can incorporate a couple of other strong temptations in your pattern of training turns and automatic sits. Work without varying the new procedure until the dog seems to take the very pattern, as well as the points of temptation, as a continuous reminder to think of you.

Don't quit before your dog is earning praise by working with the relaxed response that comes from complete absence of contention; otherwise you will lose the character benefits of the lesson. Generally this objective can be accomplished within an average-length training period. However, if your dog takes more than average convincing, work until you are successful, then praise him, exchange your leash for the long line and, with the word "okay," let him drag the line about while he has the usual enjoyable but controllable break before going back to his everyday life.

About this time in your dog's training program you may get an unexpected thrill and reward. Though your dog has been given the "okay" release, and you may have occupied yourself with munching an apple or studying the clouds, your dog may still be keeping his full attention on you. Or, as he enjoys exploring the nearby area, unbothered by his dragging line, you may notice that he is well aware of your position as you stand or saunter along. Here, without the slightest effort on your part, your dog is giving you attention that you were never able to get back when you used to "flog him with phrases."

It may be that you are lamenting, "He won't take his eyes off me." If your dog is one of the hunting breeds that needs lots of initiative, or a show-dog that should have animation, observers may be saying, "Now you've done it," as they see a dog whose actions seem to orbit around you. Give those "experts" caramels to occupy their mouths until those mouths are opened in surprise as you show them how wrong they are.

You will see that this remarkable attention that you are instilling in your dog is the foundation of the equally remarkable accomplishments to follow.

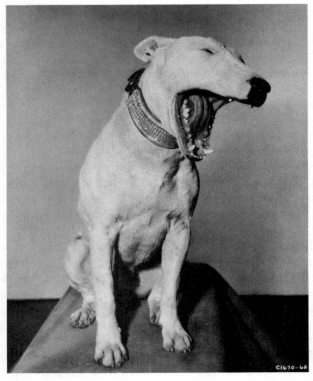

Metro-Goldwyn-Mayer

"Wildfire" (in private life, Cadence Glacier, C.D.X.), star of *It's a Dog's Life*, demonstrates that a trained dog is a happy dog.

LESSON VII

THE SIT-STAY

Before you finished the preceding lesson, your dog was sitting automatically on all stops and was taking your working pattern as a reminder to be attentive. Let's see how well he has retained that lesson —whether your work resulted in a permanent impression or a temporary influence.

Bring your dog, at heel, from his place of confinement. Stop just as you leave the area. If he sits without the slightest cue, he is ready to learn the next exercise. If not, he may need another lesson on the automatic sit before he can pass the test of responding without any preliminary warm-up.

The sit-stay, as the words would imply, is that exercise where the dog, when told to "stay" while sitting, holds his position until another command, or release, from his handler causes him to move. He is no more to be permitted to stand up, lie down, or scuttle around on his backside than he is to walk away. He is to be taught that the sit-stay demands an exact position as well as an exact location.

So that you might better see the logic of the technique we'll use to teach the exercise, let's perform an interesting experiment. Carry a light chair or stool into a room that is equipped with a solid door. Set the chair down, go out and close the door. Now imagine that the chair is your dog and that the dog is on a sit-stay. Imagine further that he is one of those dogs that has been taught that breaking from a stay position will bring nothing more than a repetition of the command. How would you know when to repeat the command?

Tell the dog to stay before you take the pivoting step in front of him.

Keep the correct angle on the leash.

"That's a stupid question," you say. "You wouldn't know when to repeat the command unless you could see him, and you can't see a dog through solid walls."

You're so right. What you are admitting is that a stay which a dog holds only when constantly reminded or threatened is useless when the handler is out of sight.

Perhaps you would prefer the useful sit-stay—the type that will control a dog whether the handler is in sight or out of sight. If so, you must start right. And "right" bears no resemblance to the common, pathetic routine of starting the command by pushing the dog back as he moves from position, and repeating, "Stay, stay, stay, stay," while you shake your finger at him.

Instead, we are going to introduce the dog to the sit-stay by a method that will encourage him to resist temptation from the beginning.

The technique of teaching the sit-stay is a series of mechanical steps that must be followed exactly as described if you and your dog are to progress with a smooth confidence. If you have difficulty using written instructions, read and, without your dog, rehearse these steps until the order of procedure is sharp in your mind.

First, just before making a routine stop, reduce the amount of slack to about ten inches. After you've stopped and your dog has sat automatically, raise your right hand smoothly, *without* jerking, to apply sufficient tension to encourage the dog to remain seated. (See illustration on page 76.) Next, give a command, "Joe, stay," and as you speak, extend your left hand, fingers fully spread, to a position a few inches in front of your dog's face. Hold that hand in position as you take a single step with the right foot, pivoting on the left foot toward the dog, so that you are facing the dog from a location one step in front of him. (The illustration on page 77 diagrams this pivoting step.) While the leash should not be vertical as when making an actual sit correction, the tension should be at such an angle as to encourage the dog to remain seated, rather than to move toward you.

It is known that animals sometimes instinctively understand positive gestures and you may be pleased to see your dog regard your extended left hand as if he knows what you want.

Now, as you continue to hold that left-hand gesture, without letting the tension go completely out of the leash, increase and decrease the pressure in a series of weak, unemphatic tugs, which, because of previous experience in sitting, your dog is certain to resist. Also, the angle is such that the dog would have to defy gravity in order to move in the direction of the tension, so he could hardly do other than resist those unauthoritative little tugs.

Now with the restraining tension still in the leash, reverse your pivoting step so that it puts you back in your position at the side of the dog. Now you can release the tension in the leash and lower the left hand to pat the dog as you praise him for resisting the temptation of your movements and the tugs on the leash. The exercise finished, heel him back into your pattern of work.

About one dog owner in a hundred will experience difficulty in starting the sit-stay. That person will be one of two types. He will be one of the "kindlies" who has practiced pussy-footing around his dog's showings of disrespect, believing that some miracle will change his own status from that of a doormat to that of the dog's master. His dog, true to form, may lunge in any direction, hook his feet over the leash, or try one of the other "brat routines" that no properly disciplined dog would dare attempt. The correction is almost the same as that recommended for controlling the dog that rears and paws when the heeling exercise is started. Grant him his wish to become "airborne," keep him elevated until he has neither the strength nor the will for further rebellion, and when at last, with grateful heart, he is returned to earth, keep the angle of the leash so steep that sitting, not moving, will be uppermost in his mind.

The other type of dog owner that is apt to have trouble with the sit-stay is the "carrier type." This type generally owns a small dog, often a Poodle, that has been picked up on dozens of excuses, ranging from a cold pavement to the owner's teddy-bear complex. This dog regards everything in the way of word and gesture as an invitation "to arms," and the left hand position and leash tension are sure to find him standing on his hind legs, front paws outstretched in anticipation.

To correct this problem, keep the tension straight up, so that the dog cannot move toward you, but finally dangles back to the sit position. If he should panic, as is often the case with those dogs that have been shielded from reality, the panic can best be drained off by slowing the "dangle." If the "dangle" is slow enough, the panic will not recur. Be consistent and he'll soon realize that he's more comfortable when his rear is on the ground. From then on, he can be handled on the sit-stay as easily as a dog that has lived in a favorable environment.

During this first period of work on the sit-stay, you will probably repeat the exercise at least fifteen times. Within the training time of

By the end of the fourth day's work on the exercise, your dog should hold for five seconds with the handler several feet in front of him.

After seven days on the exercise, return to the
dog using the counter-clockwise pattern as shown.

the next three days, your dog, if effectively worked, will understand his obligation on the sit-stay and it will be time to correct any disobedience to the stay command.

Naturally, since training in reliable obedience can best be done in situations which the trainer sets up or rigs to his own advantage—never by a catch-him-if-you-can method—you must get the dog to disobey in a situation which you can control.

Start the training period of the fourth day by reviewing the exercises of heeling, sitting automatically, and the start of the sit-stay. Then, on about the fourth automatic-sit, give the usual stay command and hand gesture as you put tension on the leash and take that pivoting step that puts you in front of and facing the dog. Remember—give the command as you leave, not after. Now, release the tension by letting the full amount of slack come into the leash. Be certain to keep an unbreakable grip on the hand loop. With that belly of slack in the leash, take another step straight backward, which will put you four or five feet from your dog.

There are two things to remember about the stay command—give it before you leave, not after, and then keep your mouth shut.

Furthermore, since you have given him a hand signal to stay, you can relax that left hand and let the dog do all the "remembering" about the command.

Possibly you did such a good job of acquainting your dog with the meaning of the stay command that he seems to comprehend he should stay, even though you are five feet away and nothing is restraining him.

To ask him to hold for more than five seconds on this first trial is possibly to miss an opportunity to reward him for his good judgment, so retrace your steps, pivot back to position at his side and praise him.

Be certain not to let the dog use the action of your return nor your praise as an excuse to move before the exercise is finished. Now, end the exercise with a heel-command and start back into your working pattern of heeling and automatic sits.

By returning and praising the dog after he held for even such a short time, you will eliminate the possibility of confusion and give the dog an important feeling of accomplishment—showing him that he was right in believing that even though you stepped back farther than usual, he did right to stay.

And what if he didn't stay, but, tempted by the new situation, moved before the five seconds elapsed, when you praised him, or before your heel command ended the exercise?

In any case, keep your mouth shut and move very, very fast toward the spot where your dog should have stayed sitting. As you move, gather the slack with your free hand so that you will have just enough to take up with a two-handed corrective jerk that propels—not leads —the dog back to his proper position.

You will not be confused, nor confuse your dog, if you remember that the correction should jerk the dog from where he moved, back to where he should be, and that the path of the correction should be the exact reverse of the pattern the dog followed when he moved. It is vitally important that the correction be in the direction from whence the dog broke. This rule applies whether the dog broke when you were out in front or when you returned to his side.

People of normal intelligence are aware that a dog generally moves because he wants to, and for a trainer to merely lead him back to where he was left and to tell him to stay would result in a reward not a correction. So, if you are one of those who would lead or push the dog back and then repeat the word "stay," the chances are you will be regarded as quite a curiosity.

Whether your dog comprehended from the first that the new situation, with more distance and a slack leash, would be no excuse for moving, or required many corrections to convince him that "stay," meant "stay," regardless of your position, when he has held several consecutive times for at least five seconds, it will be apparent that he understands his obligation and is ready for a program of stability-building temptations.

The second day's training, after you have started the stay corrections, will begin with a review of your pattern of exercises. Work on heeling, the automatic sit, and the sit-stay. When your dog has held two sit stays for five seconds each, begin to lengthen the period you remain standing in front of him. Progress from five seconds to longer periods, using properly timed and applied praise and corrections, until, by the end of the session, your dog will stay for at least a half minute with you standing a loose leash length in front of him. Remember—the word was "progress," not "jump." Gradually increase the time.

Proper timing is vital to your success with the stay exercises. After making a correction, insist that the dog hold his position until you finish the exercise. And your responsibility is to watch for any sign of willingness or resignation that shows your dog is ready to cooperate, and to get back and show him with praise that his change of viewpoint is a good thing for both of you.

To get full benefit from your corrections and to avoid confusing the dog, make this your rule: following any correction, take the dog's first sign of cooperation as the moment to return and praise him for proper response.

You might wonder why, if the "break" and correction came after only a few seconds of the exercise, the dog's quick change of heart should merit praise instead of a demand that he finish out the rest of an average period.

There is good reason for our procedure. If the dog were honestly confused and in doubt as to the proper action, your prompt appreciation would show him that he had made the right decision. This opportunity might be lost if you required him to hold past the first sign of willingness after the correction. There is nothing inconsistent in your action since, should he move as you return to praise him or break when you again leave him, he will again be corrected. If your correction and praise are the inevitable results of his own actions, his resistance to time and other temptations will grow naturally.

However, if you have a tough and cagey dog that you know deliberately breaks a stay, taking the correction, so that he can earn praise and quick release by holding only a short stay, you'll have to outmaneuver him by making him extend his brief periods of willingness into longer periods. He'll quickly figure out that he'd just as well hold the required length of time when he's first told to stay, because the period that follows the correction will be just as long as the first period you had planned.

Continue to lengthen the stay periods until, by the end of the sixth day's work on the exercise, you will be requiring the dog to hold as you stand a leash-length in front of him for a full minute.

Though the average dog easily reaches this goal of minute stays by the end of the sixth day's training, there is some variation in the rate of progress between individual dogs. When your dog has held the minute sit-stay five times in a row, you'll know that you are prepared to add another temptation. This is the temptation of motion.

The next training period, after you've proven your dog's readiness, should begin with the customary review of all exercises to date. The third time you face him on a stay, take a step to the right. Next, take a step back to the left. Reverse the order by taking a step to the left, and then back to the right. If your dog holds in the face of this distracting motion, return to praise him and finish the exercise. If he doesn't want to hold, follow through with corrections until he does.

Work on heeling and sitting for a minute or two, then do another stay. This time add a forward and backward step to the pattern of sidesteps. After consistent praise and correction has taught your dog to ignore your steps, try dropping on one knee, sitting on the ground in front of him, then jumping up and down. On all of your movements, be careful not to jerk on the leash.

Any tempting activity in which you might engage, from standing on your head to frying hamburgers in front of him, is fair temptation so long as it is not personally addressed to your dog. Quite probably, in everyday life with your dog, you will sometime have to make a fast or exciting move while he holds a stay. Certainly, if your dog is to be with you as a pal, there will be times when you will want him to stay while you or others eat. No—there is nothing unfair about asking your dog to be obedient in the exciting situations where obedience is most needed.

Having convinced your dog with praise and correction that your stepping, kneeling, and jumping are not an invitation for him to move, you will be prepared to start a new route of returning to your dog from your position out in front.

From now on, as you return to your dog when he has been left on a stay, walk back in a counter-clockwise pattern that takes you past the dog's left side, around behind him, and up to a stop beside him so that you are standing with the dog in a heel position at your left side, ready for the heel command that ends the stay. Don't circle widely as you return in the new counter-clockwise pattern. This could confuse the dog by causing a pull sideways. Let the leash hang freely from your left hand as you return in the manner illustrated. Gather the leash up only as you give the heel command that ends the exercise.

If he holds from start to finish, praise him and finish the exercise. If he breaks from the position, correct him. And remember—it is a break of position if he lies down, stands, or scoots or pivots on his backside in order to watch as you move around him. It's all right for him to swivel his head around a bit, providing his feet do not move. Don't forget—the correction should always oppose the direction of the dog's movement. For example, if he spins to the left, your jerk should spin him to the right, back to his starting position.

The often-made mistake of spinning a dog completely around, back to position, in the direction that he had chosen to break, instead of back the way he came, can delay progress in getting your dog to hold solidly as you return to finish the stay exercises.

We've been concentrating mostly on your dog's performance and how to control it. Let's take a look at yours. It may be that you are guilty of that common blunder of stepping away from your dog and then telling him to stay. Though the procedure sounds a bit insane, it is not unusual for a trainer to work at teaching his dog to hold on one stay-command, and then forget his own obligation to give that command before, not after, he leaves. In the name of fairness and common sense, give the command and gesture just before you leave, not after you've gone. And do your stepping away on the right foot, instead of the left foot, for association has taught the dog to take your stepping away on your left foot as a cue to heel.

Before you start waving a rule book, let me assure you that I am well aware that my instruction to use both the dog's name and the word "stay" in combination with a hand signal is incompatible with The American Kennel Club's rule for leaving a dog on a stay in an obedience trial. I am also aware of some other things relative to the teaching of the stay commands. I know, for example, that dogs are instinctively comprehensive of hand signals on the stay exercise. When used in combination with the verbal command, they can do much to endow the word with meaning, to assure emphasis and clarity of command so often lacking in amateur handling, as well as to lay the foundation for future use of hand signals, should your success inspire you to the challenge of advanced training. You will find that once your dog is solid on his stays, it's an easy task to conform with the rules. Until then, make your teaching job easier by using the combination command as described above.

When you are certain that you know how to leave a dog on the stay, to correct if he disobeys, as well as to return to him properly, and your dog holds consistently for as long as three minutes, you are prepared to commit the exercise to your training pattern for further perfecting along with the other exercises.

To avoid confusing you and your dog and to assure the correct foundation for each successive training step, we have dealt with the exercises singly and in the most effective order, and have developed each to a reasonable degree of non-contention before turning attention to the learning of something new. My constant reference to "the pattern of your work" should indicate that each exercise as it is learned should be committed to that training pattern for further development. By practicing obedience, your dog will become ever more happily adjusted to an obedient way of life.

Your pattern of work will divide time equally between the exercises except in instances where a dog's confusion or reluctance indicates that an exercise needs more than average effort.

Do not let the dog's obstinacy deflect your efforts from an exercise he dislikes to another he does willingly. Stay with each bone of contention until you've won your point and can praise him for cooperation. Then go to another exercise. The sometimes recommended technique of sneaking around an exercise has never helped a human or his dog. If you quit before you resolve an issue, your dog will know you for what you are—a quitter.

In a later chapter, after all basic exercises have been learned, they will be studied and developed with an eye to extending reliability and usefulness. So, when you are certain that you and your dog each know what is supposed to be done on the sit-stay, add the exercise to the heel and sit, for the benefits of practice, and we'll turn to the learning of something new.

Margaret Pooley, of the famous Rocky Reach Kennels, obedience trains all of her dogs before they are shown in the conformation classes. This kennel is the leader in dogs that have obedience degrees as well as championships.

Study this drawing carefully.

THE DOWN

You may have seen the method of starting a dog on the "down" exercise through forcing his head toward the ground by means of the trainer's foot on the leash. There are many ways in which this technique is unfair to the trainer and the dog. Count them.

First of all, a dog's attitude toward the down is not going to be one of willingness if his first association with the command is the pain of being strangled into a position that he does not understand.

Confused, as he probably will be, by the strange position and unfamiliar request, he is very apt to rebel—and rebel successfully, for this is no pull forward to make him walk, nor jerk up to make him sit, where he has only his weight with which to resist. Here, when pressure is toward the ground, the dog can brace against a force that is many times his own weight by stiffening his front legs, just as a ten-year-old boy can kneel on all fours and, with stiffened arms, easily support several hundred pounds in a gym-class pyramid.

You may be sure that the success of his rebellion will teach and condition him to resist further instruction, as well as to fight corrections when, finally, he does learn the significance of the command.

From the fact that he can brace solidly with stiffened legs, against the downward pull, it is evident that this pressure imposes many times more strain on the dog's anatomy than is ever applied by forward or upward force, where he can resist with no more than his own weight.

There is also more strain on the trainer. Standing balanced on one foot, the trainer is hardly in position to protect himself against a fall or a bite, should a big dog use all of his resources in a violent struggle. And if he does resist, the dog could hardly be punished with a sense of fairness. After all, he was not resisting a reasonable request to do something that he understood.

Even those who most dramatically assume the foot-on-the-leash stance will quietly admit that there are some dogs on which their method doesn't work.

From the moral and mechanical truths stated above, it will be obvious that there is nothing contradictory between the advice, previously given, that it is correct to establish your authority by forcing your dog into the natural action of walking with you, and the statement that you are obliged to acquaint him with the down by placing him comfortably in position until he knows what you desire him to do, without giving him the desire or the technique of bracing against it. We followed this fair procedure on the other stationary exercises, and we'll follow it on the down.

Prepare for the first lesson on the down exercise, which generally starts with the fourth week of training, by a careful study of the drawing on page 88, so that you will memorize the step-by-step procedure for properly placing your dog in the down position.

Notice how the left hand grasps the running part of the collar, that part which runs from the leash through the noose-ring. If your fingers got into the noose of the collar and your dog tried to spin or whirl, your fingers could become entangled and severely injured, so keep them in the proper position.

Without hurting or choking the dog, your grip should hold the collar snugly enough to keep his neck from sliding and turning. The reason for keeping the back of your left hand up will be apparent: the left arm can be swung over the dog to bring your weight—all of it, if necessary—to bear on his back in order to push him down as you move his front feet forward from under him and place him on the "down."

When you can close your eyes and visualize each step of the technique given in the illustration, you are ready to acquaint your dog with the down.

Begin by bringing the dog, at heel, from his place of confinement and reviewing all exercises learned to date. When you reach a point where there is not the slightest contention on any exercise, make a stop and after the dog has sat automatically, give the one command, "Joe, down," and place him in the down position exactly as shown in the illustration that you have studied.

90

Remember to keep the downward pressure of your left arm on the dog's back as you move his feet straight forward from under him—we want to get both ends down at once. If his legs are small enough so that you can hold them both in your right hand, there will be little chance of his out-maneuvering you with his feet; otherwise, you will have to grasp his left leg at a point high enough to prevent him from raising his right leg above the path of your arm 'as it moves forward to carry his feet from under him.

Do not be one of those strange individuals who try to bulldog their dog over onto his side. Nothing in the illustration is remotely similar to such an action. Again—the picture shows the collar held in the left hand, as the trainer kneels on his left knee, with the left arm bringing his weight—as much as is necessary—to bear on the dog's back, while the right hand and arm move the dog's feet forward and from under him.

Praise the dog immediately when he reaches the down position, and let him get up. As in the case of the sit, it's the down not the down-stay that we're working on.

Walk off with the dog at heel and practice the other exercises once or twice each, then repeat the placing and praising on the down.

If your dog gives you a bad time by sliding sideways out from under your arm, you can end his sliding by working with him trapped between a fence or building and yourself.

The average training period, with time spent on practicing exercises and meeting a dog's occasional challenge, will find you placing your dog on the down from ten to fifteen times, depending on whether you train for one long or two shorter periods a day.

And what if your dog isn't average, but fights against your placing him down the first time?

Consider for a moment that in using our chosen technique on the down, instead of the foot-on-the-leash, our first concern was with the dog's physical and mental comfort. We have attempted to introduce him to the down exercise in the fairest and most pleasant manner. As to the reasonableness of handling a dog against his protests, remember that, aside from training, we are still obligated to touch and handle a dog's feet, if only to treat him for an injury or to cut his nails. Thus, even the spineless ones to whom a dog's violent, screaming protests might appear to be a real problem are left no morally correct solution other than to continue handling the dog against his wishes.

And, alas, since it is impossible to be more gentle, the troubled handler can only proceed with a deliberate fairness until the dog's

The text describes the necessary amount of slack for the down correction.

Make certain that the first correction does the job.

93

rebellion against the reasonable action leaves no course but to end the dog's protests in the very definite manner prescribed in "Lesson IV" for dealing with the "protest biter."

Even though "pussyfooting around points of contention" has made the job of establishing authority much harder on both you and the dog than if you had met your obligations at the proper time, the task can still be accomplished.

For your assurance of this fact, take a look at what can be done when trainers are faced with the absolute necessity of overcoming their dog's objections to being placed on the down. There has been a rule in force in all the obedience classes that I have run that each trainer in the class will follow through on his first attempt to place his dog on the down, regardless of the animal's protest against his reasonable action. Any objecting dog is to be thoroughly convinced that he will be handled at any hour of the day or night that his master might choose. Now take a good look at the affidavit on page 7. This shows that your chances are very good. And when the dog knows that his master is going to follow through, the job is not very difficult.

Sound cruel? Would it be kind to avoid trimming and shoeing the hooves of a sore-footed horse because he didn't want his feet handled?

During the training periods of the first four days spent on the down, continue to place and praise your dog in the down position. If you've done a good job of pleasantly associating the exercise with the command, your dog should be "melting" cheerfully down into position by the end of the third day's training. By the end of the fourth day's work on the exercise, you may be sure that you have given him ample time to learn the significance of your command and that, beginning with the next training period, you will be acting reasonably if you should correct him for failing to respond to the word.

To make the process of enforcing the down easy on you and your dog, the drawings as well as written descriptions are provided. Study both until each step of the mechanics and the reason for it is clear in your mind.

On the fifth day, bring your dog from his place of confinement and go through the usual pattern of reviewing the exercises. After placing him on the down once or twice, make a stop and, after the dog has sat automatically, step out to where you can face him from a position that is about twenty degrees to the right of the direction in which the dog's body is heading.

With both hands grasp the leash about six inches from the collar. As a rule, this is enough slack to permit a jolting surprise on the down correction without the risk that the trainer's hands will hit the ground before his jerk can tighten the leash. For extremely short-legged breeds, such as the Dachshund, the amount of slack must be reduced accordingly.

As the drawing shows, both hands are locked tightly on the leash for maximum purchase, together with the feeling and attitude of absolute finality that is vital to an authoritative correction. Now, with the above-mentioned amount of slack hanging down in the leash, move your hands up close to the dog's neck so that your jerk will have distance to develop full momentum and explosive power before the leash can tighten and cause the dog to brace.

Next, give one—and only one—command to down: "Joe, down!"

If your dog goes down on the command, praise him warmly.

If the dog doesn't respond immediately, use your arms, shoulders, and back in a chopping stroke that jerks the leash at an angle that is down, a bit forward and enough toward the dog's right side so that all of the force is centered on his right front leg.

Why? Simple mechanics.

Since the downward pressure prevents the leg from moving to balance or brace, the forward pressure causes it to buckle at the joint that God put just above the dog's front foot, and the dog will crumple downward and forward over his foot with very little strain on the neck.

Give him a pat to let him know that there's a pleasant reception awaiting him on the down; then let him up again. Remember—it's the down, not the down-stay that you're working on.

The enforcement of the command was accomplished because you took the dog *off balance* with a technique based upon proper mechanics instead of trying a slow, steady, downward pull that gave him time to brace with his front legs while you bleated, "Down, down, down, now down, down," or applied insipid tugs that nagged him into greater resistance, thereby increasing the strain on his neck.

For the benefit of the more tentative members of my obedience classes, I have suggested hundreds of times that they obtain their veterinarians' opinions as to the worth of my instructions, relative to the dog's physical welfare, for correction on the down exercise. The method has received unanimous endorsement from the veterinarians they have questioned.

So, in the name of truth and simple laws of mechanics, if you should still insist on using the tugging, swinging, "bell-clapper" correction, do not call your action "kindness."

Until told differently, each time you intend to down your dog, be out in front ready to back up your command with the proper correction if your dog should be slow or uncertain in his response. Your readiness will make you an effective handler; consequently the dog will soon realize the futility of delaying his response and will be spared the large number of corrections that is the sad lot of the dog who has been nagged into resistance.

So be ready. And be just as ready to sincerely praise your dog when he goes down on a word of command. After a few days' training periods have proven that you are always ready to correct or praise, he'll probably settle for the praise.

"And," you may be asking, "what do I do if he won't down on command, but drops just ahead of the correction?"

I'll tell you what you can do.

If your dog should work this "ha-ha, beat you to it" racket, make certain that you correct him more emphatically than usual.

"Why?"

If he has so much intelligence, initiative, and coordination that he tries to turn the exercise into a competitive game, you may be sure that he may be fairly corrected for failing to down on command. Your dog must learn that he is to down on a word of command or face the correction that will surely come, regardless of his attempt to throw you a herring by downing just ahead of your movement.

"And how can he be corrected when he's lying on the ground?"

Easily. Hold a six-inch length of leash in the regular manner for correction, then lift upward until the dog's neck is raised high enough to permit a regular down correction before your hand hits the ground. Don't worry that your dog will be confused by your action of pulling him up from the down position and then correcting him. Generally, with the dog that plays the game of downing just ahead of the correction, it's the trainer who is confused, not the dog.

When the dog has gone down on command, willingly, at least twenty-five consecutive times, you'll know that he's past the point of all-out resistance and that it's safe to risk giving a down command while you are standing upright beside your dog, just as you are when he sits automatically.

Without stooping, curtseying or bowing, give a single command and, if the dog does not respond immediately, turn toward him, grab the leash within six inches of the snap, and drop your weight in as forceful a down-jerk as your position will permit. Once more, don't be slow or inhibited in your correction or your dog will be encouraged to resist.

Of course, as soon as he goes down on command, he'll be getting praise instead of correction.

If he withholds response until after you've moved to correct, be certain to follow through. An obedient dog should down on a word of command without any nod or other physical cue from his master.

Few things are more pathetic than a so-called trained dog that won't down because a stiff neck or sore back prevents his master from nodding or bowing to him.

When your effectiveness as a handler has caused your dog to perform reliably under ordinary conditions, work until you get the same reliability in more distracting situations.

This second stage of reliability generally comes within three days after the first down corrections are started.

When your dog has been taken past the point of contention or argument, you can add the down exercise to your pattern of work for further practice and polishing and consider that you and your dog are ready for the next exercise.

Cadence Topsy is the first Bull Terrier to earn the titles of Champion, Utility Dog, and Tracker. She belongs to Carol Taylor, Riverside, Cal.

"Duke" defends his family in *The Swiss Family Robinson*.

Lesson IX

DOWN-STAY

You are about to start one of the most valuable exercises in basic obedience. Since it requires not the slightest physical strain, the down-stay can be used as a convenience for keeping the dog in one place for a long time. Also, because it brings no discomfort, there is nothing inhumane about increasing the dog's capacity for restraint and emotional stability by requiring him to hold the down-stay for long periods.

The down-stay differs from the sit-stay in position, but the teaching of it is much the same—only easier. Experience on the former exercise has taught your dog that "stay," means "don't move," and this combined with the fact that he already knows the down position, justifies a correction if he disobeys when placed on a down and told to stay.

For your assurance of how easily and speedily your dog will learn the down-stay, I shall mention that in most obedience classes the exercise is regarded as so easily comprehended that no class time is alloted for demonstration. A handler is simply told to put his dog on the down, tell him to stay and use a regular down correction if he gets up. Along with this brief instruction goes the usual warning against "under-correction."

Begin the lesson with a few minutes of review on the familiar exercises. When you and your dog are performing smoothly, down him in the usual way, give a command such as, "Joe, stay," and step out to face him from a location identical to that you used for making your first down correction, which means no more than one step away. In fact, the corrections used when a dog breaks the down-stay are exactly the same as those used when he fails to respond to the down command.

Be sure that you step out right-foot-first. (When the left foot moves first, it means "heel" to the dog.) The signal you give with your left hand should be open-fingered, palm toward the dog, and as emphatic as the firm tone of your voice. Again, I am aware that the rules governing obedience trials do not permit the double command. Don't worry. Any handler capable of training a dog to stay is certainly able to limit himself to the proper command when the vividness gained by using the two in combination has caused the dog to associate each type of command with the act of staying. In the meantime, the handler, whose dog has learned that the hand motion has the same significance as the word, has a good foundation if he should ever be interested in trying the "signal exercises of advanced training."

As you stand facing the dog from a step out in front, have a few inches of slack in the leash. Previous practice in correcting the dog for failure to down on command has shown you how to get your arms and back into a correction of maximum effectiveness, so, if your dog should move from the stay, use the same technique to jerk him back to position. If he crawls toward you, or crawls in any other direction, use a jerk that sends him skidding back to the exact position where he was told to stay. It is a pitiful sight to see some dull handler pull a dog back down to position, or "tow" a crawler back to a spot, in the belief that this comfortable means of returning a dog will somehow accomplish the work of a correction.

And keep your mouth shut while you correct him. You told him once to down and once to stay. That's enough. If he disobeys ten times, give him ten corrections, but not another command.

When your dog holds for as long as ten seconds, move back to his side by the same route you came, and let your praise tell him what a wonderful job he did. If you ask him to hold too long on his first experience with the new exercise, he'll be confused and wonder just what it is that you want.

Do not permit him to use the motion of your return, nor the action of your praise as an excuse to move. Make a quick correction if he gets up before you end the exercise. When he has held a few seconds, following the praise, give a heel command, start off on the left foot, and spend a minute or two on the practice of other exercises before repeating the down-stay experience.

With these short periods of reviewing familiar exercises between the repetitions of the down-stay, you will probably repeat the new

100

exercise ten times the first day. That's enough. By the end of the day's training, he should hold for at least twenty seconds. Again, don't ask for more nor settle for less.

The second day, after moving out to face your dog on the down-stay from a step out in front, you may add the distraction of a bit of motion by taking a short step to the right, and then a step back to the left. If he holds the position as you take the two steps, move back to his side and praise him. If he takes your action as an invitation to a game, correct him and repeat the tempting step.

As with the sit-stay, it is fair for you to make a distracting move so long as it is not addressed directly to the dog. *To address an inviting action to the dog, and then correct him when he responds, would destroy confidence.*

Remember, the substance of the exercise is for your dog to remain lying in the exact spot where he was told to stay. While it is desirable that he be relaxed to the point of turning his head about, or shifting his weight a bit, the turning and shifting should not move him one inch from where he was told to stay.

Don't let him get you off balance with a program of "swim-like crawling," or "progressive stretching" that takes him five or six inches from the spot where he was left. Give this kind of dog an inch and, truly, he will take a mile. Beware of the dog who raises up from the down-stay, then, as the handler moves to correct, drops back down, thinking to avoid correction. Obviously, since it is a stay exercise, such a dog is even more deserving of correction than if he had not returned to position—his return to position proves he knew better than to break.

In a case such as that above, where the dog toys with his mentally inferior handler, the restraint-developing values of the exercises were lost. Do not merely teach the dog the meaning of the exercises—use them to make him a better dog.

On the second day of work on the down-stay, repeat the distraction of side-stepping back and forth in front of the dog. When he is holding well, take a step farther away from him, then a step back toward him. Completion of the second day's training should find the dog holding for thirty seconds while you leave him, do the distracting steps, and return to his side.

On the third day you can enlarge the pattern of your steps until you are moving sideways and backward and forward the length of a slack leash from your dog. Lest you confuse the dog, be careful that your steps do not tighten or jerk the leash.

About this time, you may face a pit-fall. There may be a temptation to try a down-stay without the leash, or with your end of it lying on the ground. Keep a good grip on that leash until you are told to do differently.

From now on, return to your dog's side by circling around behind him as you did on the sit-stay. The hand should hover at a constant level over the center of the dog's back as, with full slack in the leash, you travel around, close to the dog, in a pattern that ends when you are in proper position to start off with the dog at heel. Only as you take one step to "break the dog loose" do you gather in the slack and re-arrange the leash in your right hand. Later, when we work on another type of stay position, you will see that this technique of handling the leash on a return to the dog is not merely important— it's vital. So practice it.

By the end of the third day's training on the position, you should be able to leave your dog on the down-stay, stand facing him a slack leash length away for one minute, return, and praise him without his moving until you break him loose with the heel command.

Always be certain, when your dog breaks, to make your correction at that point where the disobedience occurs. For example, if he breaks immediately when you step out to face him, correct him from out in front, and continue on with the exercise. Don't go back to his side and start the exercise all over. Likewise, if your dog turns to face you as you are moving around behind him, on your return to the heel-position, snatch him back the way he came. In this "turning instance" make doubly certain that you keep your leash-jerk horizontal, not up. When he holds the position, resume your movement from the point of correction on to the completion of the exercise. Don't correct the dog and then repeat that part of the exercise which he may have done perfectly well. Make it a firm rule to always correct and continue on from the point where the disobedience occurs.

By the end of the fourth day, after beginning the down-stay, your dog should hold for three minutes even though exposed to the temptations of people and animals walking nearby. Once more, do not let him consider your praise as a reason to move before you take the heel-step that ends the exercise.

By now, you will find that the increasing capacity for restraint and steadiness that you are building into your dog with the down-stay, will manifest itself in seemingly unrelated situations. You may notice a tendency for him to grow more resigned and relaxed, regardless of his surroundings. Later, you will learn how the stays can be used systematically to work miracles in the calming of a "geared" or restless dog. By the end of the week, the down-stay should be as familiar a part of your pattern of work as the other exercises. Your dog should now be holding for five minutes. Most important—you will be convinced that the benefits of reliability and character development obtainable from the down-stay are limited only by your own determination, constant effort, and correct technique.

Even a large dog can be lifted into a standing position.

Stay close when you begin the counter-clockwise return.

LESSON X

STAND-FOR-EXAMINATION

Unless you are above average in discernment, you might make the common mistake of thinking the STAND-FOR-EXAMINATION is merely a formal exercise for dog shows. The error of such thinking becomes apparent when you consider that of the 11,500 dogs referred to in the affidavit that accredits this book, approximately fifteen percent were placed in training as biting problems, yet fewer than nine dogs so much as threatened the strangers who touched and examined them when they graduated from classes. Watch carefully, as we work on the STAND-FOR-EXAMINATION, and see how the exercise should be used to stop indiscriminate biting, and to make a dog emotionally stable when approached by strangers.

Since there is no confusing similarity between the trainer's actions on the down-stay and the stand-for-examination, the two exercises can be conveniently started in the same period. (You will see the start of the exercise demonstrated in the illustration on page 103.)

Set the stage with the usual review of previously learned work. When your dog is performing smoothly, make a stop and acknowledge his automatic-sit with a bit of praise so he'll know you like what he's been doing, and will not take your action of placing him on the stand as disapproval.

Change your grip so your right hand is holding the leash close to the dog's neck, as shown on page 103. This will keep his front end from drifting about as you work with his rear, and at the same time prevent an accidental upward tug which would give the dog a cue to sit.

Next, adjust your position so that you can extend your left arm across the small of the dog's back beneath his loin, as shown in the picture.

Give a command such as, "Joe, stand," then gently raise the dog to a standing position.

Remember, if you let your action, or your dog's, cause any upward tension on the leash as you work on the stand, your dog will think you a fool. And he'll be right. What word could better describe a person who would tell a dog to stand and, at the same time, cue him with a tug?

When he is standing, move your left hand from under him and gently stroke his side and his back in the area of his shoulders. For the time being, keep away from that area where you pushed when you taught him to sit. If the dog tries to shift from position, you can trap his movements between your arm and leg. If he sits back down, raise him up again. When he has stood for ten seconds, show your approval with praise as you heel him one step forward to where he should sit automatically. This definite ending of the exercise is to discourage the dog from ever sitting back down on the spot where he was placed on the stand. If he should try to sit before this terminating step, raise him back to a stand. If he makes 501 attempts to sit, raise him 502 times.

It is obvious that, when you finish your praise and stroking, your heel command, the slackening of the leash, and the forward step must flow into one smooth operation. Certainly, it would confuse your dog if you were to stand motionless beside him while you go through the process of arranging your leash. Again, give the command, take the step, and do your leash arranging as you move.

Another method of placing the dog on the stand is to give the command, then move the leash, which is held closely and at neck level, straight forward a distance sufficient to cause the dog's front feet to adjust a couple of steps ahead as his rear end is raised to a standing position. After the praise and stroking, he is "broken loose" with a forward step, as was explained in the first example.

Because, in this second method of placing a dog, he is being stopped at the same time he is told to stand, there is a bit more possibility that he might be confused and try to sit back down. For this reason, the first procedure of standing the dog, without moving him forward, is probably better for most trainers. An exception would be the handlers of German Shepherds. Their dogs, due to singular qualities of conformation, must move their front feet forward in adjusting to their extensively angulated stance. *Whether you use the first or second*

106

method, remember two things: never let the leash pull upward; and never let the dog sit back down until you have heeled him forward a step.

When he has been worked on the exercise about ten times each day for five days, your dog should hold a stand for half a minute as you lightly stroke his back. By now you should be ready to begin conditioning him to the approach and touch from all angles, as he holds the stand, in preparation for later accustoming him to strangers.

Before we begin this conditioning process, it might be well to mention that your dog does not have to learn to stand up on command. Even in the novice obedience competition, you may place him. In fact, there is no provision made for giving him a higher score if he were to assume a standing position when he hears your command. The exercise is graded solely on what he does after he is placed in the position.

Begin the sixth day of work on the stand by placing your dog in the usual way. Let all of the leash, except the grip, fall from your right hand, even though it means that several feet will be lying on the ground. This is to make it impossible for you to accidentally tighten the leash as you begin to work your way around the dog.

Give a stay command, and, with your left hand lightly stroking the dog near the shoulder, begin to sidestep around him in a counterclockwise pattern. Don't edge along apprehensively; move smoothly and confidently. He may be a bit distracted by your changing position and try to turn to face you, or sit. Use one hand on the collar to turn him back to position and use the other hand to re-stand him. As you pass in front of him, you will find it convenient to change the leash grip to the left hand and do your stroking and re-standing with the right. As you pass down his left side toward his rear, your unfamiliar presence at that point makes it probable that he will try to move from position. Again, one hand should go to the collar to turn him back to position and, if he should sit, the other hand should go beneath him to do the re-standing. If he's a big dog, when you've worked your way around to his rear, you'll no longer be able to reach the collar, and you'll have to rely on your hands to thrust him back "the way he came" each time he turns or moves. Do not drop your grip on the leash as you use the "leash hand" to handle the dog. At times, you may have to move fast to head him off. After a correction, always continue your progress from where you were when the dog "broke."

After you've passed behind the dog and are moving back along his right side toward the starting point, you'll find it necessary to switch the leash grip back to the right hand and do the handling with the left. When you've worked your way around the dog to the place where you started, immediately give a heel-command, take a step, straighten up, and adjust to the proper leash grip—all in one motion. As you practice your exercises, periodically repeat the standing and conditioning to touch routine at least ten times each day. Three days from the time you start the circling, your dog should know the score so well that he'll stand solidly while you sidestep around him an arm's length away. This will condition him to stand while you're at a distance, yet you'll be close enough to touch him occasionally, and to correct.

Always move confidently while you travel around the dog, and when you're back at the starting point don't invite confusion with an interval of "squaring up" as you stand beside him fumbling with the leash. Stop a little farther to the right than your usual heel-relationship, pause for a second with the full amount of slack still hanging in the leash, then break him loose with an angling step that brings you closer together even as it ends the exercise by heeling the dog forward. Adjust to the proper leash grip after you've started the step forward —not before.

After two days of moving around your dog at an arm's length, change that circling pattern to an oval that keeps you the arm's length from his sides and rear but lets you move out to face him from a distance of three feet in front. Face him casually; don't stare at him anxiously, or threateningly, as though you were about to bear down on him. If you have to move in for a correction, re-stand him calmly and smoothly. There are individuals whose brain waves and physical manner can prod any dog into confusion, making him take refuge in the most familiar exercise he knows—sitting.

Face the dog out in front for about five seconds, then pass the leash to the left hand, which should extend out at your side about chest-level. This will enable you to hold the hand at a point directly over the middle of the dog's back. Move back toward him and continue on a casual walk that takes you past his left side, behind him, and around back to the heel position. Finish the exercise by heeling him forward one step. Remember, the only time when you are more than an arm's length from the dog is during the five seconds you pause out in front.

By staying this close as you move around him, you will have no difficulty keeping your leash hand at a constant level of your chest and centered over the dog's back even though your dog is very large. Do your praising after you finish the command with the forward step. He will know why he got the praise, even though it comes after the step. The beginning experience on the stand taught him what it is about the exercise that pleases you.

The first few periods of facing your dog from out in front will be the most difficult for both of you. After that much experience in pleasing you, he'll know that, regardless of your movements and position, he's not to move his feet.

And if he doesn't seem to know what you want, but appears hopelessly confused? There are times when a dog, mired in a bog of confusion, must be taken right on through to solid ground. It is better to keep working doggedly and calmly than to follow the foolish advice of letting him rest "till his mind clears," which actually lets him sink deeper into the bog. Once more, if he sits 501 times, re-stand him 502 times. But remember, it is not only permissible but desirable for a dog on the stand to move his head and wag his tail in pleasure. However, he should not move his feet.

Four days after you begin to face your dog from out in front, he should be ready to be introduced to the "approach-and-touch" part of the exercise.

The person you get to do the touching can be a stranger or a friend so long as he is neither the timid, uncertain type, nor a know-it-all who will disregard your careful instructions. Tell your helper to stand quietly a few feet from the dog's right side until the dog has been placed on the stand and you have taken your position out in front, as shown on page 110. He should then move to the dog's side casually, with what amounts to a rather indifferent attitude. Without the appearance of reaching toward him, a hand should hang impersonally near the dog's nose so that a slight move of his head will permit the dog to sniff it. When his sniff or attitude shows he's resigned to the helper's presence, the person should touch the dog confidently on the head or neck and immediately, without the appearance of jerking back, turn and walk away. You should then walk around the dog and break him loose in the usual way.

We want the dog to be properly approached in the beginning of this conditioning, and this "oblique approach" is the method used by experienced men who work with those kinds of animals that might be "spooked" if more directly addressed by word or gesture. So, in the beginning, avoid those characters who, with their "way with dogs," would discourage the less receptive dogs and invite the over-friendly animals to break position. After the dog has had some successful experience on the stand, there will be time for temptations in the form of incorrect approaches.

After eighteen days the dog should do a complete "Stand for Examination."

When you are certain your helper will do as he's told, work a few of the stand-and-touch exercises into your practice pattern. Naturally, if the dog should break from the touch, or for other reasons, your job will be to move in, correct in the usual manner, repeat the part of the exercise which the dog failed, and then continue on to completion.

During the next two days, repeat the exercise exactly as started. By then your dog will be certain that he's supposed to remember your command regardless of distraction. Now that he understands fully what you want, you can generally increase the time he is left standing, and have your helper begin to touch his back (first in one place, then in another) as well as his head. At first, with this more extensive standing and touching, you'll be called upon to do a bit more correcting and re-standing; but within eighteen days of the time you begin to teach the stand for examination, your dog should hold for about one minute while you are out in front, while a stranger approaches to touch the dog's head and back, and you return to complete the exercise.

Cheer up, if you've been lamenting the fact that your dog holds perfectly well on the stand until someone tries to touch him, but then breaks the position. Regardless of whether he tries to play, bite, cringe, or panic, there's a solution to your problem.

The playful dog, who moves to meet the one approaching him, can generally be taught to think of his trainer, and where his own feet should be, by using a horizontal jerk that skids him back to where he should be re-stood. These forceful corrections, combined with quiet praise for a job well done, will eventually show an exuberant dog that he must still remember his responsibilities, despite that smiling eyes and a friendly tail are wonderfully appreciated. To stop such a dog from bowling over a child, or precipitating other embarrassing situations, is worth the hard work sometimes required.

If your dog is particularly difficult in this respect, you may have to stay close to him while your helper touches him, so that your corrections can be made faster and more effectively, until your dog no longer takes your helper's approach as an invitation to a romp.

With the biter, or the shy or panicking dog who is invariably a potential biter, your responsibility to work on the stand becomes greater.

"But I don't want my dog to let people touch him. I want him to be a watch-dog."

If you were about to utter the above inanity, don't. In most home situations, the indiscriminate biter is the least satisfactory watch-dog because he must be closely confined, and so is not ready for action in emergencies, as the properly discriminating dog would be. A ready example of how discrimination makes for the best protection-dog is seen in the case of the thoroughly disciplined police-trained dog. He cannot promiscuously bite the citizens who might approach him.

There is a second fact which we must recognize. It is almost impossible to administer the all-out jerk, necessary to discourage the determined biter, without using a leash angle that would confuse the dog into thinking you might want him to sit. But there's an answer. Give your dog lots of preliminary experience in being approached and touched while he's on a sit-stay. Then, if he backs away or whirls to bite, you can get your back and arms into a sit-stay correction in a way that convinces him it's just not wise to move in any direction, regardless of anyone's approach. When he's had enough convincing corrections, he'll be loath to invite another by risking a bite that might pull him out of position.

Suggestions for dealing with unusually dangerous dogs are included in the chapter entitled "Problems."

Whether your dog is a biter or a "shrinker," don't kid yourself into believing you can solve the problem with the old "understanding and sweet-talk" method. Many of the misinformed have gone this syrup route only to find that their impression wasn't permanent enough to protect a person who approached their dog ill-advisedly, but in friendly innocence.

You may wonder why, since he can be corrected with so much more effectiveness on a sit-stay, the stand-for-examination is ever used to condition a dog to being approached. There is a good reason. The very fact that the stand does not offer the threat of an inevitably effective correction means that it calls upon the dog to practice a greater degree of involuntary restraint. So, while the groundwork on the sit-stay may be necessary for a time, ultimately the greater good will come from being touched while on the stand. Then, too, your dog may sometime be standing or walking among a group of people when he is approached, so he should learn to control himself even though he is not influenced by the threat of a sit-stay correction. Lastly, the stand is the position in which dogs are presented for examination in the obedience and the breed rings.

Whether your dog agreed readily to the stand-for-examination or required the greater effort, within twenty-one days from starting the exercise he should hold reliably when a stranger touches him while you are standing a slack-leash length out in front.

Practice the exercise faithfully, having your helper approach the dog from all angles, touch him on the head, the back, the tail, and on the sides. You will find that the benefits of the stand-for-examination were not promised idly. There will be increased security for you; your dog will be happier and more confident; and should a veterinarian ever have to care for him, the task should be much more pleasant for the doctor and your dog.

As to indication of when you will be ready to start the next exercise—the background of experience which you and your dog have acquired through weeks of training makes it certain that you can begin another exercise seven days after the time you began instruction on the down-stay and stand-for-examination.

Obedience training is becoming popular in Mexico. American and Mexican Ch. Merrywood's Candy of Pintura, American U.D. and Mexican P.U., is the first Shetland Sheepdog to achieve all these titles. Candy is owned by the Lydon Lippincotts of San Bernardino, California.

Your dog must hold the sit-stay until you call him.

114

Lesson XI

RECALL

If you were to walk through a residential district and ask the first ten dog owners you chanced to meet how they would feel about turning their dogs loose in an unfenced area where there was danger, or great distraction, you would find few who would be willing, and the rest would regard your question as ridiculous. You would get all kinds of reasons for declining your proposition. You might learn of ordinances against having a dog off-leash; find that some "love their dogs too much" to risk their being unrestrained; and be informed that some dogs have always been confined, and there is no intention to ever risk the chance of a runaway.

On the surface, the above, like many similar lines of reasoning, does sound creditable. Lots of cities do have leash-laws—and with justification. It would be cruel to free an uncontrollable dog in a dangerous situation. But these facts don't make a point. They point to a weakness. Doors and gates are left open. Dogs do get out. Emergencies do occur—often to the injury of the dog or the embarrassment of his master. Then, too, it is a sad thing for a dog, when a vacation takes his family to the outdoors, to have to remain on leash because he might "run away" or meddle in the affairs of others. Such a dog is generally deprived for life from sharing the freedom of new places with his master, who might have been "too kindly" to earn the dog's respect.

However, regardless of how restrained the life a dog might be forced to live, there is still a reason, or rather an absolute obligation,

115

Your dog must hold the sit-stay until you call him and bring him in, hand over hand.

Bring him in, hand over hand, to a sitting position in front of you.

to teach a dog to come unfailingly when called. It is the obvious fact that there never can be full understanding between a master and a dog he cannot control.

So, you may ask, with safety, convenience and understanding all demanding that a dog come when he is called, why is it that so few owners teach dogs obedience to the command?

These individuals, who are unable to teach their dogs to come when they are called, can be divided into three general classifications: the lazy handlers who won't make the effort; the misinformed; the pig-headed persons. Typical of the third classification is the person whose thoughts are so occupied with trying to describe what he thinks is an unusual or exceptionally difficult problem that his mind is a solid wall of obsession which no ray of enlightenment can penetrate.

If you are not lazy, and will keep your mouth shut and your mind open, I can provide you with a method of teaching the recall that will eventually result in a reliability of performance which will amaze you.

Though the goal of the *recall* exercise is to be able to control the dog off-leash, it is vital to work toward that goal a single step at a time even when some of those steps seem unrelated to controlling the dog at liberty. The first of these steps is a groundwork of experience where it is mechanically impossible for the dog to fail to respond to the recall. This is another way of saying that he must always be on leash when he is called, until that specific time when you will be told to remove the leash. Until then, by confinement, or other measures, avoid those booby traps where you demonstrate your ineffectiveness by calling the dog when you cannot make him come back. This job of avoiding difficult situations until you are prepared to cope with them, may take some planning, but it will make your job easier.

Let's get started on that groundwork of experience. For a few minutes, review all exercises previously learned. Now ·comes our first problem. Not with the dog. With you. You'll probably want to explain that your dog knows enough to always come perfectly when on leash; it's off-leash that he doesn't obey. That's fine. Let's just continue to have him "come perfectly" a few hundred times while he's on the leash. Or perhaps you will argue that there's no connection between the precision of a dog sitting in front of you and reliability of performance. There is a connection. And before we're finished, you will see it. A dog, like a man, rarely gives more than you ask of him. The dog that's asked to do something as sloppy and indefinite as merely coming back to his master, soon will lapse into a pattern where he comes back to a point just out of the handler's reach.

After throwing his master the "herring" with a few of these token recalls, the dog will probably make a game of dancing about just a bit farther away. This is especially probable if his competitive spirit has been kindled by having his handler make a few lunges at him. Now you know why we're going to ask more than for the dog to merely come back near his master. We're going to teach him that "come," means all the way back to a definite sitting position in front of the handler.

Even then, the exercise won't be finished, nor is the dog to relax his attention toward his master. He must be alert for the command that tells him to do the "finish," at which time he'll be required to move to the heel position, and there to await either a final command or a release.

Always bear in mind that this formal recall is not window dressing, nor eye-wash, but a procedure that requires so much of the dog that should he, man-like, give less than his best, he is still so occupied with doing a specific thing perfectly that his "less than best" brings him close to the proper position.

Further, by having to concentrate on perfectly executing the finish of the exercise, which ends only when he has moved around to his master's side, he is not given opportunity for the mental lapse, and consequent unreliability, as is the case when he is asked to perform a casual recall which does not demand his full concentration.

Now back to laying that "good foundation" for the later, off-leash enforcement. Leave your dog on a sit-stay and face him from a slack leash length away. As you may notice in the illustration on page 114, the hand loop of the leash is held in the left hand. This is because most handlers can more efficiently reach out to grip and reel the slack with the right hand; and, as you have learned by now, indefinite, fumbling movements do not give the dog a sharp picture of what you want.

Don't do any clasping and reeling until the dog has held his sit-stay for at least half a minute. The mistake of bringing him to you immediately would cause him to take your action of facing him as an invitation to break the stay and come to you. After he has resigned himself to waiting for the required time, give a recall command, such as "Joe, come," then instantly reach out and reel the leash, hand over hand, until his head is directly in front of you and approximately a foot and a half distant.

Though you move swiftly to let him know that he should not delay in starting or coming, your actions must have the smooth clarity of instruction, not the sharpness of a correction.

When your dog has reached the proper spot in front of you, give a command to sit and, if he fails to do so, give a light, upward correction. Light because this may be the first time he has been asked to sit facing his master, and honest confusion must not be treated as disobedience.

The moment he's seated squarely in front of you, reach over and praise him. Then give a heel-command as you make a right-about turn, and adjust the leash in a manner that brings the dog into the proper position for walking. Spend some time, where you think it is most needed, on the practice of other exercises, and then repeat the instruction on the recall.

Don't permit the dog to take your act of stepping out and facing him as a cue to break the sit-stay and come to you. It is disobedience, not obedience, if he comes to you before he is called, and he should get the usual correction for breaking the sit-stay. *The probability of his anticipating and "jumping the gun" will be lessened if you will vary the time he has to wait for the command, thus showing him the exercise is not a rhythmic routine of staying and coming.*

Guard against becoming one of those compromising characters that blurts "Come," as he sees the dog about to start, thinking that this changes the dog's disobedience to obedience. Such a person is fooling himself, not the dog. Now and then you'll get a bad break when the dog starts before the command is completely spoken but is too far completed for you to withhold. In these rare instances, you can only follow through and bring him on in to a sitting position in front of you. This "coinciding" of the command and the dog's anticipation will occur less often as your dog gains experience in holding for the varying periods. In a later lesson, we'll discuss measures of correcting this "trigger-happiness" when the dog is sufficiently seasoned to permit their reasonable use.

It is important to the growth of his reliability, and to the preparation for the finish part of the exercise, that your dog sit accurately in front of you. If he persists in sitting out of position, you may be required to lean out swiftly and guide him into position with either your right or left hand as the leash enforces the sit. At first, the hand in his side is just a gentle instruction, but if his inaccuracy continues, let its speed increase until it becomes a sharp chop that reminds him he'll be much more comfortable if he concentrates on sitting properly.

Control on the stay, certainty of response, and accuracy on the sit —are three reasons you should continue practicing the exercise on leash even though it means reeling fast to keep ahead of a dog that seems to have learned the exercise perfectly.

On the average, a handler will practice the recall ten times each day. By the end of the third day, your dog should be so responsive to the pattern of "stay," "come," and "sit," that you will feel prepared to begin the "finish," which is that part of the exercise where the dog moves from his position in front of you around behind you to complete the exercise at your left side.

From "Big Red": © *Walt Disney Productions*

Walter Pidgeon and Gilles Payant chat on their way back from a fishing trip.

From this position your leg thrust would have enough power to move an automobile.

Lesson XII

FINISH

You may be surprised to find that your dog has already made considerable progress in learning the finish.

"How could he have learned what I haven't taught him?" you ask.

You've done some teaching when you didn't realize it. You can prove this with a simple experiment. First, let's take another look at the specific action of the finish. It is that pattern where the dog, after coming and sitting in front of the handler, takes a command to travel clockwise around behind the handler until he is able to sit in the correct heel position at the handler's left side.

Back to that experiment. Place your dog on a sit-stay, and call him in the usual way. After he has sat in front of you for a few seconds, instead of turning right-about and walking off with the dog, as you formerly did, give a heel command, and, without any hesitation, walk backward four or five steps. Then stop just as confidently as you do when walking forward. When you walked in reverse, your right side actually became the "heeling side" in the mind of the dog, and he walked and sat automatically at that side just as he does at your left when you're walking forward.

Let's carry the experiment a bit further. Leave him and call him again. As before, after he has sat properly, give him a heel command and walk backward. Then, without a halt, pass the leash behind your back, and take a few steps ahead, shifting to the correct leash grip as you do so. You'll find that as you changed the direction of your walking from backward to forward, your dog, working to keep you on

Give the command, "Heel," and take a backward step.

124

Pass the leash around behind you and step forward.

If the dog fails to sit automatically as forward
motion ceases, give the usual sit correction.

his own right side, moved around behind you to your left. Remember, to the dog your correct heeling side is that which is to the right of him when he is walking. That's why, when you change from walking backward to forward, he adjusts by crossing behind to keep you on his right. Again, when you stop, he sits automatically.

Your dog's response to your actions will show that you achieved more than you realized during the time you taught him to heel and sit automatically. It was your principle of demanding attentiveness and instant response that will make the movements of the finish seem logical to the dog and the teaching quite easy. Logical because the finish will be addressed to the dog in a manner based on the heel and sit, two exercises with which the dog is already familiar, and quite easy because you will use leverage to lessen the physical task if your dog should offer resistance.

When the time comes that your dog has learned the finish, he should perform the exercise on a command, without any movement from you. Consequently, the logic of our "walking and stepping approach" must progress to a point where we can pass the initiative and responsibility for acting on command to the dog.

To most fully appreciate the physical help you'll get from the correct technique that we'll use for instruction, try this procedure. Park a car in neutral, with the brake off. Hook your leash to the bumper or bumper guard. Stand facing the car two feet back from where the leash is attached. Have just enough slack in the leash to permit the hand holding it to be firmly locked behind your right leg.

I repeat, "behind your right leg," because experience has shown me that a large number of handlers become very confused as to right and left, to say nothing of the exact position of the hand.

Step back with a bend in your right leg, and dig your toe into the ground. This action will take the slack out of the leash but not pull. Now straighten the right leg and rock yourself backward with a push of the left leg. It may be that the leverage of your body against the fulcrum of the low-held leash actually moved the car a few inches.

It should occur to you that the drag of the car is heavier than that of a dog—even the biggest dog.

Now try the wrong technique, with your arm extended out from your body, in the manner in which unthinking handlers will often try to move a big dog. The arm of a powerful man, when extended out from the body, can be restrained by the single finger of a person with much less strength. From the foregoing, you will see the stupidity of trying to move the dog around with a backstroke of your extended arm.

Now let's apply our technique of logic and leverage to the dog.

Do the recall from the sit-stay in the usual way, and after the dog has come and sat in front of you, wait a few seconds, then arrange the leash-hand behind your leg exactly the same as when you pulled against the car.

Give an emphatic command such as "Joe, heel," and take a single step backward as you did against the car, but, as the step moves the dog from his position to a point at your right side, pass the leash behind you to your left hand. Without stopping or slowing your movement, reach across your body with the right hand and add its grip to that of the left as you take a single, strong step forward that encourages the dog to heel around behind you to the correct spot at your left side. The accompanying illustrations demonstrate this correct technique. If the dog fails to sit automatically as forward motion ceases, make the usual sit correction.

Study the drawings carefully, and work to get a rhythmic effectiveness into the pattern of stepping back, passing the leash behind you, and stepping ahead. Practicing the leash handling and stepping routine without the dog will sometimes smooth out your actions so that you can handle him more smoothly. When properly executed, the completion of the backward step and forward step should place you in the same location as when you started the exercise, except that now the dog is sitting in the heel position at your left side. A bit of practice will enable you to apply the technique efficiently.

Here are solutions to some of the minor problems that might arise.

If there seems to be a confusion—real or phony—that causes your dog to delay in his start, or to sit down before he gets completely around to the left side, there is a trick you can use to set him right. About one out of three times, as you do the finish, instead of following the back step with a single step forward, follow it with several running steps forward before you stop. If your dog delays his start, because he felt you "really weren't going any place," this will convince him that he'd better get started for that "heel-side." And if he should attempt to lag, or sit before he gets around to your left, your momentum plowing into the leash will show him that your heel command might mean that you're going farther than one step, and he'll be much more comfortable if he gets clear around to where he's ready to go with you.

If he fails to sit when he gets around to that "safe spot," correct him; however, don't worry about a crooked sit or a position that's a bit far ahead or behind. Just see that he gets completely around and sits, and that you show your appreciation when he does. Ways of tidying up his performance will be dealt with in the lesson on polishing.

The average trainer will repeat the recall and finish instructions about ten times a day. After seven days of work on the recall, the last four of which included the finish, you may feel that the period of instruction has been completed and the period of correction may be fairly begun.

Henceforth, while practicing the fundamentals of the recall, call the dog from the sit-stay as usual, but instead of reeling the leash to prevent his delay in starting or coming, give him a full second to make his own decision. Then, should there be a lag in his response, correct him with a stiff, two-handed jerk that propels him all the way to the proper position in front of you.

If this "propelling" is the immediate and inevitable result of each failure to respond, failures will soon be eliminated. Do not make the attention-dulling mistake of repeating a command or reminding him of your existence with little tugs. Give one command and see that he obeys it.

Let your praise for a good performance be just as emphatic as your corrections. It's the emphasis on each that makes the contrast between the two.

At the same time you begin correcting for disobedience on the foregoing part of the recall, you can begin to enforce the finish part of the exercise. Why you may reasonably do this after only four days of instruction, as against seven on the first part, is at once apparent when you remember that in comprehending the finish, your dog was merely required to perform the familiar exercises of heeling and sitting in a pattern your instructive steps showed. Four days is ample time for him to learn the meaning of your command, and to justify your correction if he does not respond to the single word.

As always, preparedness is the key to an effective correction.

The illustration on page 122 shows a dog that has been called to a sit position in front of his handler. Notice that the hand is locked securely, well around behind the leg. Now, however, allow a sag of six inches of slack to fall into the leash, instead of having it taut as shown in the illustration of the back steps being used for instruction. More than six inches of slack would cause the corrective action to be expended without its full effect reaching the dog; a lesser amount would not permit the momentum of the correction to build up into an authoritative jolt.

When your leash has this proper amount of slack, give a single command for the dog to heel. If he takes the initiative and responds promptly, and without further cue, praise him when he gets around to your left side. If he does not respond immediately, thrust your right leg backward in a step that jerks the leash in an effective correction and starts the dog on his path around behind you. Pass the leash behind you to the left hand as you take the forward step back to position; then you will be prepared to take a few running steps if he tries to sit down before he gets around you.

The fast, jolting step backward will show him that he can't beat the correction once it starts, and the only way to avoid discomfort is to respond the moment he hears the command. The occasional practice of taking a few running steps forward will deter him from the "out-of-sight-out-of-harm" maneuver of sitting down before he gets around to the proper spot.

Sometimes it takes many corrections to convince a dog that it's better to start promptly than to risk a correction that he cannot out-maneuver. On this particular exercise, there is a great danger of a trainer spoiling his dog's progress by withholding correction because ten or twelve efforts have failed to influence the dog.

If you have done an average job of working on the four days of "instructive steps," your dog should be walking freely through the pattern of the finish, which is evidence that he knows what you want. This being the case, do not relent if ten corrections in a row get you nothing but shrieks of protest from the dog, and castigations from spectators who would brand you "beast."

Determination and the proper technique will make it certain that your dog will be doing the recall and finish reliably and smoothly within four days after starting the corrections. In fact, he may be working so smoothly that you might be tempted to try a little work off-leash. Don't do it. Don't gamble. One loss is sure to cancel out any number of wins. You'll proceed much easier and faster toward your goal of off-leash control if you will concentrate on perfecting each exercise on leash. When the time comes, we'll start the off-leash work the right way, which means without a gamble.

There—you've started the last of those exercises commonly summed up as "novice obedience." You've learned that demanding response to a command does more than merely control a dog on a leash. Practice of the exercises has developed your dog's sense of responsibility and increased his emotional stability. Magically, it seems, his confidence, reliability, and happiness have increased. This is natural. As his performance improves, he gets more and more of your praise.

130

Keep this fact in mind as we begin the next lesson, which will be devoted entirely to practicing and polishing the exercises your dog has learned, so that you might be prepared to get the fullest benefits when the time comes to start work on the off-leash control.

Until now, that piece of equipment called a "tab" has remained unused. You may have wondered just why you have it. But you'll come to agree that it's one of the handiest articles you own. In order to use it most effectively, you must familiarize the dog with the feel of the tab hanging on his collar. For the rest of your training program, see that it's attached to the dog's collar, as shown, for two hours of his leisure time each day. Make sure, if you have a short-legged dog, that the tab is not so long as to catch his feet, but don't concern yourself if it swings against his legs.

Presentation of The American Humane Association's 6th Annual PATSY (Picture Animal Top Star of the Year) Award to "Wildfire," Bull Terrier dog, for his work in the M-G-M production, *It's a Dog's Life.* Pictured are owners Lillian Ritchell and Claudia Slack, trainer and handler William Koehler, and Mr. B. Dean Clanton, President of the American Humane Association, March 1956.

Henry C. Schley

Children are proud to win in "Novice Y" competition which features the on-leash exercises. Here is Raymond Koehler, son of the author, with his first trophy.

Lesson XIII

POLISHING

Up to now, your dog has learned seven exercises. Through the practice of them, he has become a bit more easily managed on leash, and is somewhat improved in general conduct. This happened within eight weeks of training. If you are thorough in your efforts, your dog will gain more in obedience and character within the next seven days than he has to date. More—you'll both be ready to start the fundamentals of off-leash control. This degree of "readiness" must never be guessed at. That's why you'll have need of an unusual bit of equipment—a piece of common store string about a foot long. Nothing stronger will do.

HEELING AND SITTING

Because the heeling and sitting exercises are nearly always practiced and used together, the techniques of polishing them will be dealt with in a single section. Before you begin, turn back to page 40 and check the leash grip and manner of starting. It may be that you've developed a bad habit or two which review will help you correct.

When ready, bring your dog from his place of confinement, and lay out a pattern of distracting points, such as you have been using in conjunction with your right-about turns. Don't use the same ones. This is to be a test of response in strange situations. If your training area permits, use at least three temptations, and be certain that they are as appealing as those you have been using. Here are a few examples to add to those that might have occurred to you: another dog, possibly one in training, so that each could serve as a distraction for the other; the open door of your automobile, which will show you whether you have brought him to a state where he would decline a stranger's invitation to jump into a car; people in unusual positions and engaged in unusual activities, such as playing games.

When your distractions are arranged, bring your dog into the area at heel, and start using them in the usual way, making momentum-packed right-abouts at the instant the dog indicates his attention has been drawn from you. Because of previous experience, he'll soon be showing a strong disinterest in all of the temptations. At this point, you can alternate your right-abouts with left turns. Here's how you can do so most effectively. Move toward a distraction in an extremely fast walk, or a trot. As you draw near it, slow down and make a left turn. If the dog's interest had left you, he was unaware of your action, and was made quite uncomfortable by your left knee. The big difference between your present use of these turns and your early practice is one of degree. Now, when your dog apparently cannot be distracted, the pattern of temptations you'll use during your week of "polishing" will give him hundreds of opportunities for doing the "right thing." This means hundreds of opportunities to strengthen his character by resisting temptation. And you'll have hundreds of opportunities to show him that, when temptation is resisted and he turns his mind to you, the result is praise.

Each day, during the week of polishing, you should work to increase the strength of distractions just as consistently as a guide-dog trainer works to assure that the temptations he supplies in training are stronger and more unusual than any of those which his dogs meet when they are guiding the blind on dangerous streets.

In addition to the technique of using temptations and turns, there is something you can do to increase your dog's attentiveness, and, in addition, assure that he will heel in the proper position. Twenty seconds' use will convince you of its effectiveness. If you are skeptical, have someone time your actions, and see.

Walk along with your dog at heel, and turn, as if for the usual right-about. But now as you pivot, take three running steps, then slow to your normal walking gait and continue on your way. There was no slack-off of the leash, so if your speed at the time of the turn was doubled, your dog had half of the usual time in which to change direction and avoid a jerk. Do not confuse this "jerk" which is the natural result of your suddenly increased speed, with an argumentative "arm-jerk." The first supplies the dog with a reason for increasing his speed. The second supplies confusion.

Make three of these turn-and-speed-up maneuvers, then make a turn at your normal walking speed. Amazed? It appears your dog might be pulled by a magnet, so increased is his attentiveness and the speed with which he reverses direction. But he wasn't pulled by anything. Certainly not the leash. He has simply learned that your turn might be followed by increased speed, and was headed in the right direction long before the leash tightened. As your "timer" will verify, the time on the actual turns and running steps amounted to less than twenty seconds.

For the rest of the week let all of your right-abouts, and right turns as well, be of this speeded-up variety. With the right turn, as with the "about," the speed-up is made just as direction is changed. Practice making some turns without a dog, handling your feet in the manner shown in the foregoing pictures until you have a feeling of well-balanced emphasis. If you do your part, the dog will turn good "square" corners and heel attentively in the correct position.

AUTOMATIC SIT

The automatic sit, used in the pattern of distractions, along with the about-turns, will make another contribution to your dog's character. Intersperse your turns with stops, particularly at those points where the dog seems a bit inattentive. If he fails to sit immediately, correct him so that he'll be reminded to always take distraction as a cue to think of you.

If your dog is one that sits out of position, approach the problem by admitting the truth. If he is heeling in a correct position and sits instantly when you stop, it stands to reason he will be sitting in proper relation to you. If he is *heeling* improperly, there is small reason to think he will sit properly. Further, if he is heeling correctly, but you make the mistake of giving him time to take a step or two after you stop, he is certain to move ahead. No more can be, nor need be, said on this fact. Possibly your dog might heel and sit correctly, but then "scootch" ahead, or around in front so that he can look at you. "Unscootch" him with a jerk that brings him, airborne, back to where he knows he should be sitting.

"Scootching" backward can generally be corrected by reducing the leash-slack just as you stop, so that the dog can't back up without tightening the collar on himself. Of course, if he's a wise guy that defiantly moves back, even though he knows the right spot is beside you, you might have to "unscootch" him with a stiff jerk that brings him back into the proper position.

Alignment, because of the way the dog is facing, is a bit more difficult to correct. Speedy success depends on how well you follow instructions. If your dog regularly swings his rear away from you, and faces you as he sits, bring the side of your stiffened left hand down in a sharp chop that would be certain to catch your dog in the loin if he were following his usual habit of swinging his rear away from you. If the rear were not swinging away, the loin would not get out where the descending hand would hit it. Instead, the hand could be used to give him a pat in appreciation of his good performance.

Do not make yourself ridiculous by working to push or hammer the dog into position after he has sat. Catch him on the way down. Three or four experiences will reveal that your dog is becoming aware that the hand is ready to meet any "sidewinding." And you'll be quite impressed by his efforts to keep himself in line.

If those efforts should cause him to turn too far the other way, you'll face a problem common to all who train animals: that of counter-correcting when a correction has influenced the student past the desired point. If so, counter-correct with a leash jerk, so that he's turned back into proper alignment.

Whether you are using your hand to catch his loin, or a leash jerk in the other direction, your dog must never feel you are exasperated or angry when you make the correction. So keep your action mechanical, not emotional.

There is a never-failing way to discourage a dog from "scootching" around in front of you. Stop, and give him plenty of opportunity to get all the way around and into your path. Give a heel command and start out with the biggest, most powerful step you can muster —and straight ahead. Feel no compunctions if a big dog receives a solid thump or a smaller one is knocked out of the way. There is plenty of room at your side, and it was the dog's foolish decision to move into your path, so don't cheat him of the consequences of his mistake. Don't be a spaghetti-spined handler who stupidly detours when his path is blocked.

Herbert Spencer said: "The ultimate effect of shielding men from the effects of folly is to fill the world with fools." The same truth applies to the world of dogs. Let your dog learn.

136

THE DOWN

Just as is true of all other exercises, the benefits to the dog's character are greatest when he is required to down promptly when subjected to distraction. If a particular kind of temptation, at first, seemed to make your dog inattentive when heeling or sitting, follow through by requiring him to down in those same distracting situations.

You may also find it necessary to do a bit of work on the down position—your position first, the dog's second. If you have continued to stoop, gesture, or curtsey when giving a down command, stop that bad habit during the week of polishing. Really, you might sometime want him to down when your back is too sore to bend. Show your dog that, if he waits for a movement from you when he's told to down, he's waited too long, for your only move will be to correct. And, if he tries to "beat the correction," snug up the leash until it is taut and give a hard jerk down regardless of how flat and apologetic his belated down places him. Your dog will be likely to down accurately if he downs promptly. If he should twist or "swim" from position, after he has gone down, move him back with a snatch or jerk on the leash. Don't use a pull.

The technique of giving a heel command and plowing straight ahead, as you did on the sit, will show your dog that he'll be uncomfortable if he allows his down position to slop over into your path.

Often, when speed and accuracy on the down are being emphasized, a dog will anticipate a command and immediately after sitting will drop in what amounts to an "automatic down." Though this is undesirable, your dog is actually attempting to please you; and with cold mechanics and in such a way that he'll not feel you are unappreciative of his efforts, you must arrange for him to break himself of the fault. Provide enough slack for him to start down, but not enough slack for him to get there. Unconcernedly, let him run out of slack a few times, and he'll start to wait for the command before downing.

SIT-STAY AND DOWN-STAY

Because the same principles of polishing apply to the sit-stay as to the down-stay, we can deal with both exercises in this one section. At this point in his training, to have your dog do a sit-stay, and then follow immediately with a down-stay, can cause confusion. Often a dog will break the sit-stay by lying down or the down stay by sitting up. Corrections for such disobedience will be much less apt to confuse your dog if, after you finish one of the exercises, there is an interval of work on other things before you practice the second stay position. So, by time intervals, or by interspersing other exercises, keep the stays separated until the exactness of each is clearly in the dog's mind.

You may find when you start polishing the dog's stay positions, that previous experience with your pattern of distractions has made him quite suspicious of temptations, and that he seems very willing to keep his attention on you and the job at hand. By the end of the first day's work in that pattern, he should be holding a sit-stay for two minutes and a down-stay for five minutes, while you face him from a leash length away, and then return by circling around behind him to his right side in order to finish the exercise by breaking him loose with a heel-step.

From this point on, you'll gain reliability by having your dog do his stays in proximity to new distractions. By now you have doubtless become quite expert in obtaining strange people and animals to walk and run near your dog, so we will leave the procurement of the distractions to your own ingenuity.

Perhaps you would like to know the point of distraction beyond which even the best training and conditioning cannot assure a dog's reliable performance. The point might be said to coincide with that where the "instinct for self-preservation" would logically take over. Certainly, it would be unfair to ask a dog to hold when it appeared that he was going to be struck or attacked. However, don't let your dog bamboozle you with a lot of phony fears. Noises of cars back-firing, and traffic roaring, such as a guide-dog constantly experiences, are not reasons for disobedience or panic. Nor is the fact that another animal is running in close proximity justification for your dog to move from a stay. Licensed judges do not regard a dog running wildly about a ring as a reason for dogs doing stays in that ring to break their positions.

Here is a bit of magic you can use, along with your distractions, to make your dog wonderfully solid on his stays. Select a building with both angles of the corner unobstructed for at least ten feet (bushes or other objects might entangle your leash or hamper your handling). Place your dog on a stay about two and a half feet back from the end of the building. Then step around the corner so you are standing a loose leash length from the dog and hidden from his sight.

From the dog's standpoint, you have now disappeared. Chances are he'll break. If he comes toward you, you'll see him. If he goes away, the leash will tighten. In either case, you will be informed of his break and can move to correct him. Since he cannot see through the building, he won't know how far away you are, but experience will show him that you can certainly get to him in a hurry.

Unfortunately, the leash movement will not inform you if the dog should go down from a sit-stay or sit up from a down-stay. If your dog should give you trouble in this way, your chance to make the necessary correction will depend on having a properly placed mirror to let you see his actions, or having someone to watch and signal you.

Gradually increase the length of these corner stays until, by the end of the week, your dog will hold the two minutes on the sit-stay and the five minutes on the down-stay with you hidden from his sight.

There is another effective way to make your dog more reliable on his stays. This is especially useful in dealing with the dog that tries to run away, or in other ways dodges from correction.

After the end of your longe line has been tied to a post or tree, the dog is brought to the area, and placed on one of the stays about three feet from where the line is tied. After the snap has been fastened to the collar, the leash is removed, and the handler gives a stay command and walks away. Though tied, the fifteen-foot line provides so much slack that there is no feeling of physical restraint.

Actually, in even the most limited direction, the dog could run twelve feet. But if he did break, there would be no opportunity to avoid correction by running. The line would bring him up short and hold him, even though the handler was returning from a great distance. The more you use this facility, the more you will understand that your dog is being restrained, not physically, but by his recognition of the inevitability of correction. Progressively increase the distance and time you are away from your dog, and you'll see immense growth in his capacity for restraint on both stay positions.

As always, insist that your dog hold until you have finished the exercise in the proper manner. It's his turn then: show him with sincere praise that you understand what a wonderful guy he really is.

RECALL

You can forget the use of distractions while polishing the recall. As you will see—and you certainly will see—your dog will lose his interest in distractions in a matter of seconds after using the implement described in the next lesson. Now we're concerned solely with obtaining the utmost in accuracy, so that after his "conversion" assures response on leash or off, you may be certain that he'll respond accurately, too.

This working for accuracy means that you'll have to be very consistent in the use of your leash and hands. Each time your dog sits (after *recalling*) too far away from you, snub him closer with your leash. As mentioned earlier, a good distance is so that his head is about a foot and a half in front of you. You should be ready to lean forward and, with your most convenient hand, cut off any attempts to sit to one side or sideways. Previous experience on this correction should have made you quite expert at getting enough force into these "side chops" to make the dog aim for the comfort and praise that awaits him in a position directly in front of you.

FINISH

The corrections explained in the lesson teaching the recall and finish should be used, when needed, to encourage a prompt and accurate finish. In addition to the jolting backstep (used when a dog is slow to begin the finish), and the gimmick of breaking into a run to correct the dog that stops half-way around you can now use your practiced hand to straighten up his final sit position at your left side. As on the recall, those hand movements should progress from the first gentle reminders to the final, sharper encouragement.

STAND FOR EXAMINATION

No distractions should be used, while polishing the stand for examination, which will turn the dog's attention from the person who approaches and touches him. The more fully conscious the dog is of that person's actions, the more the purpose of the exercise is fulfilled. The actions should now be varied somewhat in manner and extent.

Having had considerable practice in holding the stand with you out in front, and while your helper approaches from a few steps away, your dog should now hold while the approach is made from as much as fifty feet away. From this distance your helper comes to the dog more as a stranger would approach, which would not be true if the dog had been eyeing him from a short distance away. Since the approach takes longer, the dog gets practice in holding for a greater period.

You can see the importance of having your helper vary the direc-

140

tion of his approaches—strangers, who blunder up to gush over your dog, do so from all directions. They will also come toward him at varying speeds, so have your helper move both slowly and rapidly—but never threateningly.

Another change: the dog may now be "gone over" more thoroughly, being required to hold while he is touched on the head, shoulder, back, and under the chest.

Here is a very useful procedure, especially if you should want to exhibit your dog in the obedience or breed rings. Have your helper push down, but without authority, in the region of the dog's hips, just hard enough so that the dog must tighten his muscles and resist a bit, but not so hard that the resistance will be over-ridden. As the dog's resistance to the hand is felt, the person should smoothly turn and leave the dog; you should return in the usual way and praise him. By very gradually increasing the hand pressure in a way to encourage resistance, your dog will be brought to understand that you are very pleased with the way he "pushes back up," and in other ways works to resist pressures that might move him from the stand position.

Want to prove this to yourself? Watch the utility exercises in the obedience ring and see the trained dogs in this class as they stand, off leash, minute after minute, while part of the time a strange man examines them. Compare this demonstration of control and concentration, achieved through training, with the manner in which the handlers of dogs in the conformation classes of the breed-ring must "finagle" and fuss to keep their dogs standing in one place when the judge wants to examine them.

Any disobedience on the stand should be met with the corrections given in the lesson devoted to that exercise, but met a little more forcefully. By now your dog should have enough experience on the stand so that a hand raising him "sharply" will convince, not confuse. Notice, I said "a hand," not the leash. He will still be confused by any upward tug on the leash.

The piece of string, described at the start of this lesson, will show you how well you have done the week's work of polishing. It will also show you some very interesting things about yourself and your dog.

The ends of the string are tied together, the loop put through the collar ring, and then passed back through itself to form a second, six-inch loop to which your leash can be snapped. If a chain is "no stronger than its weakest link," your leash and collar unit is not stronger than the string that joins it. That's the way we want it.

Start your first training period, *after your week of "polishing" has been completed,* by joining the leash to the collar as you've been told. Do not substitute anything stronger than the store string regardless of the size of your dog. We do not want a string strong enough to hold your dog—you should no longer have to hold him, nor even lightly cue him—but only strong enough to serve as a symbol of a relationship you have established.

When collar and leash are linked with the string, give a heel command, and go on a "Cook's Tour" around the premises, using a few random distractions en route.

House doors, gates, and car doors are particularly good places to check and see if he sits automatically. Give him a trial on all the exercises learned thus far, including a change of pace on the heeling. If your dog does them all, and seems to take the temptations as cues to be even more attentive, it shows that you have taken him past the "point of contention," and have laid the groundwork for the wonderful accomplishments to begin with the next lesson.

If your dog failed to perform any of the exercises—if the string broke—if you side-stepped or leaned to keep the string intact—or if you gave double commands—your position is not one of authority. You are not the boss. *You had better return to the practicing of your leash work until you are.*

When you and your dog are able to pass this string test, there is one thing you will have learned—an important thing: "the meaning of training a dog so that he comes to take the strongest distraction as another reason for thinking of you . . ."

And then you'll be ready for the next lesson—

C. Lydon Lippincott

Trained dogs are good citizens.

C. Lydon Lippincott

Roy Rogers' "Bullet" was one of the dogs that participated in a "Fun Frolic for Dogs" to raise funds for the children at Casa Colina Home for Crippled Children.

144

LESSON XIV

THE THROW-CHAIN

It is true that obedience is most needed during times of emergency. It is equally true that obedience, like all insurance, must be obtained before you need it. On this premise, our training has progressed to a point where your dog, when on line or leash, takes distractions as a cue to be even more attentive to you, having found that it is at such moments that you are most likely to act.

The time has come for him to learn that you can act with something besides a leash. However, one of the most important progressions of dog training is the proper transition from on-leash to off-leash control, so keep that leash on your dog until you're told when and how to take it off. Right now, we'll use the leash to introduce your dog correctly to the throw-chain.

Until told differently, don't even have the chain in your hand unless the dog is on the leash. While the throw-chain will cause an amazing response, it is instruction through the leash that determines the pattern of that response.

Before you begin the lesson, arrange for two temptations in your training area; or, better yet, take your dog to a fresh area. If possible, have someone go along as your helper.

Whether you score a "miracle or a miss," depends on how well you learn and observe each of the rules for using the throw-chain, and the principles underlying its use.

FIRST: Don't let your dog see you throw the chain. This should pose no problem. Your dog has eyes at only one end. Throw at the other. There are four reasons for this rule. (A) It's impossible to injure an eye when the chain strikes the dog on the rear. (B) He certainly won't try to dodge the chain if he cannot see it coming. (C) If he doesn't see your throwing motion, the chain will not be associated with a threatening action that would seem a gesture to drive him away. (D) There will be benefits from mystery and surprise if he sees no contributing action on your part.

SECOND: Don't miss the dog. Be sure you're so close that you won't. There's no need to worry about your ability. Cold mathematics will show that if the leash runs to his neck and he's facing away from you, the dog's rear cannot be very far away. The most important reason for this "no-miss rule" will be emphasized by your own experience in using the chain. Simply stated, he won't know you *can* miss him if you don't. Have no wild ideas about getting someone else to throw the chain for you. Many who say they are unable to throw, have tried this stunt, only to find that they end up with a confused dog.

THIRD: Don't let him see you pick up the chain. Your dive to grab it would show him that you have only one, and you are emotionally and physically off-balance without it. That's why you have someone along. Have your helper quietly pick up the chain and place it in your throwing hand, which should be held behind your back to receive the chain. While your dog is well able to follow this round-about method, the system makes for more poise and proficiency on your part. And if no one is around to help you? Simple. Just leave the dog tied behind a wall or building while you pick up the chain. Or, better still, use several chains, mark where they fall, and then collect them all at once. Two or three chains may give an opportunity for another shot that could be missed if you had only one. A four-inch strip of cloth tied to a chain makes it easy to find even in high grass.

When you are certain you know all "the rules and reasons," bring your dog into the training area and, holding only the loop of the leash, release him from command with an "okay." Regardless of whether you're right-handed or left-handed, hold the leash so that your throwing hand will be free to handle the chain, which should be clenched so snugly that it will not rattle.

Let your dog relax and enjoy himself on the full length of the leash if he chooses. In fact, go with him so that the leash will not tighten; as you do so, maneuver so that you stay directly behind him.

When your dog is deeply occupied with a distraction, or something else of interest, it is time for you to act. Act in a fair and proper order.

Since you gave him his break, it would be unfair and cruel to correct before calling him. Call him in a normal way. If you "overpower" him with volume, you might waste an opportunity for correction. If the dog turns from the point of interest and starts toward you, complete the recall and finish in the usual manner, and praise him.

If he delays as much as one-half second in his response to the command, throw the chain sharply at his rear. Sharply. It will not hurt him unless you toss, lob, or shot-put it so slowly that he has time to turn his face to the impact. Also, if the chain is thrown slowly, he may have time to walk out of its way. When the chain strikes his rear, reel the leash in swiftly and sit the dog in front of you. Postpone the finish until you've given him the most convincing praise possible. After the finish, take one step with the dog at heel, and then release him with another "okay."

As before, do not let the leash interfere with his pleasure as you try, quietly, to steer his course back toward the same temptation.

It's now that you may get your shock. That same dog who has been jerked, shoved, and shamed away from such temptations, with no avail, now, even though not under command, might shun the situation where he had been corrected only once with the throw-chain. But keep trying. Let your relaxed attitude show him that you have no objection to his "going visiting," which, in truth, you haven't. Your concern begins only when he dares to delay a half second in his response to your recall command.

You may be very lucky and almost immediately get a second opportunity to use the chain. More likely you'll have to wait at least five minutes before his renewed interest will lead him back into the situation, and longer before he will delay his response to your command. Difficult as it now may be to dull his attentiveness to you, saunter, relax, and keep trying.

While you're relaxing, make certain there is not the tiniest sound from the throw-chain.

Finally, if you are skillful and patient, you should get the second opportunity to use the chain. Be sure that the calling, throwing, pulling and praising are done in the proper order. The author has often seen a person of confused or compromising nature actually work to make his movements known to his dog, then, in weird order, pull the leash, give the command, throw the chain at the dog's head and then scramble to pick it up while the dog watches. In obedience classes, this individual can be heard lamenting: "The chain doesn't work with my dog."

If, after you use the chain the second time, your dog will not even face the same distraction, change to another tempting situation. Even in new situations your opportunities for correction may depend on letting the dog become engrossed before calling him, instead of giving the command before his interest has a chance to fully develop.

One half of the session where the throw-chain is introduced should be spent on the throw-chain and half on reviewing previously learned exercises. When you've finished, take your dog to a different area for his after-training break on the long line.

Your first experience with the throw-chain might cause you to wonder why dogs that will ignore the discouragement of a sharp leash correction can be so affected by the slight discomfort caused by the chain. Obviously, the reason must be more psychological than physical.

Parallel your dog's situation with a conceivable experience of your own. If you were to watch an expert archer shoot, consecutively, ten arrows into a target, would you bet that he couldn't do it on the eleventh try? Or that he couldn't repeat the performance from a ten-foot greater distance? And why wouldn't you wager? Because you had no previous experience to indicate any probability that he would miss, nor that there were any limitations of distance.

YOUR DOG WILL NOT BET AGAINST YOU IF YOU DO NOT PROVIDE EXPERIENCE THAT SHOWS HIM YOU CAN MISS.

Elementary, but often overlooked, is this fact that most creatures make their "bets" or decisions by previous experience. Hence, all of those important rules, particularly the one about "not missing." Study them again.

Though there's no great discomfort in the procedure, the fact that you can contact him at a distance is mysterious and impressive—and amazingly effective. That this effectiveness causes a response in the right direction, when the instinctively distasteful "throwing at a dog" would ordinarily drive him away, is predetermined by the leash control, and then justified in the mind of the dog by the praise you give him. When the response has been justified often enough, it becomes a trait of the dog's conduct, and of benefit to his character. And while the appeal of the "right thing" is increasing, the appeal of the "wrong thing" is diminishing. The dog is changing. It is as true of the dog, as of yourself, that each time a temptation is overcome, it is overcome more easily.

If you have one of those unusual dogs that reacts to the throw chain in a frightened manner, keep on using it. It would be a disastrous thing to stop using it, or to use it in a watered-down way. Recall the

148

many situations in which you have been, that seemed startling and unfair, but which, through constantly pleasant experience, become no longer startling, but actually inviting. And, after all, it's the dog's decision. If he does nothing to cause you to throw the chain, he'll be getting praise in its place. Would you pity a sore-footed man who insists on running barefoot through briars? There is only one way in which the throw-chain, properly used, could cow your dog. That is when his "pitiful cringing," whether real or phony, "cons" you or a soft-headed member of the family into commiserating with him so that your coaxing and tears convince him that, indeed, he's just had a most unusual and terrifying experience, and his fears or "nerves" are perfectly normal. They're not. And neither are you, if you think you can beef up his spine with syrup.

Two days after you begin to use the throw-chain to correct his disobedience on the recall, you can start to use it to increase your dog's reliability in heeling.

Hold the leash so that your throwing hand is kept free for action. A "right-hander" can hold the leash in his left hand, thumb in loop, in a way almost identical with the regular right-hand heeling grip; but with a little more slack so the dog will have opportunity to disobey.

Now, with the leash arranged and the chain bunched and ready for throwing, give an ordinary heel command, and start walking. Avoid any sharp turns or emphatic maneuvers which would cause the dog to be particularly attentive. Keep walking casually along toward any area which you think would invite the dog to drift away from the proper heel position.

Obviously, if his drifting should cause him to lag behind, you could not use the chain—he would see you throw.

THE THROW-CHAIN SHOULD NEVER BE USED TO CORRECT LAGGING. And don't try to get around the rule by having someone else throw the chain. However, if you play your dog against the point of interest in such a way that he angles away from your side, there will be a split second in which you can throw. And that's long enough for an alert and ready handler. The problem of throwing is even simpler if the dog's interest takes him out ahead of you so that his rear is exposed.

When the moment comes, throw. Hold your mouth shut. Keep on walking. You told him to heel when you started moving, so why should you repeat the command?

And, if he should break, why should you call him? He was at heel, and heeling has nothing at all to do with the recall.

If, when hit with the chain, he moves back to "pleasant haven" of his own volition, or if your movement snubs him back into line, praise him without breaking your stride. You can have a helper get the chain, or walk the dog around the corner and tie him up while you retrieve it. Naturally, the relative positions of you and your dog, while heeling, will provide fewer opportunities to throw than you will have on the recall exercise. This means you will have to work more carefully to observe the rules. Take courage from the fact that, all the while his attentiveness is denying you opportunity for correction, he's getting loads of practice in "being good." So there is no justification for hurrying into throwing in a manner that would violate the rules for the throw-chain's use. Be careful.

When your dog has reached the point where he is very respectful of your ability to contact him at a distance, you can begin to use the throw-chain on a third type of situation: as a correction for wild charging, inside and out. An example of each should be sufficient to demonstrate how useful the chain can be.

Outdoors, a common source of embarrassment to his master is the wild-eyed, indiscriminate charger who rushes the gate, or streaks along the fence, gouging a groove through the landscape. In contrast to a qualified watch dog, this gouger is likely to charge the same mailman or garbage man who has been serving the house for years. Probably his pathetic master's futile efforts to head him off have increased the dog's speed and zest for the chase. From his owner's vocal and physical exercises, he has learned two things: the master doesn't like it; he is too slow to do anything about it. Your dog may soon learn there is something that isn't "too slow."

By now you know that the working premise of dog training is a situation which will give the dog an opportunity to show his disobedience and, at the same time, provide you with a definite opportunity to correct him.

If it's the garbage man your dog charges, meet the man a couple of doors down the street and arrange for him to make five or six noisy arrivals spaced a minute apart. You'll find when he learns your purpose that he'll be most cooperative. He'll be a grateful man. Be sure to have your longe line fastened to your dog's collar before the man's first arrival.

The many times you've watched the dog travel his frenzied path should tell you just where to stand to get a shot at his rear or side. Yes—obsessed as he is—you can risk a shot at his side as he tears past. Don't call him before you throw. It's not a recall. He's to be punished for doing something that a hundred ineffectual reprimands have told him is wrong. Besides, you want him to refrain from chasing garbage men even at times when you're not around to call him.

Watch, when he starts his run, for that right moment. Then throw. Grab the line and snatch him back to where you are standing. Don't praise him. The jerk is to show him that, while you can't outrun him, you can interrupt his idiotic dash from a distance and make him end up in front of you.

After this first "interruption," it may be that he won't turn his attention from you until it appears that the garbage man has faded from sight and sound. If necessary, disappear from the dog's point of view so he'll relax before the man's second arrival. When the rattling and clanging announces the man's return, casually drift back into position for action. As before, throw when you can; then grab and reel in the line. After a few repetitions of the "arrival, chase, and chain routine," your dog might appear to lose interest in garbage men.

Tell the garbage man to give it everything he's got on the clattering and banging so that the activities are as inviting as possible. Let the man know that he should not watch the dog as though directing his activities at him in a teasing way.

When your dog has been worked to a point where he will no longer show an interest, stage a few more arrivals to give him an opportunity to practice being good.

Possibly it will take several sessions with the garbage man before your dog is cured of harassing this familiar caller.

If you have one of those rare dogs who can only be discouraged by heavier artillery than the throw-chain, rest easy. When you read the lesson on "problems," you will learn how to use equipment that will bring about the dog's conversion in a matter of moments.

The damage he does outside is small in comparison to the financial havoc that a charger can achieve indoors. Here, upon hearing the approach of a familiar service man, a well-practiced dog can roll up a throw rug, knock over a small table, and damage blinds or drapes in a single, floor-scratching scramble.

The mailman's arrival makes an exemplary situation in which to demonstrate how well we can cope with this problem of charging inside the house. The mailman, like the garbage man, will brim with gratitude when you ask for his cooperation. After all, the sounds have made him expect the dog to break out through the wall of the house at any time.

Arrange to signal the man with a porchlight or the movement of a curtain when you want him to approach and start the action.

If you have furniture that might catch and interfere with your long line, use a piece as short as six or eight feet. Without a knot or hand-hold in the end, it will slide right over things without catching.

When your dog is equipped and relaxed, ease into a strategic position, and be ready with your throw-chain. You will handle the chain and line on these indoor set-ups exactly as you did the outdoor situation. This means timing your throw to hit the dog when he starts his charge, and using the line to flip him away from the direction of his rush so fast he'll practically face himself in mid-air. The more startling, uncomfortable, and conclusive the experience, the greater its benefits.

If you have to retrieve the chain yourself, tie the dog in another room while you pick it up.

Give your dog the advantage of as many "approaches" as possible. Keep in mind that when he's denying you opportunities for correction, he's getting more and more practice in "being good." Again, it may take several sessions with the chain and line before he swears off mailmen, but repeat the performance until the sound of the man's approach causes your dog to turn from that direction as though suffering acute nausea.

Ridiculous as it seems, many inexperienced trainers are slow to adopt the principles that apply in one situation to another similar situation. What works in the case of the garbage man and mailman also applies in the case of the gas man, milkman and other callers who come to your house so regularly that any discriminating dog should know their presence is legitimate.

Work carefully and consistently on the three aforementioned types of situations in which the throw-chain might be used for correction: recall, heeling and charging; and add new distractions as your dog grows in reliability. Be equally consistent in taking advantage of any situations that develop without your help. To work successfully in those situations which you set up, and then to let the dog get away with a charge because a chance opportunity has caught you flat-footed, is to cancel out much of your good work. In short—keep that line on the dog when he's in the house and at such times as there is the least possibility of someone approaching to tempt him. And keep that throw-chain in a handy pocket. Lay for him.

The time spent each day for working with the throw-chain on the problems of the recall, heeling, and charging will probably average about fifteen minutes. Spend an equal amount of time on your regular, routine exercises in a definite effort to increase your dog's accuracy and reliability. Your dog will be rigorously tested for these qualities at the start of the next chapter.

Within two weeks from the time when you began work with the throw-chain, you should feel like wagering that no distraction will tempt your dog. That is, unless you have that "one-in-a-hundred" dog that is so tough he ignores the chain. As has been said, we'll discuss his type a bit further along in the lesson on "problems." You may be certain there is something he won't ignore.

The American Humane Association presented "Sam" its PATSY Award for top animal picture star of 1959 in recognition of his role in *The Shaggy Dog,* and awarded "Asta" its Television PATSY Award for his work in *The Thin Man.* One of the important functions of the American Humane Association is to protect the welfare of animal actors through consultation and advice offered by experienced representatives present during the filming of all pictures featuring animals.

YANKIE

154

LESSON XV

THE LIGHT LINE

The ease and certainty with which a dog, trained past the point of contention on leash, may be made to perform with equal reliability when free of restraint is sometimes a source of embarrassment to those who had fearfully approached what they thought was a gamble. Properly achieved, the control of an unrestrained dog is so simple that they are embarrassed because they "didn't think of it." Yet, simple though it is, there is an occasional person who does not grasp the underlying principle and so fails to get the fullest benefits from the technique.

Just "why" the method works on a dog is more easily understood when you see that it would work on a person—even a very intelligent person. So you'll have the best possible understanding of our procedure, borrow an "intelligent person"—preferably one who's good at mathematics, such as an engineer or accountant, and we'll see how he can cope with the principles we'll use.

The implement that bridges the gap between control on the leash or longe and control when the dog is physically free will be a piece of light line, different in appearance from anything you have used thus far, particularly in its length. It should be very strong, very long, and very light: so strong that your dog couldn't possibly break it; so long that, regardless of his great speed and your slowness, you would have no difficulty in grabbing the trailing end; and so light that its weight and length would be almost imperceptible—certainly offer no discouragement to the dog's attempts to run.

You'll be surprised to find, with a little investigation, that there are lines made of newly developed materials which have tremendous strength and little weight. For example, there are salt water fishing lines of very small diameter that can stop the wildest rush of the biggest dog. Lines that will hold the medium and small-size dogs are not much larger than string. To make absolutely certain the line is correct in strength and weight, question a fisherman or other expert.

As to length, you're the sole judge. If you have a fast dog that you feel is going to try to bolt away, and you are mentally or physically slow, get a line a hundred feet long—or longer. Remember this—you can get a line that's hundreds of yards long, and two or more can be tied together. Certainly, then, neither your dog's speed nor your slowness poses a real problem.

If your line is bright and easily seen, dull it down by dipping it in dye or left-over coffee.

Leave your dog in the yard, bring your "intelligent human" and the line, and a pocket knife, and we'll go into an open area for a few interesting experiments. Start by unwrapping about ten feet of line from your roll, and then walking along with the ten feet dragging on the ground. With its smoothness and small size, you'll hardly feel its drag. Now unwrap another ten feet; walk, and try to feel the difference. Chances are you'll be unable to feel any more drag from the longer length than from the shorter. Unwrap another ten feet, and walk. Again, the additional length has caused no difference in the feel of the line.

KEEP FIRMLY IN MIND THE FACT THAT IT'S IMPOSSIBLE FOR A PERSON OR A DOG TO ESTIMATE THE LENGTH OF A VERY LIGHT LINE FROM THE FEEL OF ITS DRAG.

Next, ask your "intelligent human" to face straight ahead while you drop a noose of string over his head. Cut about thirty feet of line from the ball and string the thirty feet straight out behind your friend. Now, ask him to try his best to run away while you try to grab the line and stop him. The answer will be a "no." Let's look at the thing from his viewpoint. You didn't tell him how long the line is; he couldn't estimate its length when he saw it wrapped in a ball; and, even if he should whirl around to look at it, he would need considerable time to locate its end. And, as you found, the drag on the ground will tell him nothing.

So how could he possibly know how long the line is? Or how much time you would have to make your grab? How can he possibly figure his chances for running away from you?

Now your helper, even though he may be a brilliant engineer, is standing there with a line on his neck; and, for all he knows, it may be a hundred yards long and strong enough to hold a bull. And he doesn't want to find out the hard way.

After he's had a few of the right experiences, neither will your dog want to find out the hard way.

"But," you're sobbing, "what happens when the line comes off?"

Let's find out. Again we'll use your human helper. After you assure him that you have no intention of stretching his neck, ask him to walk about, letting the line drag from his neck. Walk along about ten feet behind him and, without letting him know what you're doing, quietly cut the line.

Ask him to run. He won't. Because there is so little feel to the drag, he won't be aware that he now has a short line and a good chance of getting away. And, after he's had the right experiences, neither will your dog.

To go further, enough of the right experiences can make both a human and your dog refuse to run from you even though the line is completely off from their necks.

Now that we've proved that neither man nor dog can calculate his chances of running away when he doesn't know the length or strength of the line on his neck, let's see how we'll use the line to give your dog those "right experiences."

It's most important, if you are going to get the fullest benefit from your first session with the light line, that it be fastened to the dog properly. Keep in mind the "why" as well as the "how" of the procedure.

Stretch your line out conveniently in the training area, making sure that it is free of knots and snarls that would offer resistance when dragged. Once more, the length of the line must be your decision. No one else knows how fast you think and run in comparison with your dog.

When you bring your dog into the area, have both the tab and leash fastened to his collar. (Illustration on page 154 shows properly attached tab.) Spend a few minutes reviewing with the dog on leash. Arrange to finish the practice with an automatic sit at one end of the line.

Carefully, so as not to inform the dog of what you are doing, tie the end of the line to the loop in the tab with a good, firm knot. One of the several reasons that we use the tab should now occur to you. By wearing the device during some of his leisure time, your dog has become accustomed to the tug of its swinging and bobbing, and will hardly notice the additional tug of the dragging light line. In case you make him suspicious with a big, fumbling production of tying the knot, a bit of heeling and sitting while you still hold the leash will make him forget the line is attached.

After a few starts and stops, place your throw-chain in the proper hand for action. Remove the leash, being very careful not to entangle it with the line and cause a "reminding tug." Throw the leash a few feet out in front of the dog. Give a heel command and start walking.

If you are lucky, the discarded leash and weightlessness of the line will give him such an unrestrained feeling that he'll break, expose his rear, and give you your opportunity to use the chain.

Throw. Then get one foot, or both feet, on the line to slow it down before you grab it. This is not difficult when the dog's break occurs from the heel position because the line's length should give even a slow handler time to grind his heel down upon it. To grab the line bare-handed, before it has been slowed down, is like stroking a power saw. A thin glove is a good added precaution.

Reel in the line without a word as you keep right on walking. However, it's almost certain that your surprised dog headed back to your side the moment the tightening line told him that he wasn't quite as free as he felt.

After all, your groundwork with leash and chain had taught him the whereabouts of "pleasant haven," and the line showed him you needed no leash to make sure he'd get there.

At this time you will feel very thankful that your groundwork took him past the point of argument, for, unbreakable though it is, the light line does not give the good hand grip necessary to setting a pattern with an argumentative dog.

Definitely stated, the line is an unfailing assurance that a dog will perform in a pattern that has been established: it is not a comfortable nor an effective implement for establishing a pattern. Your leash should have done the establishing weeks ago.

When your throw-chain has been recovered, re-attach your leash and then repeat the procedure of holding the leash and line together, as you do starts and stops. By thus focusing his attention on the leash, you will recreate the feeling of freedom when the leash is removed and thrown in front of him.

Possibly, his first experience made such an impression that when the leash is again thrown on the ground, he'll check his inclination to break and will be quite content to heel respectfully along beside you. This is the moment to stop, and regardless of how he sits, show him with sincere praise that he's doing exactly the right thing in obeying as though you held the leash.

Whether he shows this cooperativeness the first time the leash is removed, or after experiencing correction with the chain, make certain you show this approval.

Do not make the mistake of asking the dog to heel interminably without telling him he's doing the right thing. This would confuse him; and when he finally breaks, he might be doing so because he didn't know what you wanted. If you praise him for a little heeling, he'll be apt to give you a lot more; and then, when temptation finally causes him to break, your correction will be justified because he's experienced the pleasant results that came from doing the right thing. So praise him now and then as you keep working and waiting for that second opportunity to correct.

Whether you get the one correction or many, when you've worked as long as fifteen minutes on the light line procedure, put the throw-chain back into your pocket, remove the line, and with both the leash and tab fastened to the collar, use the remainder of your training period to increase accuracy and reliability by practicing the routine exercises.

While you're practicing, it may help you to keep in mind that you are using a wonderful formula for controlling a dog's attitude toward a situation. This is the almost magical effect of utilizing the feeling of competence and confidence that comes from doing a familiar exercise by backwashing the feeling into a preceding situation wherein the dog felt less competent and familiar. To follow the new and strange with a review of the familiar can do much to establish your dog's proper attitude for the new thing he is learning, which in this case was response when off-leash. Deliberately use this principle to make your dog confident and happy in his work.

After your training period is finished, replace the leash with your longe line, give your dog an "okay" release and a bit of relaxation as the two of you saunter around the area.

Later on in his training, when you feel complete confidence, your longe will be replaced by the light line during the after-training break period. To make the change too early would be to invite a line-burn on your hands.

Your dog has done a good job and deserves a break period uninterrupted by distractions or commands. As it is, his experience with the light line may have left him so concerned that you'll have to work to get him to relax. He'll learn, eventually, that the line not only signifies authority, but can provide fun, as well.

Put him back into his yard when the break is over, and leave him alone for awhile.

It may be that instead of performing in a manner similar to that described, your dog acted differently. You could have made a fumbling production out of tying the line, entangled it with the leash, or in some other way aroused his suspicions so that he never for a moment felt free enough to run. Or possibly he is one of those that stands still when the leash comes off, having stopped himself by stepping on the line. In any case, the problem is the same: the dog must be made so familiar with the presence of the line that he will forget or ignore it. You can accomplish this by giving him lots of walking on leash while he drags the line, which should be tied to the tab in the usual way. This will accustom him to moving even though the line slides between his toes or brushes on his legs. After a few of these "conditioning sessions," he'll hardly be aware of the line and tab. Then you can return to the main project of using the line to establish off-leash control.

After two days of using the light line to assure response on the off-leash heeling, you should have enough confidence to use it in one of those situations where the dog is at a greater distance from you. You will find it particularly useful for correcting the dog that does a good sit-stay and recall, even at considerable distance, as long as the longe line is fastened to his collar in the manner described earlier, but, when that authoritative weight is gone, sits staring confusedly.

Here's a way to blast that "mental vapor-lock." Before placing your dog for a recall, lay out your line so that it can run from where you plan to leave him to a point a few feet straight behind him, and from that point circle back to where you intend to stand. Fasten the tab to his collar; then bring him into the area on leash, and stop where you planned to leave him. Try to join the line to the tab so smoothly that he will not even know you are doing it.

Because the line is laid out to circle around behind him, there will be nothing visible in the dog's immediate foreground to make him expect a set-up. Place him on a sit-stay, then move to the other end of the line and casually pick it up.

Due to the fact that the operation has been much smoother than if you had fumbled around at laying out the line after it was tied to the tab, your dog will probably not be aware that you are prepared to correct him if, without the reminder of the longe line or the leash, he should hesitate in coming when called.

160

After facing him for a few seconds, give a recall command. If he responds promptly, praise him as he starts toward you; thus he's getting praised for his decision to come, not merely for sitting in front of you. Remember, there is a difference between praising and coaxing.

If he doesn't respond promptly, jump backward in a way that tightens the line in an unforgettable jerk.

Properly given, the correction should convince him that he had better move when he hears the command, even though he hasn't been reminded by the weight of the leash or the longe line. Repeat this set-up a few times each day until the dog responds promptly.

If your emphasis on a fast response causes him to anticipate and come before he is called, the line will again be an asset. It can stop him cold if he tries to run off or bolt, as you charge back to grab the tab and make your stay correction. As you grab, you'll realize that along with making the dog forget the line, the tab makes a very good hand-saving handle. Your persistent efforts with the line will show your dog that, regardless of the absence of weight on his collar, or the distance from you, he had better stay until called and then come immediately.

While the throw-chain can never be used in situations such as the afore-mentioned, where the dog is facing you, it can be used to settle the hash of the smart aleck, who takes off in a wrong direction when called.

AGAIN—CAUTION. DON'T EVER THROW IF HE RUNS BEFORE HE IS CALLED. THIS MEANS THAT HE BROKE THE STAY, AND ONLY THE USUAL SIT-STAY CORRECTION SHOULD BE USED.

If your dog is an "artful dodger" who bears down on you and then scoots to one side, or if he makes a game of shooting past you and circling back, tag his fanny with the chain as he flashes past. This, and the solid jolt of the line, will make him believe that the best way to make sure his rear is away from you is to keep his head toward you.

On the more important informal recall, where the dog is called away from a distraction you have provided, or an emergency that occurs naturally, the throw-chain will be used in conjunction with the light line. Follow exactly the same procedure as when you used the chain in conjunction with the leash and heavy line. Of course, experience gained from working with the heavier equipment should have increased your proficiency with the chain, and made such a pattern of the dog's response that he reacts without any thought of argument.

The difference and advantage of the lighter equipment is the fact that it is the bridging step to the technique of controlling the dog when he is entirely free of restraint. The previously discussed case of the indiscriminate charger who harasses the garbage man, mailman, and other familiar callers, will also require work on the light line if off-leash reliability in those situations is to be achieved.

Again, the technique of using the line in combination with the chain will follow the pattern of the earlier work with the heavier equipment. Naturally, the increased length of the line over the other equipment will provide control at a greater distance. He can't tell the length by the weight, so set up your situations in such a way that his mad dash takes him quite a distance before the line and chain remind him that there's absolutely no way of telling how far away you can control him. If he's charging inside the house, you may find it convenient to use a shorter line than the one you use outside.

To increase your dog's reliability on the sit-stay and down-stay, you can quietly attach the line to the tab before you remove the leash and soon convince him that he had better hold his stays when he's not reminded by the weight of the leather and snap.

Within a week after you begin to use the light line, you'll find that your dog has changed. He will no longer disobey the heel and recall commands. The greater the distractions you provide to encourage his "charging," the more he seems to turn his attention back to you. At least, that's the way it is when he's on the line. You wonder what would happen in those same situations if the line were not on him.

There's a way you can arrange for a preview of what will happen when the line finally comes off. First, make sure that your dog has had sufficient periods of the right kind of work to make him infallible when he's on the line. Before bringing him out for his trial, equip yourself with a small scissors or knife. To fumblingly untie the line from the tab in the nervous manner of one removing the detonator from an explosive, is to tell the dog that you are no longer confident and neither your commands, nor actions, are to be respected.

Work with the full length of light line and the throw-chain on the heeling exercise until his attitude tells you that distractions are only making him more attentive. Now is the time to stoop over and, without any fumbling around, reach back and cut the line about four feet from the dog's collar. Let both ends lie where they fall. Give a command, and start off with your usual confidence.

Your dog will respond to your command and actions in the usual way.

"Why shouldn't he?" you protest, "there's still some line on him."

162

And then, as you walk along, it hits you. Physically, that four feet of line is hardly better than nothing. It would be almost impossible to grab that short line in time to stop him from bolting, but your dog is walking along as resignedly as though it were forty feet long and his chances of breaking were nil. He does not take pencil and paper and compute his chances of outrunning you, considering the factors of your relative speed against the reduced length of the line. A dog's arithmetic is not that good. He does not even turn to look at the end of the line.

And, aware of the consequences previously experienced, no properly trained dog would ever dare to run without being certain of the length of line attached to his collar. For that matter, neither would a human. Not even an accountant or an engineer—remember.

THE PRINCIPLES OF THE LIGHT LINE NEVER FAIL. AT TIMES, A TRAINER, THROUGH LAZINESS OR LACK OF IMAGINATION, WILL FAIL IN HIS APPLICATION OF THOSE PRINCIPLES.

In your command there was no quaver that would let your dog know that you weren't fully prepared to cope with him. Come to think of it, you didn't feel like quavering. You didn't feel a lack of confidence. Strangely enough, though it was only four feet long, that line not only did something for the dog, but also did something for you.

Rather mysterious, isn't it?

You'll come to find that the line will keep doing that "something" for you and your dog when it's only five inches long. And when it's gone.

You've now seen how your dog responds on four feet of line. That was to demonstrate the method of your progress. In the actual practice of good training, we wouldn't reduce the working length of the line to four feet in one step. Rather, we'd cut a few feet from the dragging end every few days providing, of course, that the dog continued to reach new levels of reliability when tested in situations of increased distraction. This testing will prevent you from making the serious mistake of reducing the line length too fast.

The next session, after you've had your "preview" on the four-foot length, should feature, in addition to your leash work, practice with the light line on all previously discussed exercises.

This means practice on the full length of line, not the four-foot piece.

At this time, which generally comes after three weeks of working with the throw-chain, and one week after beginning to use the chain in conjunction with the light line, we're going to add something to the training procedure.

You will recall how you were instructed to finish your training periods by letting your dog drag the longe around for awhile as he relaxed, uninterrupted by distraction or command from you. You were probably pleased to see how quickly your dog came to enjoy these "breaks." The procedure blended into a companionship that is most enjoyable for you and your dog. You can both benefit still further from these interludes.

It is now that we will start giving the dog his break periods on the light line instead of on the longe. In addition to the regular after-training breaks, two or three times a week attach the line to your dog's collar and without any preliminary work take him on a sauntering walk in an area he will enjoy. It would be a special treat if one period should be a long hike on a week end, with a car ride to and from the location.

It would add to your confidence if, occasionally, you were to grab the line to enforce a recall or to get your dog heading your way if a stray dog or cat beckoned his attention. Be careful never to restrain him. Use the slack and a right-about to bump him and emphasize the merit of heading your way.

But, primarily, try to make your dog feel that the purpose of these walks is your mutual pleasure, not his training.

You now have the information necessary to use your light line and throw-chain as a bridging step to off-leash obedience in the exercises of heeling and recalling, and in the correction of problems that have to do with bolting or charging.

You have seen how the line can cause a dog to resign himself to holding a stay position by showing him the consequences of trying to run from correction when something, often quite unnoticeable, just might be tied to his collar.

You have found how your dog, already appreciative of the after-training breaks on the line, can be made much happier by the combination of control, confidence, and pleasure that the light line brings.

The light-line work, which should occupy about a third of your training time, will provide control and mutual confidence when your dog is at a distance. The remainder of the time, spent on leash work, will increase the dog's accuracy and promptness. The leash, with its positive grip, provides such an authoritative correction it discourages arguments and gives a great many opportunities for praise, thereby progressively instilling in the dog a greater compliancy of mind.

It is the function of the light line to show the dog that he can be held accountable for the qualities of control and character gained through the leash work, even when the leash is not present.

Within two weeks from the day you begin work with the line, you'll find that both you and your dog have changed. You now feel very confident that he will obey under any condition on a line which your week of "testing and shortening" has reduced to two-thirds of its original length.

Exactly how long is the line at this time? That you'll have to gauge against your own confidence and the work you've done. If your confidence has shortened along with the line, you'll know you've cut too much too soon. Play it safe. Let your confidence be your guide.

From this two-week point on, you may be able to reduce the length of the line gradually, until by the end of the fourth week, you feel qualified to work the dog with only one foot of line hanging from the tab—or a few inches—or nothing.

Possibly, your dog may be one of those that needs the influence of the tab and one or two feet of line even after a month of line work. Or it could be that he is one of the erratic type that appears reliable, but is ready to take a tight situation, or tension in your voice, as an inspiration to try to outwit you. If the shortness of your line has enabled him to outmaneuver you, sneak a long line back onto him, put him back in the same situation, get the same tension into your voice; and then, when he breaks, give him an experience that he'll never forget. By dumping him end over end, after he's been tagged with the chain, you may make an indelible impression that could sometime save his life. It is probable that the influence of the throw-chain will have him back at your side even before you can begin to tighten the line.

After this "experience," lay for him by alternating between short and long lines, giving him the greatest distractions when he's on the long piece. Another valuable procedure is to let the dog drag the light line around in the yard, or house, and then open the door and bring him under command. He's almost certain to bolt out a few times and give you a chance to use the chain. Eventually, an open door will be a cue to think of you.

Regardless of your own abilities and the peculiarities of your dog, one thing is certain: the line will give you an unfailing means with which you will ultimately accomplish his off-leash control. What an accomplishment! Not only will your dog obey your commands off leash, but you will have laid the foundation for the solving of problems that might occur later.

C. Lydon Lippincott

The right kind of training brings control and security to all situations.

166

LESSON XVI

DON'T LOSE IT—USE IT

You have spent the training periods of many weeks teaching your dog exercises that are essential to his control, are fundamental to future training, and will assist in correcting problems of conduct and character. You are now at a point of decision—a decision that will determine whether you acquire control as infallible in the demanding situations of daily living as you demonstrated among the strong distractions of your formal training periods.

Before your previous success and confidence causes you to dismiss the question with a "Why not?" let's consider the case of the top obedience trial winner who appears faultless during training and competition, but seems to revert to an almost undomesticated state on the street or in the home. In the same ring with such a dog may be others who might score lower, but maintain their reliable conduct when they leave the ring, and whenever they're seen on the street or at home.

This second type debunks the statements of the ignorant who say, "Show obedience is like an act—just a routine." Remember, too, the atmosphere of a dog show is not always the same solidly familiar bedlam. Strange things often happen. The judge is nearly always a stranger. Runaway dogs bolt into the ring. Canvas fences flap and blow down. On the sit-stay and down-stay, the dogs are placed by others they have not seen before. Certainly, the formal obedience ring is a pretty fair test of behavior amidst strong distractions, as you would find if you were to take a dog who is "just kinda trained to mind a little around home" into such a situation.

Why is it, then, that dogs which are so reliable among the distractions of the obedience ring are not equally reliable in the more familiar and less distracting situations of home and street?

Simple enough.

Their masters just didn't work as consistently to create a pattern of unfailing obedience in the other situations as they WERE FORCED TO DO to meet the demands of the obedience ring. Obviously, the masters and dogs had the qualities to assure the reliable behavior under extremely tough conditions. Any failure to benefit fully from the dog's training was caused by a decision—or, rather, a lack of decision.

If, in your daily living, you use the control developed in your formal training, it will increase and become permanent. If you fail to use it, it will deteriorate and be lost. The decision is whether you will "lose it, or use it."

Don't depend on luck to give you the opportunities you'll need to transfuse your authority from the training area to the realm of everyday living. Follow the dependable technique of creating tempting situations which you can control. These situations should typify the incidents that are apt to occur in your everyday relationship with your dog.

You will have the most association with your dog at home, so let's start the transfusing process there. But first it would be well to take a look at the mistakes of another handler, which might reflect your own failure. Two things have prevented this handler from fully appropriating to home use the training he has given. First, the home distractions he created were not similar, nor as strong, as those that commonly occurred. Second, he failed consistently to take advantage of chance opportunities to use the obedience. Inevitably, his dog quickly sensed the difference between his attitude of preparedness when in the "set-up" situations and his inconsistency when occupied with guests, or with other activities.

You can avoid such a person's failures. When you have completed all of the assignments of the preceding lessons, devote ten minutes a day for a week to practicing all of the exercises in every part of the house where your dog might be given a command. So that you are equipped to make the most effective corrections, the dog should be on leash during these periods.

During other times of this week, let him enjoy his home life in such ways as you feel proper, but make certain that the tab, or, if it seems advisable, the tab and a piece of line are fastened to his collar. Have the throw-chain in your pocket, ready for use. Once every hour or so, when you are occupied with tying your shoes, talking on the phone, reading, visiting with company, or some other typical activity, place your dog under command by calling him to you. If he fails to respond, let the speed of your correction prove you are willing to interrupt any activity at any time to back up your command with action.

This procedure will work wonders unless you keep "washing out" your progress by reacting differently when good fortune sends an unplanned occurrence. Throw down the paint brush, jump off the ladder, and, even though a visitor stands open-mouthed, let your correction show the dog that, regardless of how busy you are, what position you're in, or how you're interrupted, you'll enforce obedience to your command. And as for being prepared to deal with these unexpected occurrences, I have never heard why, unless he is wearing a Bikini bathing suit, a person couldn't have a throw-chain in his pocket.

And please don't tell me a few feet of nylon line fastened to a dog's collar will "catch on everything." It won't.

If your house is filled with knick-knacks and you'd like added assurances, use a suitable length of the new plastic-coated clothesline that's on the market. You'll see why it can't snag or tangle. Its slick surface won't give you the hand-grip you'd need for winning an argument with your dog, but he should have been past the arguing point long ago.

By now, your own experience has shown you that, when the line has given you control of a situation, a good hand-hold on the tab is your best guarantee of being able to make the final effort necessary to bring the dog into the proper position. Even when you no longer feel the need for the light line, you'll gain much by continuing to have the dog wear the tab in all situations. You'll feel authoritative, knowing that you won't have to seek out the correct collar ring, and then handle the dog with an ineffectual grip on the slippery metal. Further, the tab's presence will remind the dog of your authority. Leave it on until you feel your dog is past the need of a correction. As always, you have a responsibility to see that there is no hazard to the dog in the form of objects that could entangle the equipment and choke him.

Once you've decided to do so, there's no great difficulty in applying the authority established in the training area to the situations of the home. The foundation of routine practice in the house, the creating of incidents similar to those likely to occur, and the consistent use of obedience when unplanned occurrences give the opportunity, will increase the pleasure and security you and your dog share during your home life.

If properly photographed, the gymnastics of a driver as he copes with a "screwball" dog while driving down a freeway or through downtown traffic might be quite a comedy sequence. That is, it might be a comedy to all but the driver whose neck is at stake. If you, too, are often cast in the dual role of driver and dog-fighter, there is an answer to your problem other than leaving your dog at home.

As in the house, the precedent of obedience in the situation is set by practicing routine training in the very place where you will use it. This means in proximity to the car as well as in it. It should be "on-leash" practice when the car is standing still, so you are in a position to back up your command with an effective correction regardless of the dog's maneuvers.

Have your car parked in your drive with a door on each side open. Bring the dog, at heel, to a halt within a step of one of the doors. If, instead of sitting automatically, he tries to barge right into the car, you will be in good position for a sit correction. Good car manners begin with entering in the proper way. When he has sat, give him a stay command and have him hold it for at least a minute. Then order him to enter. "Okay, in," seems to convey to the dog that he is released from the stay and can follow the suggested tug of the leash into the car.

In the way that is most convenient for you, maneuver him to that place in the car where you prefer him to ride, and put him on a down-stay. Leave him with the leash attached to his collar, and stand a few feet from the car, with the doors still open, so you can see if the dog breaks. If he does, move to correct him. After he has held five minutes on this first experience, return, recover your grip on the leash, and bring him from the car by recalling him to a sit position in front of you. After the finish, move off with the dog at heel. Incorporating the car into a pattern of obedience practice will cause your dog to regard it as a place where you might be able to enforce your commands, instead of a situation where he can dazzle you with his foot-work, as he's done so often before.

While you wouldn't want your dog to stay rigidly motionless during hours of riding, these long, formal stays are still the best foundation for his later, more relaxed, but controlled conduct in the car.

After a few days, he should enter the car properly on your command, and hold a down-stay for at least twenty minutes, with the doors wide open, while you work at trimming a hedge, or at some other activity which would make him think you're much too preoccupied to do anything about his breaking. Don't let him break the position until you call him from the car and have him finish in the proper manner. KEEP IN MIND THAT THIS FORMAL TREATMENT IMPARTS TO THE CAR AREA THAT ATMOSPHERE AND SIGNIFICANCE CREATED BY ALL OF YOUR PREVIOUS TRAINING ROUTINES. The dog is made to feel that the area of the car is indeed a place where he should mind.

After the first few days, you can vary the procedure by entering the car and sitting down while the dog holds a sit-stay outside. If he should attempt to break, jump out and correct him; then return to your seat. When he has held a full minute, call him into the car, place him on a stay, and get out. After he has held for a couple of minutes, call him out with a regular recall and finish. This waiting for the command to get out, as well as to get in, will be a great convenience, and may sometime save your dog's life.

When he's holding well prior to getting in and out of the car, you can introduce the less formal stay, which does not require such a definite position, but still keeps the dog in that area of the car you desire. Your longe line will be useful for this job. Bring the dog at heel to the car in the usual manner. After the automatic sit and stay near the door, give him an "okay in." Leave the car doors open and your mouth shut. Don't tell him to stay, but if he leaves that area where you want him to remain, grab the longe and pile him back to where he should be. The line will be long enough to foil him if he tries to dart past you, go out the other door, or jump over the seat.

Let your jerk take him all the way back, and he'll soon learn that, though you didn't tell him to stay, he had better not leave his "riding area" until you tell him to do so. He will learn this in the same way a dog learns to stay in one room of a house, or a farm dog learns to stay away from certain sections of a barn: by the bad consequences of his action.

If you have a "geared" or restless dog, he may need the restraint of the formal stays for several days before you go to the relaxed control that only required him to stay in an area. On both types of control, the dog will be made more reliable if you have animals and other temptations brought into the vicinity of the open doors. Now, when the car is motionless and you can correct him, is the time to subject the dog to such distractions.

Now for the next step, which is dealing with the dog when the car is in motion. Get someone to drive for you so you can move right in if

171

the dog gets out of line. As always, have your dog wait for your command to enter the car. If you think he needs the stabilizing effect, put him on a formal sit-stay or down-stay, and as your helper drives along make sure that he holds it. If your previous training has provided enough distractions to make him solid on his stays, your task shouldn't be difficult. Otherwise, you'll get plenty of exercise twisting and leaning as you bounce him back to where he should be. Remember, even though he may not have been on a formal stay, you can still snatch him back to the place where you want him to remain. Act, don't talk, and he'll soon know he'll be more comfortable in his own area.

Give him a few of the short trips with someone else driving; then, if his attitude seems right, head for an untraveled road, change places with the driver, and convince the dog that you will turn to correct him even when you're occupied with driving. On a quiet road, with your helper ready to grab the wheel, you'll be reasonably safe in whirling around for a correction.

Your program of training and practice will soon make your dog a better traveling companion. Be sure to hold your gains by guarding against sloppy handling on your part. Consistently require your dog to enter the car properly, keep his own place, and leave only on command and under full control.

Naturally, the precept of doing some foundation training in the same area where you might sometime need to control the dog applies to those situations in your yard and away from home. As you were reminded earlier, the statement that you "don't want the dog to leave the place" doesn't eliminate the possibility that someone might leave the gate open, or you might have to take your dog with you, if only to the veterinarian's. Leash laws and regulations against dogs running at large can best be observed by the owners of those trained dogs which, when accidentally given their liberty, can be brought back under control. So with the dog on leash, practice the routine exercises in the yard, in all types of street situations, in stores and other places, until he seems relaxed and reliable regardless of the situation.

Since much of your away-from-home work might involve the use of the car, use the opportunities to emphasize that, when you stop, he should never come through the door except on command and under control. Permit no moment of horseplay or indecision while he looks around. Such a moment has caused the death of many dogs.

When you and your dog are performing confidently on these tours, go through the same program, step by step, with your dog on the light

172

line. Be certain that it's long enough and strong enough to keep you capable and confident. This experience will assure you of control, and protect the dog against panic when emergencies find him off-leash in strange places.

The light line can be particularly effective in straightening out the bratty dog who, when an open door or gate has provided liberty, dances coyly just out of reach. Set up this situation a few times, preparing carefully with a line long enough to really surprise him. In the case of a dog who is slow to come when called from his liberty in the yard, stack the cards in your favor by leaving the line attached until such time as he's been shown the error of his ways. Then, turn him out on gradually shortened lengths. Don't take the line off completely just because he has responded reliably a hundred times in a row.

Nothing more can be gained by supplying you with any more specific examples of how or where you can use obedience. It is obvious that the methods presented in this book can be applied in all situations where there is a need.

The lesson on "problems" gives information on correcting those dogs whose wickedness is of such a specialized nature as to require something in addition to the character-stabilizing obedience work. So don't let a problem or two distract you from your immediate purpose of giving your dog experience in all of those places where you might have to control him.

And, when your work with leash and light line has shown him you're "in charge" anytime, anywhere, be consistent in handling your dog the right way. At home, in the car, away from home—don't lose it— use it.

C. *Lydon Lippincott*

As a significant part of the country's largest obedience program, the Orange Empire Dog Club pioneered street trials.

PROBLEMS

You have already learned one reason why this book maintains that your dog should be trained in his basic obedience before you make a direct approach to specific problems of conduct and character. Some of those "specific problems" have been corrected by the general benefits of training.

Perhaps not quite so clear is a second reason. This is the fact that, even when it does not completely remedy a situation without direct work on the problem, training in basic obedience makes the success of that direct effort more certain. It is very important to do all possible to assure success when you first cope with a problem, because to fail on the first attempt is to make the second effort more difficult.

Third, as common sense tells you, it is easier, physically and mentally, to make specific corrections on a dog that has been made more reasonable by obedience training.

THERE, YOU HAVE THREE GOOD REASONS FOR COMPLETING YOUR BASIC OBEDIENCE BEFORE TRYING TO USE THE CORRECTIONS GIVEN IN THIS CHAPTER.

BOLTING, OR RUNNING AWAY

Whether a dog bolts from the house, yard, or car, or runs from the master when on a recall or heeling, the fault is equally dangerous and maddening. The correction is always the same in principle. It consists of setting up situations that give him every incentive to bolt, and which result in consequences that make him wish he hadn't.

Whether your "situation" is an accidentally opened door, or the removal of your leash when in an area where strange dogs happen to be, the light line should have been quietly attached to his collar, and the throw-chain palmed in your hand before the "big break" occurs. If the opportunity is overwhelmingly apparent and the distraction great enough, he may forget, or disregard the line, and bolt. Throw the chain and use the line to make his experience a memorable one. Ideally, your jerk on the line should cause him to swap ends and bounce back to you, hardly touching the ground.

And what if the dog is so big and tough he ignores the chain? As was promised earlier, there is something he won't ignore, no matter how big and tough and unmanageable he may be. From a hardware or sporting goods store get a good slingshot and a few packs of BB shot. A *WHAM-O*, and several other commercial brands will shoot harder and straighter than the home-made ones that can be made from today's inner tubes.

If you are one of those unfortunate individuals who have never known the fun of a slingshot, don't let your lack of experience stop you. Find out from the sporting goods clerk, or an experienced friend, how you hold and shoot it. When you've learned the "grip" and "release," put eight or nine BBs into the pouch at one time and shoot the load against a box or can. You'll see that the shot spreads into a pattern that would be quite certain to hit your dog.

Here's the best way to hold the implement while loading and carrying it. Hold the pouch with two fingers behind and the thumb low down on the face so as to prevent the BBs from rolling out before the thumb and forefinger of the other hand pinch the load tight with the shooting grip. It is easy to drop the shot into the pouch by hand or with your mouth. When it's loaded, if you like, you can carry the pouch and the grip in one hand until the moment when the other hand pulls and releases the pouch for the shot. The technique of loading, carrying, and shooting the slingshot with maximum accuracy and force is well worth learning. Your dog, even though he borders on the incorrigible, is not apt to outrun, nor ignore, those BBs. If he does, the small steel balls, such as come packed with the *WHAM-O* slingshot, are procurable at many stores. Even if he has a heavy coat, the recalcitrant dog will not ignore them.

The slingshot, like the throw-chain it replaces, is held in readiness and used at the moment the dog bolts. You won't hit the dog in the eye if you shoot when he's running away, so rear back and let him have it. If you have to really sting him to make him respond when he otherwise might bolt into traffic, console yourself with the fact that the positive control you are establishing may sometime save him from injury or death.

Provide your dog with opportunities to bolt until it seems they only serve to turn his mind back to the light line and you.

And, when good fortune causes a friend to open a car door, or a gate, with your dog in a position to bolt, don't miss your chance because "the line wasn't on him." In the house and out, leave a piece of line on, for the influence it exerts, until an open door or gate seems only a cue for the dog to look at you. And, even when you reach this point, don't suddenly take it off. Use the technique, explained earlier, of shortening the line bit by bit, corresponding with your own confidence. When the last of the line has been removed, let the dog wear the tab for a while longer. It will serve you well.

Work consistently, using the line to guard against bad breaks, and your dog will come to agree that, regardless of "opportunities" and "distractions," he's much better off staying with you.

FENCE RUNNING AND GATE CHARGING

If your dog persists in fence running and gate charging even after he's been "dusted" repeatedly with the throw-chain, you'll have to resort to the heavy artillery of the slingshot. This is in conjunction with the light line, of course. Whether he runs a fence race with the neighbor's dog, convoys a person along a walk, or runs without a visible provocation, it is your job to give him an incentive, and then stake out in a convenient spot.

If you have practiced, you'll be able to give the miscreant quite a surprise. The range and impact of the slingshot is much greater than that of the throw-chain. With a good load of BBs in the pouch, you can fire through an open window and across a yard with an effectiveness that leaves the dog remarkably quiet. When the "quiet" comes, continue to let him drag the line, gradually reducing the length until finally it is lost.

Where landscaping, or other physical factors make the use of the slingshot impossible, results can sometimes be obtained by fastening three or four feet of light line to the dog's collar, and attaching a "drag" consisting of a piece of two-by-four to the other end. The size

177

of the dog will determine the length of the wood. Three to eight inches seems to cover the range of sizes pretty well. Drive a staple in the middle of the wood, or bore a hole, so you can attach the line.

When the dog runs, he causes the two-by-four to bounce in a crazy, jerking pattern that will give him some most discouraging whacks. By gradually reducing the size of the drag, some dogs can be brought to the point where a piece of light line, or the tab, will serve as a reminder of what their running can bring.

If there is danger of the dog becoming entangled and choked, use a line that is strong enough to pull the drag, but which will break in an emergency struggle.

STAYING HOME

A surprisingly large number of dogs, if sufficiently grounded in their response to light line and throw-chain, can be taught to stay within the boundaries of an area, even if those boundaries are marked with only a low fence, a hedge, or a flower row.

If you feel that your dog is intelligent and well-grounded in obedience, you might enjoy the challenge of breaking him to boundaries.

With the light line attached, take your dog into the area where you would like him to remain, and with an "okay" release that suggests an attitude of relaxation, not horseplay, encourage him to go where he likes. Try to keep the line from tightening until he gets within a foot or so of the boundary line; then, without a word, stop him by turning or by holding solidly on the line. Give him a word of praise for his turning, and then let him know it's all right for him to return to his own interests. When he again reaches a point near a flower bed or fence, which would be a route out of the area, let your turn, or jerk, tell him that "he's gone far enough in that direction." As common sense should tell you, concentrate on those places where the dog is most likely to exit. Don't waste time turning him away from a boundary that consists of a building or a twelve-foot wall.

Persist in this pattern of encouraging him to relax, but at the same time making him conscious of the area wherein you wish him to remain. It requires a program of consistent work, free from the setbacks that would occur if the dog were given opportunity to cross the boundaries between your training periods; but eventually his actions will show you that he knows where you've "drawn the line."

Now, while you watch, let him drag the line around as a reminder

178

of the times he's been turned away from certain places. If he ventures across the boundary that you've taught him to observe, a carefully timed shot with the slingshot will show him life is better when he stays within his own area.

Next comes the critical part of this particular training. You've shown him where he should not go. Now you must supply temptation to cause him to cross the boundaries so you will have opportunity to correct him at those times when he has THE STRONGEST POSSIBLE INCENTIVE TO DISOBEY.

Another dog, or a cat, on the far side of the hedge or fence should cause him to forget the boundaries and give you your opportunity. As in every case where you use the technique of maximum temptation and correction, the greatest benefits are obtained through repetition of the procedure when it seems that the dog can no longer be successfully tempted.

Each time he turns away from these strong incentives to disobedience, his quality of obedience grows stronger. Soon, even the fact that you're not around will not be sufficient to make him cross the boundaries.

There is something you can use for protection, if you feel that he might hang himself when he is dragging the line around while you're gone. Since the line at this time is a reminder and a symbol of authority, more than an implement for physical correction, you can join the line to the collar with a few inches of "break-away section" that is strong enough to drag the line, but not strong enough to hold against the dog's weight, or a struggle, if the line should catch on something.

There is almost no limit to the reliability that can be obtained by this principle of supplying the absolute maximum of temptation when you are set to correct the wrongdoer. If you have the determination, you can make "not crossing the boundary" almost a religion with your dog.

If you are short on time or ability, you might find one of the following "mechanical aids" useful where you have a fenced area.

Here's a way you can make him feel that he's jumped from confinement into closer confinement. Fasten a line, a strong one, to his collar and tie the other end in such a way that the dog can reach only one of the routes he commonly takes over the fence. The line should be long enough to permit the dog to jump the fence without the possibility of hanging, but so short that he has only a few feet of movement when he lands. You can help him to see that he's jumped into a worse situation if you are hidden out in the neighbor's yard, or a nearby car. Descend on him, blister his bottom, and pitch him or drag him back over the fence.

Work the set-up on all boundaries where the dog might consider jumping, adding to the surprise and unpleasant landing in every way possible. A bunch of BBs from a slingshot will contribute greatly to his reception on the wrong side of the fence.

So you've got a smarty who won't try to jump until you drive off in your car, and you don't want to give him the chance of jumping and strangling when you are gone. There is a simple and safe solution. Drive half a block in your car, switch to a friend's, and come back and park. Enough of these situations, and automobiles as well as the line will be a reminder to the dog of your omnipresence. Even a stupid dog, if he jumps into bad situations often enough, should come to prefer the larger area of freedom and comfort of the yard he's been leaving.

When you feel it's safe to try him when you're going to be gone for a while, do so by letting him drag the line with the "break-away section." That drag on his collar is quite a reminder of the horrible messes he's jumped into.

Some jumping-jack dogs, given to leaping over a fence or beating themselves hysterically against it, can be discouraged by a simple device consisting of a block of wood fastened to a line that is attached to the dog's collar. The line should be long enough to permit the block to drag on the ground at a point about halfway back on the dog. A hole bored through the block, or a staple driven into it, will serve to fasten the one end of the line. The block should be of a weight to drag easily, and still be heavy enough to flip against the dog with a good whack each time he jumps. In addition to supplying the whack, the block serves to throw the dog off-balance when he jumps. If, before giving up, he decided to chew free of the block, you can always substitute a length of light bronze or steel cable, obtainable at your hardware. Even with this unchewable, unbreakable material there need be no danger of hanging or strangling. Simply join the cable to the collar with a break-away section that is so close to the dog's neck that he cannot chew it.

The unbalancing, along with the whacking, usually convinces the dog that the discomfort caused by the block dragging is not nearly so great as what he experiences when jumping, and soon he'll ease up in his attempts to clear the fence or beat it down with his lunges.

The critical time on the foregoing correction comes when it seems that the dog has quit altogether. To remove the block at this point would be to invite failure. Instead, use the principle of the "gradually diminishing reminder," which is another way of telling you to change progressively to lighter blocks until it seems that something the size of a clothespin, and finally the line itself, is an efficient discouragement to the dog's jumping.

This procedure of attaching a block can be used even more easily on a dog that crawls under or through a fence. In this case, the block should be longer than the width of the opening through which the dog crawls, with the line attached to the middle of the block so that it becomes a drag that will not follow the dog through the opening. If properly equipped, it's almost inevitable that the dog will learn his exits lead, not to greater freedom, but to closer confinement. If, when he finds he has tied himself into a bad situation, he tries to chew, remember to replace the first five feet of light line with the metal cable. As always, it's your responsibility to take precautions against his choking.

Whether your dog goes over, under, or through a fence, be slow to remove the line and quick to re-attach it, block and all, if there should be a recurrence.

As in all types of corrective training, you must provide temptations and incentives to cause the difficult dog to disobey, and consequences so discouraging that he'll wish he hadn't.

In cases where a dog is a veritable escape artist, and still, because of traffic or other hazards, must be made to stay within an area, an electrically charged wire can sometimes be used to advantage, just as it is used to keep cattle, horses, and hogs confined to pastures or pens. This, of course, is the current that comes through a battery powered "fence unit," or another safe shocking device, and not the house current which would be dangerous to humans and dogs alike. Commonly, these devices have about six volts' capacity and simply startle the animal that comes in contact with the charged wire, but are in no way harmful.

In most instances, even if there is a wide fence, it would be impractical and expensive to electrify it; so it is nearly always better to follow the same procedure as is recommended when the fence is wood or brick, or when no fence exists.

This consists of stringing one or two strands of light, inexpensive bare wire on laths, or other dry, non-conducting sticks which are stuck in the ground along the boundaries of the area where the dog is confined. You will be the judge of how high the wires should be. Naturally, the dog should not be able to walk under the bottom strand, nor step over the top strand, so the difference in set-ups for a small dog and a large one would be great.

If any green foliage, or a tree touches the wire, your circuit will be grounded out, so check it carefully before putting your dog into the area.

Even when you use the "charged wire" treatment, it's best to have your dog drag his light line as a reminder of what is right and wrong.

Possibly you've got one of those ingenious dogs who seems to know instinctively how to get past the wires without making contact. If so, try this technique. In addition to his light line, fasten a piece of wire to a ring of his collar. It should be long enough so that a few inches of the wire drag on the ground. Now, when your dog crosses the charged wire, this trailing piece will drag over it and at the moment its end leaves the ground your dog will get a jolting surprise.

If the wire is too long, part of it will always be grounding out. There must be a moment when the end rides over the charged wire, completely free of the ground.

Even though a six-volt circuit, such as the above, does not offer the slightest danger to the smallest baby, there are sometimes ordinances against "electrified fence," so check with the authorities before using this method.

Persistence in applying one of the above techniques will convince even the most recalcitrant dog that his home area is a pretty good place to stay.

Some dogs seem more concerned with getting into the house than getting out of the yard, much to the damage of doors, and even windows. You have probably heard various suggestions for correcting this screen-scratching, door-damaging activity. One of the most common suggestions is "a pan of water in the face." While the water-throwing works in some cases. I've found it to be quite ineffective in the cases of dogs that were exceptionally stubborn or spoiled.

Here is a correction that often gets results, particularly when the dog has been very receptive to obedience training. Fasten your longe line to his collar; then, with music, laughter, and other inviting sounds, make him think he's missing out on a big party. When he starts belaboring the door, rush out, grab the line, and snatch him away from the door. In the same snatching motion, put him on a long down for about twenty minutes, insisting that he hold until you come back and break him loose. If the consequences of each of these yipping, scratching demands for admission is a jerk and a long down, he will eventually conclude that life is better when he waits for an invitation.

182

If your dog seems completely obsessed with getting into the house regardless of rebuffs, you may save your property and your time by using the battery powered shocking device described above.

This correction has the advantage of being effective even when you're not home. With a little ingenuity, it can be adapted to any door, or situation, regardless of material and the dog's footing.

For the most logical example, let's start with the simplest one: the screen door with the wooden frame, faced with a porch of cement or other grounding material. Hook your charged wire to the screen, making sure you get a good contact. Give your dog a good incentive to jump against, or scratch, the door. Unless he's an idiot, one experience should show him he's had it.

But what if the door has a metal frame?

By using tape, either adhesive or the new industrial variety, cover the vulnerable area of the door with cardboard. Now, onto this "insulating face," tape a strip of copper window screen, which can probably be bought as a scrap at your hardware or building materials store. Thread your charged wire into the screen, and you are ready.

"And what if he scratches a wooden door?"

Wood is a non-conductor, and you can stick your screen right to the surface in the dog's scratching area. You'll be ready for action as soon as you attach the charged wire.

Used consistently, one of the foregoing methods should serve to keep your dog in or out of any area you desire. But don't make the mistake of taking the early results as an indication of permanent impression, and slack off too soon. Control the situation until it seems the dog has a genuine aversion to "going out" or "going in" before he is asked.

DESTRUCTIVE CHEWING

Whether a dog chews shrubs, shoes, or household treasures (and there are specialists in each field), the depredations end in one of two ways. The dog is made to stop chewing, or is exiled to a situation where there is nothing to chew. The "companion" who must be exiled may sometime be accidentally left in a chewing situation, and for this reason is not nearly so satisfactory as the one who is taught to respect property.

Before going into methods of correction, you must carefully consider the possibility of a mineral deficiency in your dog's diet. Such a deficiency can cause destructive chewing that appears sheer deviltry, but in reality is done to satisfy a craving for something his body lacks.

I stated in the introduction the reasons why I would leave the subject of diet to veterinarians and pet supply stores; however, the almost universal ignorance of the vitamin-happy public on the significance of basic minerals, together with the urge to chew, so often caused by mineral deficiency, makes it advisable to discuss minerals and what they do.

You know that your dog's body, like your own, is composed of minerals. Naturally, these minerals must be replenished by what you eat and drink. When the diet fails in its assignment of replenishing, the deficiency causes many body processes to fail. Assimilation and metabolism of other food substances require an adequate supply of minerals or they remain unused by the body.

A commonly observed example of how a deficiency can cause a dog to chew, while seeking to satisfy a hidden hunger, is found in the dog that lacks the mineral balance necessary to assimilate the sulphur-bearing protein in his diet. He will actually feel a "sulphur hunger," and chew at his own hair to satisfy a perverted appetite. He'll chew other things, also, not in mischief, but in his feverish seeking, and so is brought to our consideration for correction. Further, since mineral deficiency causes deterioration of his nerve sheathing, he is apt to become nervous, restless and noisy.

The foregoing points to our obligation to make certain that there is an adequate mineralization of the dog's system before punishing him for chewing.

Don't smile pityingly, explain that your dog gets everything he needs, and read the analysis off a bottle of combination vitamins and minerals. Instead, consider the experience I have had in my obedience classes. In June of 1958, a commercial laboratory in California provided me with a large bulk sample of an organic mineral combination, together with the suggestion that I pass it on to the owners of those dogs in my classes whose nervous conduct, or unthrifty appearance, indicated a mineral deficiency.

The results were surprising to the members of the classes, and of great significance. Within two weeks there was a general, favorable change in temperament, and an improvement in physical condition. A good percentage of the chewing cases were corrected. In part, the surprise was due to the fact that many of the improvements were noticed in dogs whose owners had previously supplied them with "everything" in the form of vitamin-mineral combinations.

When the classes witnessed the results of mineralizing a dog's system, the question generally asked was: "What's the difference between the minerals in the combination products on the market and the ones in the sample?"

Nutritionists explain it this way: "In the first instance the minerals are not organically combined, but the minerals that produced the results were."

Organic in this case means minerals as naturally present in plant life. As the one plant grown in a medium where there is no mineral deficiency, this particular manufacturer chose sea kelp. The results of both government and private research support the company's claim that marine vegetation is the most mineral-rich plant life in the world. Doubtless this abundance of organically combined minerals from nature's storehouse is the reason that the sea-kelp-based formula is able to curb nervous habits and a morbid appetite more often, and to a greater degree, than other products we have tested in our classes.

The humaneness and common sense of assuring that a dog has no mineral deficiencies, before punishing him for acts that could be caused by such shortages, needs no further justification. When this consideration has been met, you can use the following corrective techniques without inhibition.

Rather than waste time on discussions of such maneuvers as pointing to the damage a dog has done and saying, "No-no-naughty-naughty," tying the damaged article to his neck, or going through calisthenics with a folded newspaper to the rhythm of "Shame-shame-shame," let's start out with some methods that the record shows are a bit more effective. So that you might better understand the aversion, and even revulsion, caused by the first correction we'll discuss, try the following experiment.

Select a food that you like exceptionally well, cram your mouth full of it, and hold it there for awhile without chewing. In a surprisingly short time, you will experience a gagging sensation and will want to empty your mouth—not by swallowing, either. This gagging sensation in association with the taste causes a revulsion. This same principle can be used to discourage your dog from destructive chewing.

The specific technique is to select a piece of the material he has chewed (and you needn't catch him in the act) and place it well back, crossways, in his mouth. Use a strip of adhesive tape to wrap the muzzle securely in front of the chewed material, so that no amount of gagging and clawing can force it from his mouth.

Perhaps you are wondering if these frantic efforts to rid himself of the material will cause the dog to scratch himself painfully. Yup.

They surely will. And the person who earned the money that bought the ruined shoe, or the long-awaited piece of furniture, now badly mauled, probably experienced a bit of pain when he surveyed the damage.

And if your doggie "didn't know any better," he'll know better after an hour or so of his mouth burden. When, after a long time, the tape is finally removed from his mouth (a bit of ether will remove it easily) you may find he seems to hate the sight of the object. Don't be fooled into thinking he's cured. His recent experience may be just a temporary influence. You want a permanent impression. You can work toward that permanent impression by repeating the "taping in" process the next day, even if he hasn't chewed anything in the meantime. Naturally, if he does chew before the next day, you should immediately tape the last-chewed object in his mouth.

Surveys made in obedience classes to check the effectiveness of this revulsion method show that if the handler will follow through with the taping-in for at least six days after the dog has apparently stopped chewing, eighty percent of these destructive chewers can be reformed.

Don't take a couple of days without a chewing episode as a sign that your dog doesn't need the clincher of the full six follow-up days. The stronger the "bad taste" you leave in his mouth, the more chance of a permanent impression.

Before you tell me your dog chews on something that couldn't be taped in his mouth, consider this example. If he chews on the corner of a house, and his chewing doesn't produce a splinter big enough to place in his mouth, stick a few strips of cheese boxes, or light crating, in those spots where he is most likely to chew. Once stuck in place with tape or a bit of glue, the boards become an inviting part of the building. It will be a "part" you can handle. With ingenuity, you can attach a convenient "part" of suitable material to anything from a sofa to a barn. *Be sure any object you might tape in his mouth is too big for him to swallow.* If he chews on an object too small to meet this precaution, provide a sufficiently large object, similarly shaped and of the same kind of material, for his sampling and correction.

For that twenty percent of the dogs which seem to feel neither revulsion nor repentance from the "taping in," but continue to destroy valuable property, more drastic measure must be taken. A wire from a shocking device (such as was previously described) can be brought into contact with the chewed object while it is in the dog's mouth. If the material is a non-conductor, it will have to be dampened so the dog will feel the tingle. *It is only in extreme cases where the dog must quit chewing "or else," that this traumatic method is recommended.* There are some dogs so destructive that no person could afford to keep them. Yet it is cruel to have them destroyed if a drastic correction can end the chewing problem.

If your dog is one who picks his "chewables" from the clothesline, your job is easy. Hang some damp clothing from a bare wire that is insulated at both ends. Connect the charged wire from a fence unit to the clothes wire, and hang some damp laundry at an inviting length. Turn on the fence unit and get out of sight so your dog will feel free to chew.

In all situations where the dog is punished, it is better to take the dog into the area where he chewed than to bring the object to him. After all, in addition to not chewing, you probably want him to stay away from the laundry, bush, or other chewed object, so let his discomfort be in those areas. When it seems like a difficult job to stop his chewing, remember that no one else can afford to keep a chewer either, so you can't write off your obligation with "free to good home."

BARKING, WHINING, HOWLING, YODELING, SCREAMING, AND WAILING

Dogs are known to emit all of the above sounds in many different keys. Unlike the chewing problem, where a loss is no concern of the neighbors, the neighbors take a heated interest in the vocal efforts of a noisy dog. Eventually, so will the law, which generally gives a choice of four procedures: (A) quiet the dog; (B) keep him in a soundproof area; (C) get rid of him; (D) move.

The fact that you realize you have such a problem makes it certain you have "reproved" the dog often enough to let him know you were against his sound effects, even though your reproving didn't quiet them; so we'll bypass the loudly clapped hands, the cup of water in his face, the "shame-shames," and start with something more emphatic.

We'll begin with the easiest kind of vocalist to correct: the one that charges gates, fences, doors, and windows, barking furiously at familiar or imaginary people and objects. A few clusters of BBs from a good slingshot, in conjunction with the light line and plenty of temptations will cause such a dog to use his mind rather than his mouth. But you won't make the permanent impression unless you supply dozens of opportunities for him to exercise the control he thus acquires. Make sure these opportunities don't always come at the same time of the day, else he may learn to observe the "quiet hour," and pursue his old routines at other times. With the help of the light line, it will be easy to follow the BBs with a long long-down to make sure he gets the most from his lesson. As was mentioned before, eliminating the senseless barking will not lessen the dog's value as a watchdog, but rather, as he grows more discriminating, increase it.

The dog who vocalizes in bratty protest or lonesomeness because you're gone constitutes a different problem. If it is impractical for someone to stay with him constantly (there are owners who cater to neurosis by employing dog sitters), you'll have to heed the neighbors and the law and quiet the dog. This calls for a little ingenuity as well as a heavy hand.

Attach a line to your dog's collar, so your corrective effort doesn't turn into a foot race around the house until you reach a stalemate under the bed. This use of the line in the correction will also serve to establish it as a reminder to be quiet as the dog drags it around when you're not present. Next, equip yourself with a man's leather belt or a strap heavy enough to give your particular dog a good tanning. Yup—we're going to strike him. Real hard. *Remember, you're dealing with a dog who knows he should be quiet, and neighbors who have legal rights to see that he does.*

Now leave, and let your fading footsteps tell the dog of your going. When you've walked to a point where he'll think you're gone, but where you could hear any noises he might make, stop and listen. If you find a comfortable waiting place on a nearby porch, be careful not to talk or laugh. Tests show a dog's hearing to be many times as sharp as yours.

When the noise comes, instead of trying to sneak up to the door so you can barge in while he's still barking, which is generally impossible, respond to his first sound with an emphatic bellow of "out," and keep on bellowing as you charge back to his area. Thunder through the door or gate, snatch up the belt that you've conveniently placed, and descend on him. He'll have no chance to dodge if you grab the line and reel him in until his front feet are raised off the floor, or, if he's a big dog, until you've snubbed him up with a hitch on something. While he's held in close, lay the strap vigorously against his thighs. Keep pouring it on him until he thinks it's the bitter end. A real whaling now may cut down somewhat on the number of repeat performances that will be necessary. When you're finished and the dog is convinced that he is, put him on a long down to think things over while you catch your breath. After fifteen or twenty minutes, release him from the stay; and leave the area again.

So that you won't feel remorseful, reflect on the truth that a great percentage of the barkers who are given away to "good homes," end up in the kindly black box with the sweet smell. Personally, I've always felt that it's even better to spank children, even if they "cry out," than to "put them to sleep."

You might have a long wait on that comfortable porch before your dog starts broadcasting again. When he does, let your long range bellow tie the consequent correction to his first sound, and repeat the spanking, if anything emphasizing it a bit more.

It might be necessary to spend a Saturday or another day off so that you'll have time to follow through sufficiently. When you have a full day, you will be able to convince him each yelp will have a bad consequence, and the consistency will make your job easier. If he gets away with his concert part of the time, he'll be apt to gamble on your inconsistency.

After a half-dozen corrections, "the reason and the correction" will be tied in close enough association so that you can move in on him without the preliminary bellowing of "out." From then on, it's just a case of laying for the dog and supplying enough bad consequences of his noise so he'll no longer feel like gambling.

Occasionally, there is a dog who seems to sense that you're hiding nearby and will utter no sound. He also seems to sense when you have really gone away, at least according to the neighbors. Maybe his sensing actually amounts to close observation. He could be watching and listening for the signs of your actual going.

Make a convincing operation of leaving, even if it requires changing clothes and being unusually noisy as you slam the doors on the family car and drive away. Arrange with a friend to trade cars a block or two from your house so you can come back and park within earshot without a single familiar sound to tell the dog you've returned. A few of these car changes are generally enough to fool the most alert dog.

Whether your dog believes you are gone anytime you step out of the house, or requires the production of "changing clothes and driving off," keep working until even your neighbors admit the dog has reformed. If there has been a long history of barking and whining, it sometimes requires a lot of work to make a dog be quiet when you're not around, so give the above method an honest try before you presume your dog requires a more severe correction.

Finally, if your dog is uninfluenced by the punishment and the reminder of the dragging line, you may be able to silence him with the mystery of a tingle from a properly used electric fence unit, such as has already been described.

Danger! If it's used as a short-cut gimmick by a handler who is lazy, or less intelligent than his dog, electricity can cause great nervousness in an animal. The current cult of "stock-prod-happy" incompetents who can't meet a dog on even intellectual terms has caused nervousness in many dogs that could have been effectively corrected with a different method. *The use of electricity is recommended only when the spanking method fails to quiet a dog that must be quieted— or else.*

As an example, if your dog does his noise-making in the yard, fasten one end of a bright shiny chain to a tree limb with a piece of rope so that the chain doesn't come into contact with the tree or other conducting surfaces. As to length, when the other end is fastened to your dog's collar, he should be able to move around in a considerable radius with the chain being free of the ground nearly all of the time. The area of movement will be quite great if the chain is tied at least six feet above the ground.

To the upper end of the chain fasten the charged wire from a six-volt shocking device. The chain will serve to conduct the electricity to the collar. Since your dog might panic, it is recommended that he be secured to the chain with a leather collar as well as the metal collar which will conduct the current.

The situation should be set up so that the current can be flicked on and off without the dog's being aware that anyone is around. If you have to drive off in the car before your dog will make a sound, hide someone in the house to operate the switch for you. Though hidden, it is very important that the person be able to see the dog.

Instruct your helper carefully. When the noise begins, he should flick the switch on until the dog gets a jolt, and then flick it back off. Most of the time this first tingle will be followed by a startled yelp and silence. There should be no more current turned on until the dog's noise begins again.

However, don't take the sounds of panic as intentional barking. Let the dog fight the panic out with the chain until he settles down. Protected as he is by the leather collar, the dog is not apt to injure himself with frantic jerking and, finding the chain unyielding, will eventually settle down. If and when the bratty noises recur, they should be met with another jolt. If there is no discomfort when the dog is not barking, the dog will be apt to remember just what he did to cause the shocking experience to be repeated. Three or four experiences should be enough to convince your dog that you can out-maneuver him whether you're home or gone.

In the house, the mechanics of the correction are a bit more complex. If you lack the technical skill, get assistance from someone who could rig a proper circuit to use the above principles in the inside situation. Undoubtedly there is someone in your neighborhood who can check your situation and figure the set-up out for you.

Once more, use the "tingle" only if absolutely necessary and then very carefully.

BITING

The small percentage of dogs that bite people is monumental proof that the dog is the most benign, forgiving creature on earth. However, embarrassment, danger, liability, and the law demand that "something" be done about the few dogs who do bite. If you have a shred of conscience, you'll find it tough to unreservedly accept that "something" as putting the dog to sleep particularly since there is a possibility that stupid handling may have implanted and cultivated the dog's biting career.

Because the motivations that make dogs bite are varied, it follows that the corrections must also differ in type and application; and we had best take each example in close association with the specific correction recommended.

THE PROTEST BITER

As was necessary, we dealt exhaustively with the "protest biter" when we started to handle the dog during the early obedience exercises. One thing might be added. Because the reasonable protest could be in peculiar situations, where the dog would attempt to avoid correction, it is wise to give him a lot of experience with a line hanging from his collar. With the line to remind him that he can't take his bite and escape unpunished, the dog will form new habits. Let him drag a short line until he no longer protests the reasonable actions of people who mean no harm and possibly are trying to help him.

THE OVERLY POSSESSIVE DOG

This extremist is more "screwball" than guard dog. Even after a person has been properly admitted to a house or room, this neurotic lies hoping they'll walk toward his fetish, which is often a silly toy, so he can justify a bite. This possession may be an area as well as an object. A corner, the "cave" beneath a table, and a closet are good examples.

With a wholesome assertion of rights, and without the slightest appearance of teasing, set up some training situations. Use a helper who is able to cooperate intelligently. For the protection of the helper and yourself, as well as a necessary facility, in the beginning have a piece of line as heavy as your longe line attached to the dog's collar. Put him on a stay, and make him hold it while your helper moves around in the "sacred area."

If the dog moves aggressively, make the correction as explained earlier, and then put him back into position. He can't very well stay and charge at the same time, and will eventually come to associate the imagined intrusion with the necessity of restraint. This is a gradual process, but nearly always effective. It seems that the dog who learns not to break a stay in order to bite, readily learns to restrain his aggressiveness when at liberty in the same situations. Work on it. Your chances of winning a complete victory are excellent.

THE CHASE-HAPPY BITER

This type of dog, with the tremendous drive he expresses in chasing and biting at people who are running, skating, or riding such things as bikes, scooters, motorcycles, and horses, needs basic obedience—but plenty. After you've added to his restraint and conscience by having him hold lots of stays while exposed to the temptations, you can stimulate him with the same distractions without his being told to stay. What you do with the stays is to make him think well before charging anything.

Be certain of two things: first, that he is equipped with a good strong line; second, that if he moves one inch aggressively, he'll wish he hadn't. Remember, you are liable if his charge, with or without a bite, should cause someone to fall and be injured. So grab the line and give him about five minutes of the hardest tanning you can administer. Use a belt heavy enough to make him really feel your efforts. Sometimes the long duration of a spanking is a big factor in making an indelible impression. *Since you're dealing with a dog that could cause the death or serious injury of a person, let there be no compassionate trembling before the necessity of stern measures.*

Truthfully, it might be well to explain your situation to the police so they'll know you'll have to make a better citizen of your dog, even if you have to do it the hard way; then they'll be prepared to answer any protest from kind folks who would rather have your dog put to sleep than punished.

When, after a few days' work, it seems that nothing can get your dog to ignore you and the line, nor react to the distractions, you may be sure of one thing. You're well started—that's all.

The successive steps that make the permanent impression are well demonstrated by the example of a dog I know in Riverside, California. This Boxer, one of the very few of her breed who seem to want to chase bicycles, was obsessed with the two-wheeled monsters. When finally, by means of the line, and effective use of the slingshot, she appeared ready to turn away from, instead of toward bikes, observers felt that she would backslide when no one was around. They didn't reckon with the determination of the mistress. Literally, the woman put a boy on the payroll to ride back and forth in front of the house. When the dog lost all interest in bikes, the owner restored it by having the boy drag a burlap sack of tin cans behind him. This swishing, clattering bicycle was much more tempting than any straight, production-line model, and when the inevitability of punishment, fortified by hundreds of times of wearisome exposure, finally caused an allergy to the ultra-attractive model, the feeling became the dog's permanent attitude toward all bikes. It was the hundreds of chances to say, "No, I won't," that actually "brainwashed" the dog.

So follow the example. When the line and punishment have caused your dog to say "No," make the attitude permanent by giving him hundreds of opportunities to repeat the "No."

THE SNEAK BITER

This dog is the type who lurks in his lair behind a bush or under the table, ready to glide out and nip a human whom his imagination has changed to a tiger. Even those indulgent folks who thought the "stalking game" was quite cute during their dog's puppyhood, grow tired of the tiger role and wish to stop the game. And it is generally a game, more than a sign of viciousness, and as a rule, not too difficult to stop.

After attaching the longe line to your dog's collar, place him on a down-stay in the lair where he most likes to lurk, and have a number of people go by at various rates of speed, but with no appearance of teasing. Make him hold for at least a half hour. The reason? There are three: first, he's developing restraint in the exact situation where he needs it; second, the continued exercising of the restraint makes the situation a bit boring and distasteful; and third, by associating the boredom with the situation where he has played his "game," he comes to regard the process more and more as a direct punishment of his sneak attacks. Give it a good try. Then you will know you've dealt fairly with your dog; and if he requires more emphatic discouragement, you can conscientiously give him a good tanning for each attempt to bite. When he no longer rises to the bait of a person walking by, continue to leave the line on while you give him many opportunities to say "No, I won't." As in all your training, find ways to show your appreciation when he makes the right decisions.

HOUSEBREAKING

For most dog owners, housebreaking begins with a puppy. Because he eats one or two more meals a day than a grown dog, the puppy requires more frequent opportunities to relieve himself. This fact is often mentioned and too often forgotten. Carefully observe your pup's digestive cycle. Try to work out a regular schedule of feeding that will permit you to take the pup out about the time he generally needs an airing, and you'll be taking advantage of the pup's instincts for cleanliness. The less your carelessness forces him to violate his precepts of cleanliness, the more control he will develop.

The second consideration in the housebreaking of a puppy is the practice of close confinement when he's out of your sight. Whenever possible, keep him in view when he's in the house, so you'll see the signs of his need, and be able to take him outdoors.

A PUPPY COLLAR WITH A SHORT PIECE OF LINE DRAGGING FROM IT IS ONE OF THE BEST ASSURANCES THAT, FEELING GUILTY IF HE STARTS TO COMMIT AN ERROR, HE WON'T TRY TO RUN FROM YOU AND COMPLICATE MATTERS IN MORE WAYS THAN ONE. THE LINE ALSO SERVES TO REMIND HIM OF HIS RESPONSIBILITIES.

When you must be out of sight of the pup, don't leave him to his own devices before he is housebroken. Confine him in a dog-crate of the proper size so that he would be soiling the area in which he is held. Dogs as a rule don't like to be in close proximity to the mess they make, and will restrain themselves until they are let out. Since it prepares the pup for later traveling, and confinement when ill, the crate is by far the best way to confine a dog. However, if you cannot buy or make a crate, tie him on a short chain on a floor that is non-absorbent. Absorbent surfaces are pretty much an invitation for a pup to relieve himself. That's why he will seek out and use the newspapers intended for the purpose, and will leave the linoleum to go to an inviting rug. So keep him confined during those moments when you are not observing him. Close observation and few opportunities for messing will get the job done much sooner than newspapers and punishment.

If your dog is a bit more dirty than the average, or your schedule won't permit close observation, you may have to use papers. Use a stack an eighth of an inch thick. Spread them out in an area where the dog will be forced to take his choice between the papers and the non-absorbent area around them. Do not give him the run of the house so he will have his choice between the papers and a softer, more inviting area, such as a rug. The closer the papers are placed to a door leading to the outside the better. Drop a few of these soiled stacks of paper in a section of the yard where you would like your dog to relieve himself. Then, when you are going to be in the room to observe him, see that no papers are on the floor; and when he appears to be seeking them for his purpose, take him out and place him in close proximity to the soiled papers. Tie him, or in some other way keep him in the area until, encouraged by the smell and his own need, he relieves himself. Show your pleasure at his good manners, and take him back into the house.

Soon he'll know that his signs of agitation, as he seeks the papers, will get a response from you. A bit of recognition, such as "Want out, boy?" or "Let's go," will help set the procedure of letting you know. Once you get him started in the right behavior pattern, his reliability will grow rapidly.

Occasionally, there is a pup who seems determined to relieve himself inside the house, regardless of how often he has the opportunity to go outside. This dog may require punishment. Make certain he is equipped with a collar and piece of line so he can't avoid correction.

When you discover a mess, move in fast, take him to the place of his error and hold his head close enough so that he associates his error with the punishment. Punish him by spanking him with a light strap or switch. Either one is better than a folded newspaper.

It is important to your future relationship that you do not rush at him and start swinging before you get hold of him.

When he's been spanked, take him outside. Chances are, if you are careful in your feeding and close observation, you will not have to do much punishing. Be consistent in your handling. To have a pup almost housebroken and then force him to commit an error by not providing an opportunity to go outside is very unfair. Careful planning will make your job easier.

The same general techniques of housebreaking apply to grown dogs that are inexperienced in the house.

For the grown dog who was reliable in the house and then backslides, the method of correction differs somewhat. In this group of "backsliders" we have the "revenge piddler." This dog protests being alone by messing on the floor, and often in the middle of a bed.

The first step of correction is to confine the dog closely in a part of the house when you go away, so that he is constantly reminded of his obligation. The fact that he once was reliable in the house is proof that the dog knows right from wrong, and leaves you no other course than to punish him sufficiently to convince him that the satisfaction of his wrong-doing is not worth the consequences. If the punishment is not severe enough, some of these "backsliders" will think they're winning and will continue to mess in the house. An indelible impression can sometimes be made by giving the dog a hard spanking, of long duration, then leaving him tied by the mess he's made so you can come back at twenty-minute intervals and punish him again for the same thing. In most cases, the dog that deliberately does this disagreeable thing cannot be made reliable by the light spanking that some owners seem to think is adequate punishment. It will be better for your dog, as well as the house, if you really pour it on him.

Some of the new "breaking scents" on the market can aid in your housebreaking program. One type discourages the dog from even visiting an area. Another encourages him to relieve himself in the area where it is sprinkled. Your pet shop should be able to supply further information on the brands available in your district.

Be fair to your dog in what and when you feed him and consistent in your efforts to housebreak him, and you'll soon accomplish the job.

THE DOG FIGHTING PROBLEM

The recommendation, contained in the introduction of this book, that all of the contents be read before the training of the dog is begun, is urgently advocated, and particularly in the case of the fighting dog. Often dogs that are bluffs or inexperienced, will become socially well-adjusted from the benefits of obedience training, with a bit of emphasis on setting up problems and using the throw-chain.

However, if your dog is uninfluenced by the ordinary approach to the problem, your concern for his safety and welfare as well as your own, doesn't leave any course but to take the necessary steps to break him from fighting. Two dogs can do so much damage to each other, or to humans who might be bitten in trying to separate them, that even the most emotionally unstable person can hardly protest any strong measure necessary to make a fighter into a peaceful citizen.

One method has been proven so far superior to others that there is hardly any reason to discuss other techniques. It is a method that I have used hundreds of times, in my obedience classes, on fighting dogs, many of which had been sent to me as a "last resort" by police departments and humane organizations.

Objectively, here is how a qualified trainer would proceed. A helper, well coordinated and intelligent, holds another dog which the fighter would likely challenge, about fifty feet away from the dog to be corrected. A hose, such as described for dealing with a biter, is held out of sight in the trainer's right hand. The leash is wound up short around the left hand.

Without a word from the handler, the fighting dog is moved directly toward the other dog until he is close enough to be tempted to try a lunge. At the first growl, or aggressive move, the hose is brought down across the middle of his muzzle. If the correction is forceful enough, it is certain the thoughts of fighting will be removed from the dog's mind for at least a few moments. Now comes the important part. The fighting dog is not held back, but actually pulled toward the dog that he tried to attack. This strange attitude, where the handler confronts him with an opportunity, instead of restraining him, is the principle that really makes the correction pay off. Even though the dog turns his head—and most do after one correction—he is pressured toward the other dog over and over, until it seems he has formed such an aversion that he does not want to see the other animal.

Consistent action on the part of the trainer tells the dog that each time he shows aggressive intent, or growls at another dog, he will get the correction on the muzzle and then be pulled up close for his "opportunities." When he realizes that the full consequence is the unvarying result of his attempts to fight, he will begin to form his own aversions to combat.

No qualified trainer would ever dream of threatening the dog with the hose, to the accompaniment of such asinine drivel as "You'd better not, or you'll get it." A trainer wants a dog to mind when he's not around to threaten. It can be stated very simply: the dog should receive the correction each and every time he makes the slightest aggressive move.

As was advised in the other two situations where severe correction has been proven the proper course to follow, if there is any doubt as to your ability to duplicate the procedure of a competent trainer, and make a safe and effective correction, do not attempt it. Nevertheless, the author has a moral obligation to inform the owners of the confirmed fighters that there is a correction which might convert their dogs from the dangerous practice of fighting, and possibly save them from being destroyed as incorrigibles.

In connection with the handling of fighters, you will be interested in reading the affidavit in the front of the book. It is certainly proof that to give up too soon on the correction of a fighter cannot be called kindness.

JUMPING ON PEOPLE

By now you know that a dog's good behavior habits around his master, and others, can generally be established by the proper use of obedience. This is especially true in the case where a dog jumps on a person. Obedience will also curb a dog's exuberance and make him feel less inclined to jump.

If your dog is one of those rare ones who continues to jump on folks, even though obedience has been used intelligently and consistently, you'll have to follow up with other methods.

The easiest situation is where your dog jumps on you. Instead of trying to step on his back toes (which can be very difficult in the case of a big or agile dog), raise your knee sharply upward so he meets it as he jumps against you. If your action was emphatic enough, he should bounce off, quite surprised. If you are soft, or poorly timed in your motions, he'll think he's discovered a delightful new game and be sure to jump on you all the more. Follow through on the knee thrust each time he jumps on you. When he starts to get reluctant, pat your chest, jump up and down, and in other ways make him forget his suspicions and venture a jump. The fact that the knee was ready will make his reluctance more permanent than if the matter had been dropped when he first grew suspicious. It would be unfair if you were to call his name when you're tempting him, but there is nothing unfair about your bouncing excitedly up and down. He'll soon get fed up with the game the way you play it.

The job of teaching him not to jump on others is a bit more difficult. Many people are loath to correct someone else's dog emphatically, and their efforts are no better than nothing at all. But you probably can find at least four or five well-coordinated friends who can use a knee effectively. Arrange to have at least two or three arrive as company, one after the other, and use the correction. The next day, invite one or two others over for the same purpose. This consolidated effort seems to be much more effective than the occasional correction interspersed with several opportunities to jump without the bad consequences. Make sure that all members of the family are consistent in thwarting the dog's jumping at all times. It is most cruel for a person to encourage a dog to jump on him when he is dressed in old clothes, and then correct him because the dog jumps on him when he is dressed to go out. It is very important to keep the percentage of times he is corrected considerably greater than the number of times he is able to jump unscathed. Be alert to use his obedience training in ways that will discourage the jumping. Remember, no dog can hold a sit-stay and jump on someone at the same time.

Another effective way of correcting the dog that jumps on people other than his master is to make sure the throw-chain is in your hand and you are standing in good position to use it every time he has an opportunity to jump. Naturally, you'll follow the procedure of having a great many people approach invitingly—never teasingly—so that there will be many opportunities to use the chain. This method is especially good for correcting a dog that jumps on children too small to cooperate by using the knee technique. Often it is a combination of all the methods that stops this bad habit.

OVER-EXUBERANCE

There is one cure for over-exuberance, and it is a sure cure. First, thoroughly obedience train your dog. Seek out situations that will

199

stimulate his exuberance, and practice your controls at the highest point of excitement. This will invariably develop his capacity for restraint, and make him take the distracting situation as a cue to be calm. A determined handler can always correct this problem.

HOLE DIGGING

After a dog has dug a few ruinous holes in a lawn or flower bed, it is almost certain his master has shown him he disapproves, and the dog has not been particularly impressed by the disapproval. Generally, the first action of the master is to focus the dog's attention on the hole that's been dug and spank him. Sometimes this procedure accomplishes the purpose, but there are other ways that seem more effective.

If you come home and find your dog has dug a hole, fill the hole brimful of water. With the training collar and leash, bring the dog to the hole and shove his nose into the water; hold him there until he is sure he's drowning. If your dog is of any size, you may get all of the action of a cowboy bull-dogging a steer. Stay with it. I've had elderly ladies who'd had their fill of ruined flower beds dunk some mighty big dogs. A great many dogs will associate this horrible experience with the hole they dug. However, to make sure of a permanent impression, fill the hole with water and repeat the experience the next day, whether the dog digs any more or not. On the third day, let him watch you dig a hole and prepare it for a dunking. Class surveys have shown that more than seventy percent of the dogs who experience this correction for as many as six consecutive days swear off hole digging. If the master takes the first sign of repentance as a permanent change, and stops the dunking after only a couple of days, failure is generally the result.

Another correction, found to be very effective and easier to administer, is the policy of putting a screw-in stake in the ground adjacent to the hole, tying the dog to it on about two feet of chain, and leaving him to meditate for an hour or so. If this is the inevitable result of each excavation, the dog will eventually turn his energy to other channels.

It is not necessary to "catch the dog in the act" in any of the above instances of correction. Be consistent in your corrections and your dog will come to find the smell of freshly dug earth quite repugnant.

POISON PROOFING

The vile names that his deeds call forth are probably taken as a compliment by the twisted mind of a dog poisoner. Convictions seem altogether too few and the sentences for the crime too light. The only source of satisfaction for a dog owner lies in poison-proofing his dog.

Because poison is so often fatal, it is unwise to risk a dog's life to anything less than the most effective method of protecting a dog. Reminding you that it's your dog's life you're betting on them, we'll dispense with such superficialities as having a stranger place, or hand, the dog some food filled with a bad tasting center, carefully placed and baited traps, or the master's babbling of, "No, no, no," as his dog seems about to eat food that is offered or found.

One method of poison-proofing far excels any other. It is also the easiest to use. If you will follow through by applying it in every type of situation where your dog would be vulnerable to a poisoner, you will be providing your dog with certain protection.

The materials you'll need are a low-priced, battery-operated fence charger, and enough light, insulated wire to run from where you will conceal the unit to the different areas where you want to proof your dog against eating food. Regardless of the spots where you set the charger, the dog shouldn't see it or hear it and be warned that something strange is taking place. Both the fence charger and suitable wire can be obtained at a hardware store for a price that is small to one who feels the need to protect his dog.

At a place where the dog is particularly vulnerable to a poisoner, we'll make our first set-up in your yard. Lock your dog up so he cannot watch. Set the fence unit in a place of concealment, attach the ground wire to a pipe or a rod in the ground, and the live wire to the place designated. Run the other end of the charged wire to the spot where you feel someone might be likely to toss a bit of poisoned food. Bare half an inch or so of the end of this wire. On this bare end, stick a bit of meat, or other moist food that would appeal to your dog. Starting an inch back from the food, bend a couple of angles in the wire so that the bare part and the food will be held free of contact with the ground. Turn on the fence charger. Let the dog out into the yard.

Eventually your dog will find the food. If you are watching at his moment of discovery, you'll see that his first sniff will be met with a fat spark. He'll not be apt to try the second sniff, but keep some bait on the hot wire for at least two days. Then change the set-up to another part of the yard. If possible, conceal the wire in heavy grass or cover it with dirt, allowing the tip to protrude to hold the tid-bit free of the ground. This will make the food appear just as though it were tossed over the fence.

When your dog has had opportunity to develop resistance to food found in all areas where a poisoner might toss it, you can supply experience that will make him form an equal aversion to any food offered by hand. You'll need an outsider to help you. Possibly you can exchange services with another dog lover who might want to protect his pet. As with the case of something being found on the ground, run the bare tip of the live wire into the tid-bit. Now, however, it is offered in the person's hand, insulated from his skin by a rubber glove or a bit of cardboard, plastic, or other non-conductive material. Change situations and strangers until you feel that in or out of the house, no one could coax your dog to eat anything he might offer.

With sufficient follow-through in applying the above method, you can be sure your dog will decline any food that might be found or offered, and eat only out of his own dish. This resistance should make him quite poison-proof.

STEALING

Canine kleptomania is entirely different from the spirit in which a dog takes an object to use as a plaything. Often one of these "light-fingered" dogs will take something that strikes his fancy—from a figurine to pruning shears—and hide it. And a puzzled neighbor may be hospitably received with a wagging rear and smiling eyes as he eases close to the dog's home porch for a closer look at a rake that resembles the one he's been missing.

Because the dog's taste and range are so varied, it is sometimes difficult to "hot-wire" or "mouse-trap" enough different objects to make him think that crime doesn't pay. However, difficult though it is, the procedure of "booby-trapping" tempting and strategically placed items is still the best way of starting to correct the stealing fault in a dog. This "booby-trapping" will make him more thoughtful in his choosing, but it's certain that he'll be able to steal some objects that have not been planted. It is also certain that you'll discover some of his loot. Whether you discover these stolen articles five minutes or five weeks after they disappeared, apply the "revulsion principle" of taping them in his mouth in the manner described in the instructions for dealing with chewing. Some of the articles will be of such nature as to make the task difficult, but for the most part the principle can be applied to things that a dog can pick up and steal.

Again, before starting, carefully review the instructions for taping objects in a dog's mouth (given in the section on chewing), and the methods of using a fence charger (given in the section on poison-proofing). Used consistently, in combination, they will convince your dog that crime doesn't pay.

THE PREDATOR

The law and the public have little sympathy for a predatory dog. In most areas, on the slightest evidence that a dog is even harassing domestic animals, a farmer may, with impunity, kill the dog. In some instances this attitude and legality may be justified; in other cases they are abused. Certainly, both possibilities, together with consideration for the animals a dog attacks, point to the need for correction. Confinement alone is not the answer. Dogs do get out.

The predatory fault is so serious that it calls for the most effective correction. Therefore, we'll merely mention the more commonly known methods, such as punishing a dog when "caught in the act"; tying the dead fowl or animal around the dog's neck until time and decay make him quite tired of the burden and its smell; beating him with the thing he's killed; and similar procedures. We'll get right to a method that has proven almost infallible. The dog who preys on chickens makes a good example with which to demonstrate principles that can be applied to all domestic animals and poultry.

Obtain a cull chicken from a poultryman or farmer. Borrow or buy a fence unit such as previously described in this book.

Begin by placing a piece of cardboard about two feet square in a suitable place for your dog to spot a chicken. Push a sharp stick down through its center so you will have a stake a few inches high on which to anchor the bird. Fasten a few coils of the fence charger's live wire to one of the chicken's legs, tie the legs together, and seat him as comfortably as possible in the middle of the cardboard. Secure his legs to the stake so his wingbeats can't move him from the insulating surface of the cardboard.

Experts tell me that it takes a lot of electricity to even make a chicken tingle, so feel no compunctions when you turn on the six-volt charger. Let your dog come into the area; then hurry to conceal yourself, so that he won't be the least bit influenced by your presence.

Even if you should miss the sight of his contact with the chicken, you'll hear the sound effects, and odds are that your astounded dog will drown out the chicken. One thing is certain—he won't be chewing on the chicken when you get back to the area. If he hasn't retreated as far as possible, he'll have pulled well back to where he can risk a safe and bewildered look.

This first experience means you're well started. I repeat, well started. Next comes the longer and more important part of the correction.

If you have a small pen, or can make one, about six feet square, place your cardboard, chicken, and fence charger set-up in the middle of it. Turn on the current. Lock your dog in the pen with the chicken. He was a dog that always liked an opportunity to grab a chicken. Now, suddenly, life is just one big, overflowing, ever-present opportunity to do just that. And if he decides to say "no," there will be hours and hours of time to repeat the "no," because the greater part of each day for at least a week should provide this opportunity to grab a chicken or refuse to do so. It is the process of this "mental laundromat," more than the initial shock, that cleanses a dog's mind of naughty thoughts toward his fellow creatures.

If it is impossible to provide the "companionette quarters" of a small pen for the dog and the object of his avowed good will, you can tie the dog on a five-foot chain, and place the chicken set-up well within the radius of his reach.

As was said before, this example of correcting the chicken-killing dog demonstrates a method that can be used to correct dogs that prey on all domestic animals and poultry. In the case of cats, rabbits, and other animals that might be hard to tie down, you can easily place the creature in a very small cage with such fine wire and large mesh that it seems openly exposed to the dog.

You can set the cage on cardboard and run your live wire to the wire on the cage. Make sure that all of the cage wire is linked together so none of it will fail to be electrified.

Your dog will feel very close to the animal in the cage. After he's had his surprise, follow through by putting him and his new-found buddy in the small pen, or by tying him so that he is constantly in grabbing distance of the other animal. As in the case of the dog that kills chickens, he needs these hours of opportunity to say "no."

Either by figuring a way to keep him away from the wires of the small cage that holds him, or by arranging to turn the current off and on, provide a means of protecting the animal from long periods of shock. Slight jolts, that would go unnoticed by a bird, would cause discomfort to an animal. Your dog, of course, brings his discomfort down on himself.

After a week during which he's had at least forty or fifty hours of opportunity, "no" will become a new way of life.

Some dogs are so predatory by nature that they will require more than the average effort. Watch your dog's attitude carefully, and be thorough in your application of the correction. Remember the law and the fact that one of the lives you save may be your dog's.

CARSICKNESS

Since continued carsickness is almost always in part due to a mental condition, which was caused by an early unpleasant experience, it follows that a change of attitude is basic to correction of this inconvenient and messy situation. The best way to bring about this change of attitude, along with a physical accustoming, is by very short, pleasant trips over a straight road, and while the dog has an empty stomach.

Literally, each ride should end before the dog has time to get sick, even if it means limiting the beginning experiences to a block in distance.

Together with a progressive increase in distance, there should be a happy conclusion to the trip, such as a walk, some play, or another bit of enjoyment which will "backwash" into the experience in a way that will make the dog regard cars more favorably.

As an aid to making these early experiences as pleasant as possible, you can procure some anti-carsickness pills from your veterinarian. However, the progressively lengthening rides are still the fundamental part of making your dog a good traveler.

OBEDIENCE COMPETITION

When, under the most distracting conditions, your dog will reliably and accurately perform those exercises which you have taught him, it can be said that he is capable of meeting the standard routine tests that The American Kennel Club uses to accredit a Companion Dog, commonly called a "C.D."

If you have a purebred dog, and enjoy competition, you can enter a new field of interest and pleasure by participating in the formal obedience of licensed shows. You and your dog will improve greatly when you face the objective of doing your best for a score.

The problem in "doing your best" is to become familiar with ring handling procedure and the atmosphere of being judged so that you will be smooth and confident in your handling and able to communicate with your dog in a way that brings out his fullest response. Regardless of how obedient his dog is, or how much a person has studied the rules and handling demands in books, there are two or more things he must do before he can expect his dog to score well in competition. He should observe, first-hand, the handling of dogs in the obedience ring, and get someone to run through the novice routine with him so he will acquire practice in giving the correct commands and properly executing the maneuvers when he is told to do so, instead of hesitating until he feels his position is better adjusted to that of the dog.

In brief summary, the regulations which are of major concern to handling are those that limit a handler to a single command each time the judge orders a test of performance, and which demand that the handler be penalized for any additional motion or sound, given intentionally, or unintentionally, which could possibly give a further cue to the dog. So, if you have any nervous wigglings, head-scratchings or other unusual mannerisms, learn to control them while you're working a dog in the ring. Remember, too, the time and manner of executing the exercises is not left to your initiative. The stops, starts, and patterns of performance must be done when and as the judge specifies. Only by this observation and practice in executing the exercises on another's order will you free yourself from compromise and develop the balance and confidence necessary to get good obedience scores.

Ask the one who runs through the routine with you to watch and listen for any motions or words that would cause you to lose points for double commands and unintentional cues. As an aid to what you observed at the ringside, you can get a booklet containing much information from The American Kennel Club, 51 Madison Avenue, New York, N.Y. 10010.

The hard-working judges, who give so much time to obedience, vary somewhat in their interpretation of the rules and the routine patterns to be used for judging, but generally the variations are not of great significance.

Watch the practice matches and novice judging at shows whenever you can. Read your rule book carefully. Practice with someone putting you through the routine, in association with other obedience enthusiasts and their dogs if possible. You'll soon be prepared to complete the requirements, as outlined in your rule book, and you'll get much profit and find a new world of fun and friends in helping your well-trained dog acquire the title of Companion Dog.

With this success, your interest in further training and showing is certain to grow, which is one of the nicest things that could happen to you and your dog.

(End of Section 2. This book, *The Koehler Method of Guard Dog Training*, contains 400 pages.)